Augusta County, Virginia

Land Tax Books

1782-1788

Ruth and Sam Sparacio

The Antient Press Collection
from

Colonial Roots
Millsboro, Delaware
2016

Colonial
Roots

Helping You Grow Your Family Tree

ISBN 978-1-68034-113-3

CONTENTS

[this page intentionally blank]

AUGUSTA COUNTY, VIRGINIA
LAND TAX BOOKS
1782-1802

(page 1.)
    Memorandum of the Quantity and Value of each lott and tract of land in the First
Battalion of Augusta County and also valuation of JOSEPH BELL, ELIJAH McCLANACHAN and
JOHN POAGE, Commissioners for the year one thousand seven hundred and eighty two

Proprietors Names	Lotts & Parts of Lotts	Quantity of Land in each Tract	Average Price p Acre	Value Sett on Each Lott and Tract	Tax on each Lott & Tract of Land
ANDERSON, George Senr.		155 1/2	20/	155...10.....0	1...11.....1 1/4
ANDERSON, George Junr.		155 1/2	20/	155...10.....0	1...11.....1 1/4
ANDERSON, Margaret (Widow)		100	13/	65.....0.....0	0...12.....0
AGNEW, James		147	15/	102...10.....0	1.....1.....8 1/2
ALLISON, William		131	10/	65...10.....0	0...13.....1 1/2
do.		32	5/	8.....0.....0	(ink blot)
ALLISON, John Senr.		212	8/	84...16.....0	0...16...11 1/4
do.		10	15/	7...10.....0	0.....1.....6
do.		62	5/	15...10.....0	0.....3.....1 1/2
ANDERSON, James (Son to James)		150	12/6	93...15.....0	0...18.....9
do.		115	5/	28...15.....0	0.....5.....9
ANDERSON (? Anot---) Capt.		482	15/	361...10.....0	3...12.....3 1/2
do.		77	6/	23.....2.....0	0.....4.....7 1/2
ANDERSON, Samuel		137	5/	34.....5.....0	0.....6...10
do.		200	11/	110.....0.....0	1.....2.....0
do.		200	9/	90.....0.....0	0...18.....0
do		200	9/	90.....0.....0	0...18.....0
do.		34	3/	5.....2.....0	0.....1.....0 1/4
ASKINS, John (Shoemaker)		200	4/	40.....0.....0	0.....8.....0
ASKINS, John		127	4/6	28...11.....6	0.....5.....8 1/2
ANDERSON, William Senr.		926	10/	463.....0.....0	4...12.....0 1/4
do.		200	2/6	25.....0.....0	0.....5....( )
ARMSTRONG, William N. Mount.		200	7/	70.....0.....0	(torn)
do.		328	7/	114...16.....0	1....( )....( )
ARMSTRONG, Able		120	7/	42.....0.....0	(torn)
do.		140	2/6	17...10.....0	(torn)
ANDERSON, Samuel Junr.		100	8/	40.....0.....0	0.....8.....0
ANDERSON, William (?)		100	8/	40.....0.....0	0.....8.....0
ANDERSON, Joseph Senr.		40	3/	6.....0.....0	0.....1.....2 1/2
ARGENBRIGHT, John		150	4/6	33...15.....0	0.....6.....9
ALLEN, William (Smokey Row)		100	6/	30.....0.....0	0.....6.....0
do.		130	7/	45...10.....0	0.....9.....1 1/4
AFFREEL, Jeremiah		160	9/	72.....0.....0	0...14.....5
AFFREEL, Daniel		400	7/	140.....0.....0	1...8.....0
do.		77	2/	7...14.....0	0.....1.....6 1/2
do. (for Son)		188	3/	28.....0.....0	0.....5....7 1/4
ABNEY, John (Hatter)		230	6/	69...0.....0	0...13...9 1/2
do.		120	3/	18.....0.....0	0.....3.....7 1/2
do.		6	6/	4...10.....0	0.....0.....1 1/4
do.	1			35.....0.....0	0.....7.....0
do.	1			5.....0.....0	0.....1.....0

(page 2. Augusta County Land Tax Return for 1782)

Proprietors Names	Lotts & Parts of Lotts	Quantity of Land in Each Tract	Average Price p. Acre	Value Set on Each Lott and Tract	Tax on each Lott & Tract of Land
ALEXANDER, James (Long Meadow)		400	10/	200.....0.....0	2.....0.....0
do.		100	2/	10...0.....0	0.....2.....0
do.		147	8/	58...16...0	0...11.....9
do.		80	2/	8.....0.....0	0.....1.....7 1/4
ALEXANDER, Fr---		265	8/6	112...12.....0	1.....2.....6
ALEXANDER, James C.		90	8/	36.....0.....0	0.....7.....2 1/4
ALEXANDER, John Senr.		100	8/	40.....0.....0	0.....8.....0
ALEXANDER, James Senr.		100	8/	40.....0.....0	0.....8.....0
ALEXANDER, James Junr.		110	8/	44.....0.....0	0.....8.....9 1/2
AILOR, Anthony		250	9/	112...10.....0	1.....2.....6
ALLEN, James Senr.		264	7/6	99.....0.....0	0...19.....9 1/2
ALLEN, James Junr.		110	8/	44.....0.....0	0.....8.....9 1/2
do.		160	4/	32.....0.....0	0.....6.....5
ALLEN, Robert Jr. (S. River)		80	17/6	70.....0.....0	0...14.....0
do.		100	3/	15.....0.....0	0.....3.....0
ALEXANDER, Andrew		204	7/6	77...10.....0	0...15.....6
ALLEN, Robert		400	10/	200.....0.....0	2.....0.....0
ALLEN, Elizabeth (Widow)		147	7/	51.....9.....0	0...10.....3 1/4
ALEXANDER, Robert Senr.		314	10/	157.....0.....0	1...11.....5
do.		50	8/	20.....0.....0	0.....4.....0
ARMSTRONG, William		200	8/	80.....0.....0	0...16.....0
do.		170	2/	17.....0.....0	0.....3.....5
ARMSTRONG, Robert		224	8/	89...12.....0	0...17...11
ALEXANDER, Gabriel		363	8/	145.....4.....0	1.....7.....0 1/2
do.		130	1/6	9...15.....0	0.....1...11 1/2
ALEXANDER, John (South River)		260	4/	52.....0.....0	0...10.....5
ALEXANDER, Andrew Junr.		194	3/	29.....2.....0	0.....5.....9 3/4
ditto		90	1/6	6...15.....0	0.....1.....4 1/4
(torn)AIN, Neal		200	4/	40.....0.....0	0.....8.....0
ditto		150	1/6	6...15.....0	0.....1.....4 1/4
ALLEN, James Junr. (for Hugh)	)				
ALLEN's Hairs	)	100	20/	106.....0.....0	1.....0.....0
ditto for do.		400	2/6	50.....0.....0	0...10.....0
do. for do.		100	3/	15.....0.....0	0.....3.....0
BYERS, David		100	10/	50.....0.....0	0...10.....0
do.		35	10/	17...10.....0	0.....3.....6
BELL, Flowrance		400	12/6	250.....0.....0	2...10.....0
do.		183	5/	45...15.....0	0.....9.....1 3/4
BERRICK, Philip		280	3/	42.....0.....0	0.....8.....5
BRATCHEY. Thomas		214	9/	96.....6.....0	0...12.....3
do.		25	3/	3...15.....0	0.....0.....9
BREDON, EDD.		200	5/	50.....0.....0	0...10.....0
BUCHANAN, Patrick Capt.		200	4/	40.....0.....0	0.....8.....0

(page 3. Augusta County Land Tax Return for 1782)

Proprietors Names		Quantity of Land	Average Price	Value Set	Tax
BUCHANAN, John Senr.		125	9/	56...15.....0	0...11.....4 1/4
BING, John		350	9/	157...10.....0	1...10.....6

Proprietors Names	Lotts & Parts of Lotts	Quantity of Land in each Tract	Average Price p Acre	Value Set on each Lott and Tract	Tax on each Lott & Tract of Land

(page 3 contd. Augusta County Land Tax Return for 1782)

Proprietors Names	Lotts	each Tract	Acre	and Tract	of Land
BELL, John (Long Glade)		400	7/	140.....0.....0	1.....8.....0
do.		38	3/	5...14.....0	0.....1.....2
BLAIR, John (Taylor)		360	11/	198.....0.....0	1...19....7
do.		40	3/	6.....0.....0	0.....1.....2 1.2
do.		60	2/6	7...10.....0	0.....1.....6
do.		19	2/	1...18.....0	0.....0.....4 3/4
BLACK, Elizabeth (Widow)		120	4/	24.....0.....0	0.....4.....9 1/2
BLAIR, William (Tanner)		150	4/6	33...15.....0	0.....6.....9
BRAWFORD, Rebecca (Widow)		200	8/	80.....0.....0	0...16.....0
BLAIR, Joseph Lieut.		300	5/	75.....0.....0	0...15.....0
BERRY, George		249	9/	112.....1.....0	1.....2.....5
BERRY, William Junr.		98	8/	39.....4.....0	0.....7...10
do.		50	2/6	6.....5.....0	0.....1.....3
BURGIS, William		240	2/	24.....0.....0	0.....4.....9 1/4
BROWN, Benjamin		100	10/	50.....0.....0	0...10.....0
do.		30	8/	12.....0.....0	0.....2.....5
do.		55	2/6	6...17.....6	0.....1.....4 1/2
BROWN, Thomas		300	9/	135.....0.....0	1.....2.....1 1/2
do.		70	6/	21.....0.....0	0.....4.....2 1/4
BROWN, Hugh		306	4/	61.....4.....0	0.....2.....3
do.		22	6/	6...12.....0	0.....1.....3 1/2
BROWN, Charles		295	7/6	110...12.....6	1.....2.....1 1/2
BURK, William		268 3/4	4/6	60.....9.....4	0...12.....1 1/4
BELL, William Senr.		200	3/	30.....0.....0	0.....6.....0
do.		217	1/6	8...15.....6	0.....1.....9
BELL, James Senr.		300	7/	105.....0.....0	1.....1.....0
do.		113	3/	16...19.....0	0.....3.....5
BELL, William Junr.		206	8/6	87...11.....0	0...17.....6
BELL, James (Capt.)		240	7/	84.....0.....0	0...16.....9 1/2
do.		80	2/	8.....0.....0	0.....1.....8 1/2
BROWN, John		155	7/	54.....5.....0	0...10...10 1/2
BAILOR, Jacob		235	5/6	64...12.....6	0...12...11
BLAIR, William	1			25.....0.....0	0.....5.....0
BRADY, James		300	1/6	22...10.....0	0.....4.....6
BOWYER, William (Colo.)		50	10/	25.....0.....0	0.....5.....0
do.	1			30.....0.....0	0.....6.....0
do.	1			35.....0.....0	0.....7.....0
do 1 acre and quarter	1 1/4			20.....0.....0	0.....4.....0
do.		146	5/	36...10.....0	0.....7.....4 1/4
BOWYER, Michael	1			20.....0.....0	0.....4.....0
BROCK, John (See J. Graham)		196	7/6	73...16.....0	0...14.....9
do.		100	3/	15.....0.....0	0.....3.....0
do.		45	5/	11.....5.....0	0.....2.....3
BASKINS, Charles (Capt.)		240	9/	108.....0.....0	1.....1.....7 1/4
BUCHANAN, David		415	3/9	77...16.....0	0...15.....6 1/2

(page 4. Augusta County Land Tax Return for 1782)

Proprietors Names	Lotts	each Tract	Acre	and Tract	of Land
BUCHANAN, Sarah (Widow and heir of James Buchanan, dead)		150	3/6	26.....5.....0	0.....5.....3

(page 4 contd. Augusta County Land Tax Return for 1782)

Proprietors Names	Lotts & Parts of of Lotts	Quantity of Land in Acres	Average Price p Acre	Value set on each Lott and Tract	Tax on each Lott & Tract of Land
BELL, Robert (W. Creek)		190	3/	28...10.....0	0.....5.....8 1/2
BUCHANAN, William		370	4/	74.....0.....0	0...14.....9 1/2
BROWN, John (C. McCUTCHINS COMPA)		252	6/	75...12.....0	0...15.....1 1/4
BERRY, Charles		426	8/	170.....8.....0	1...14.....1
BEARD, Thomas		318	5/6	87.....9.....0	0...17.....6
BEARD, William		400	11/	220.....0.....0	2.....4.....0
BROWN, Francis		174	8/	69...12.....0	0...13...11
BROWN, Hugh		174	8/	69...12.....0	0...13...11
BLAIR, William Senr.		87	6/	26.....2.....0	0.....5.....2 1/2
do.		120	4/	24.....0.....0	0.....4.....9 1/4
do.		69	3/	10.....7.....0	0.....2.....0 3/4
do.		61	3/	9.....3.....0	0.....1...10
do.		18	3/	2...14.....0	0.....0.....6 1/2
BURNSIDE, John		400	9/	180.....0.....0	1...16.....0
do.		42	3/	6.....6.....0	0.....1.....3
do.		21	3/	3.....3.....0	0.....0.....7 1/2
BURTON, Edmund		213	4/	42...12.....0	0.....8.....6 1/4
BURKET, Frederick		75	4/	15.....0.....0	0.....3.....0
BELL, William (Son to Samuel)		150	6/	45.....0.....0	0.....9.....0
BELL, Samuel (M. River)		159	11/	87.....9.....0	0...17.....6
do.		40	4/	8.....0.....0	0.....1.....7 1/2
do.		150	2/	15.....0.....0	0.....3.....0
BEARD, Edward		200	10/	100.....0.....0	1.....0.....0
BLACK, Peter		230	7/	80...10.....0	0...16.....1 1/4
BARRIGER, Jacob (B. Smith)		748	3/6	130...18.....0	1.....6.....2 1/2
BLACK, John (S. River)		210	10/	105.....0.....0	1.....1.....0
do.		54	2/	5.....8.....0	0.....1.....1
BROOKS, John Junr.		65	8/	26.....8.....0	0.....5.....3 1/4
BROOKS, John Senr.		364	9/6	172...18.....0	1...14.....7
BEST, James		275	2/6	34.....7.....6	0.....6...10 1/2
BRATTON, Elizabeth (Widow)		200	4/	40.....0.....0	0.....8.....0
do.		120	1/6	9.....0.....0	0.....1.....9 1/2
BELL, James Junr. (S. River)		247	10/	123...10.....0	1.....4.....8 1/2
BUMGARDNER, Christopher		120	6/	36.....0.....0	0.....7.....2 1/2
BURNS, Richard		280	1/6	21.....0.....0	0.....4.....2 1/2
BELOW, A.		20	4/	4.....0.....0	0.....0.....9 1/2
BOYD, Thomas		240	8/	96.....0.....0	0...19.....2 1/2
do.		80	2/	8.....0.....0	0.....1.....7 1/2
BOYD, John		115	8/	46.....0.....0	0.....9.....2 1/2
do.		20	4/	4.....0.....0	0.....0.....9 1/2
BROWNLEE, Alexander Senr.		222	9/	99.....8.....0	0...19...10 1/2
BROWNLEE, John Senr.		222	9/6	105.....9.....0	1.....1.....1
do.		62	4/	12.....2.....0	0.....2.....5 3/4

(page 5. Augusta County Land Tax Return for 1782

Proprietors Names	Lotts & Parts of of Lotts	Quantity of Land in Acres	Average Price p Acre	Value set on each Lott and Tract	Tax on each Lott & Tract of Land
BROWNLEE, William		100	9/6	47...10.....0	0.....9.....6
do.		83	3/	12.....9.....0	0.....2.....5 3/4
BROWNLEE, John Junr.		132	9/	62...14.....0	0...12.....6
do.		18	4/	3...12.....0	0.....0.....8 1/2

(page 5 contd. Augusta County Land Tax Return for 1782)

Proprietors Names	Lotts & Parts of Lotts	Quantity of Land in Acres	Average Price p Acre	Value set on each Lott or Tract	Tax on each Lott or Tract of Land
BRIGHT. George		170	8/	71.....4.....0	0...14.....3
do.		300	1/6	22...10.....0	0.....4.....6
BLACK, Cutlive		160		32.....0.....0	0.....6.....5
BRAWFORD, Samuel		410	9/6	194...15.....0	1...18...11 1/2
BURK, John		212	8/6	90.....2.....0	0...18.....0 1/2
BLACK, John		121	6/	36.....6.....0	0.....7.....3
do.		134	10/	67.....0.....0	0...13.....5
BLACKWOOD, Samuel		105	5/	26.....5.....0	0.....5.....3
BROWN, William		225	6/6	73.....2.....6	0...14.....7 1/2
do.		148	6/	44.....8.....0	0.....8...10 1/2
do.		80	2/	8.....0.....0	0.....1.....7 1/2
BARRET, Alexander (Dcotr.)		75	10/	37...10.....0	0.....7.....6
do.		66 1/2	4/	13.....6.....0	0.....2.....8
BELL, James (S. River)		300	9/	135.....0.....0	1.....7.....0
BELL, John (S. River)		300	9/	135.....0.....0	1.....7.....0
do.		130	1/6	9...15.....0	0.....4...11 1/2
BLACK, William		316	8/6	134.....6.....0	1.....6...10
BLACK, Samuel		369	8/6	156...16.....6	1...11.....4 1/4
do.		200	7/	70.....0.....0	0...14.....0
do.		200	1/6	15.....0.....0	0.....3.....0
BERRY, John (B. Creek)		398	2/6	49...15.....0	0.....9...11 1/2
BRENT, James		200	5/	50.....0.....0	0...10.....0
do.		90	2/	9.....0.....0	0.....1.....9 1/2
do.		400	1/6	30.....0.....0	0.....6.....0
CALL, Timothy		153	10/	76...10.....0	0...15.....4 1/2
CRAWFORD, Patrick		511	25/	638...15.....0	6.....7.....9
CLEMONS, John		76	20/	76.....0.....0	0...15.....2 1/2
do.		100	8/	40.....0.....0	0.....8.....0
CLEMONS, Gasper		110	15/	82...10.....0	0...18.....6
do.		80	5/	20.....0.....0	0.....4.....0
do.		60	5/	15.....0.....0	0.....3.....0
CUBB, Marquis		100	6/	30.....0.....0	0.....6.....0
do.		77	3/	11.....0.....0	0.....2.....2 1/2
CRAWFORD, James		401	13/	260...13.....0	2...12.....1 3/4
CRAIG, George		335	10/	167...10.....0	1...13.....6
do.		265	10/	132...10.....0	1.....6.....6
do.		50	3/	7...10.....0	0.....1.....6
CARSON, Isaac		132 1/2	10/	66.....5.....0	0...13.....3
CURRY, Samuel		132	12/	79.....4.....0	0...15...10
do.		35	8/	14.....0.....0	0.....2.....9 1/2
CAMPBELL, James (Trumbles Compa.)		35	5/	8...15.....0	0.....1.....9
CALDWELL, John		300	9/	135.....0.....0	1.....8.....0
CHAPMAN, John		110	5/	77...10.....0	0.....5.....6

(page 6. Augusta County Land Tax Return for 1782)

Proprietors Names	Lotts & Parts of Lotts	Quantity of Land in Acres	Average Price p Acre	Value set on each Lott or Tract	Tax on each Lott or Tract of Land
COOK, John		30	6/	9.....0.....0	0.....1.....9 1/2
COOK, Jacob		100	2/6	12...10.....0	0.....2.....6
CROW, Benjamin		200	6/	60.....0.....0	0...12.....0 1/4

(page 6 contd. Augusta County Land Tax Return for 1782)

Proprietors Names	Lotts	Lands	Price p Acre	Valuation	Tax
CURRY, James Senr.		163	7/	56.....0.....0	0...11.....2 1/2
do.		69	2/6	8...12.....6	0.....1.....8 1/2
CURRY, Robert Junr.		400	3/	60.....0.....0	0...12.....0
CAMBLE, John (Buchanan's Compa)		200	5/	50.....0.....0	0...10.....0
CAMBLE, John (do.)		195	7/	68.....5.....0	0...13.....8
CALLISON, James		266	6/6	86.....9.....0	0...17.....3 1/4
CAIL, Peter		214	6/	64.....4.....0	0...12...10 1/2
do.		122	3/	18.....6.....0	0.....3.....7 3/4
CUNNINGHAM, David		226	8/	90.....8.....0	0...18.....1
CUNNINGHAM, John (Capt.)		173	7/6	64...17.....6	0...12...11 3/4
do. as Administrator of Alexr. CUNNINGHAM)		150	5/	37...10.....0	0.....7.....6
COWMAN, John		200	7/	70.....0.....0	0...14.....0
COUL, David Senr.		30	5/	7...10.....0	0.....1.....6
COUL, Jacob		198	6/6	59.....7.....0	0...11...10
CLARK, Robert		216	9/	97.....4.....0	0...19.....4 3/4
do.		176	6/	52...16.....0	0...10.....7 1/2
do.		86	3/	12...18.....0	0.....2.....7
COULTER, Michael		436	9/	196.....4.....0	1...19.....3
COOK, James (Capt.)		420	9/	189.....0.....0	1...17.....9 1/2
CRAWFORD, William		800	5/	200.....0.....0	2.....0.....0
do.		90	3/	13...10.....0	0.....2.....8 1/2
do.		130	2/6	16.....2.....0	0.....3.....2 1/2
do.		133	2/	13.....6.....0	0.....2.....8
CRAWFORD, John (B. Smith)		390	6/	117.....0.....0	1.....3.....5
do.		201	5/	50.....5.....0	0...10.....0 1/2
CUNNINGHAM, James Senr.		90	9/	36.....0.....0	0.....7.....2 1/2
do.		26	2/	2...12.....0	0.....0.....6
CUMMINS, Robert Senr.		164	7/6	61...10.....0	0...12.....4 1/4
CLARK, John		100	6/	30.....0.....0	0.....6.....0
CONROD, Frederick (See D. KIDD)	1			15.....0.....0	0.....3.....0
CLONINGER, Valentine		16	5/	4.....0.....0	0.....0.....9 1/2
do.	1/2			40.....0.....0	0.....8.....0
do.		320	2/	32.....0.....0	0.....6.....5
COURSEY, James		196	7/	68...12.....0	0...14.....8
CALDBREATH, Thomas		240	6/	72.....0.....0	0...14.....5
do.		200	6/6	65.....0.....0	0...13.....0
do.		40	2/	4.....0.....0	0.....0.....9 /2
CALDWELL, Robert		180	2/6	22...10.....0	0.....1.....6
CALDWELL, William (T. Spring, M. HOUSE)		130	8/6	55.....5.....0	0...11.....0 1/2
do.		186	7/	65.....2.....0	0...13.....0 1/2
CAMPBELL, Sarah (Widow)		390	8/6	165...15.....0	1...13.....1 3/4
CUNNINGHAM, John		210	5/	52...10.....0	0...10.....6
CLARK, James Junr.		412	6/	123.....2.....0	1.....4.....7 1/4

(page 7. Augusta County Land Tax Return for 1782)

Proprietors Names	Lotts	Lands	Price p Acre	Valuation	Tax
CURRY, Robert (Mason's)		135	5/	33...15.....0	0.....6.....9
do.		50	2/6	6.....5.....0	0.....1.....3
CURRY, William Senr.		200	7/	70.....0.....0	0...14.....0
CAMPBELL, William (DICKEY's Compa.)		230	8/6	97...15.....0	0...19.....5 1/2
CAMPBELL, Hugh		200	5/	50.....0.....0	0...10.....0

(page 7 contd. Augusta County Land Tax Return for 1782)

Proprietors Names	Lotts	Lands	Value p Acre	Valuation	Tax
CONELLY, Thomas		186	6/	97...15.....0	0...19.....5 1/2
do.		250	2/	25.....0.....0	0.....5.....0
do. in partnership with WALKER's Heirs		97 1/2		7...19.....0	0.....1.....7 1/4
CONELLY, Arthur		280	7/	98.....0.....0	0...18.....7
do.		215	3/	32.....5.....0	0.....6.....5 1/2
do.		35	5/	8...15.....0	0.....1.....9
do.		6	7/	2.....2.....0	0.....0.....5
CAMPBELL, Robert		200	10/	100.....0.....0	1.....0.....0
do.		55	3/	8.....5.....9	0.....1.....8
do.		14	6/	4.....4.....0	0.....0...10
CAMPBELL, John (Capt.)		200	10/	100.....0.....0	1.....0.....0
do. in partnership with James COOK, deced)		250		25.....0.....0	0.....5.....0
CRAWFORD, James & George, (Exrs. of George CRAWFORD, deced.)		311	18/	279...18.....0	2...18.....0
do.		212	12/	127.....4.....0	1.....5.....5 1/2
do.		150	10/	75.....0.....0	0...15.....0
do.		200	16/	160.....0.....0	1...12.....0
do.		194	2/	19.....8.....0	0.....3...10 1/2
CRAIG, Robert		192	16/	153...12.....0	1...10.....8 3/4
do.		200	3/	30.....0.....0	0.....6.....0
CAMPBELL, Robert (Lieut.)		380	6/	114.....0.....0	1.....2.....9 1/2
COLLINS, John (Weaver)		285	6/	85...10.....0	0...17.....1 1/4
CRAIG, James Senr.		690	9/	310...10.....0	3.....2.....1 1/4
do.		450	5/	110.....0.....0	1.....2.....0
CRAIG, George (S. River)		197	6/	59.....2.....0	0...11...10
CALDWELL, John (T. Spring)		275	8/6	116...17.....6	1.....3.....4 1/2
CARRUTHERS, James		113	4/	22...12.....0	0.....4.....6 1/4
CARRUTHERS, David		200	3/	30.....0.....0	0.....6.....0
COULTER, John Senr.		200	6/	60.....0.....0	0...12.....0
do.		106		13.....5.....0	0.....2.....8
COULTER, David		114	4/	22...16.....0	0.....4.....6 3/4
CHESNUT, William		320	3/	48.....0.....0	0.....9.....7
CAMPBELL, Andrew		262	6/	78...12.....0	0...15.....8 3/4
do.		30	3/	4...10.....0	0.....0.....9 1/2
COULTER, James		300	5/	75.....0.....0	0...15.....0
CAMPBELL, James & John (S. River)		247	6/	74.....2.....0	0...14.....9 1/4
do.		130	2/	13.....0.....0	0.....2.....7 1/4
CARRUTHERS, Thomas		100	4/	20.....0.....0	0.....4.....0
COOPER, James		150	4/	30.....0.....0	0.....6.....0

(page 8. Augusta County Land Tax Return for 1782)

Proprietors Names	Lotts	Lands	Value p Acre	Valuation	Tax
CUNNINGHAM, James (Sadler)		320	4/	54.....0.....0	0.....8.....9 1/2
CARSON, Samuel (B. Smith)		175	9/6	83.....2.....6	0...16.....7 1/2
CAMPBELL, Mary (Widow)		100	3/	15.....0.....0	0.....3.....0
CAMPBELL, Robert (Heir to Robert, deced.)		100	3/	15.....0.....0	0.....3.....0
do.		150	2/	15.....0.....0	0.....3.....0
CAMPBELL, George (Legatee of Robert, deced)		140	2/	14.....0.....0	0.....2.....9 1/2
do.		50	2/	5.....0.....0	0.....1.....0
CHRISTIAN, John Senr.		208 1/2	9/	93...12.....0	0...18.....8 1/2
CHRISTIAN, Robert Junr.		208 1/2	9/	93...12.....0	0...18.....8 1/2

(page 8 contd. Augusta County Land Tax Return for 1781)

Proprietors Names	Lotts	Lands	Value p Acre	Valuation	Tax
CHRISTIAN, Gilbert		269	10/	134...10.....0	1.....6...10 3/4
CHRISTIAN, Patrick		269	10/	134...10.....0	1...6...10 3/4
CHRISTIAN, William		200	10/	100 0.....0	1.....0.....0
CHRISTIAN, John, Gilbert & Robert					
(Legatees of John Christian, deced)		338	10/	169.....0.....0	1...12.....9 1/2
CALDWELL, Robert		200	7/	70.....0.....0	0...14.....0
CAAL, James		400	1/6	30.....0.....0	0.....6.....0
COFFEY, William (B. Creek)		186	3/	27...18.....0	0.....5.....7
COULTER, John Junr.		100	3/	15.....0.....0	0.....3.....0
COULTER, Joseph		253	4/	45...12.....0	0.....9.....1 1/2
CONNER. Margarett (Widow)		116	2/	11...12.....0	0.....2.....3 3/4
CURRY, Alexander		130	8/	52.....0.....0	0...10.....5
do.		40	4/	8.....0.....0	0.....1.....7 1/4
DUNLAP, William		70	10/	35.....0.....0	0.....7.....0
do.		70	5/	17...10.....0	0.....3.....6
DICKSON, John		160	15/	120.....0.....0	1.....2.....0
do.		106	17/6	92...15.....0	0...18.....7 1/4
do.		95	5/	23...15.....0	0.....4.....0
DUNLAP, Adam		100	7/	35.....0.....0	0.....7.....0
do.		185	3/	27...15.....0	0.....5.....6 3/4
DONALDSON, Robert		235	6/	70...10.....0	0...14.....1 1/4
DORAN, Jacob		238	5/	59...10.....0	0...11...10 1/2
do.		200	2/	20.....0.....0	0.....4.....0
DICKSON, Thomas		350	1/6	26.....5.....0	0.....5.....3
DOWNEY, Martha (Widow)		700	6/6	227...10.....0	2.....5.....6
DAYLEY, John		150	7/6	56.....5.....0	0...11.....3
DOUGHERTY. Hugh		200	4/6	45.....0.....0	0.....9.....0
DICKEY, James		158	8/	63.....4.....0	0...12.....7 3/4
DICKEY, Michael & John (Capt.)		425	9/	191...15.....0	1...18.....4 1/4
do.		73	2/	7.....6.....0	0.....1.....5 1/2
DICKEY, John (Capt., Exr. to Estate of					
Archibald HENDERSON, deed.)		100	9/	45.....0.....0	0.....9.....0
DONAGHU, Hugh		179	10/	89.....1.....0	0...16.....9 1/2
do.		122	3/	18.....6.....0	0.....3.....8
DONAGHU, James		302	3/	45.....6.....0	0.....9.....0 3/4
DALHOUSE, John		400	6/	120.....0.....0	1.....4.....0
do.		175	3/	26.....5.....0	0.....5.....3
DIXON, Archibald		130	10/	65.....0.....0	0...13.....0

(page 9. Augusta County Land Tax Return for 1782)

Proprietors Names	Lotts	Lands	Value p Acre	Valuation	Tax
DAVIS, Walter		160	9/	72.....0.....0	0...14.....5
do.		322	8/	128...16.....0	1.....5.....9
do.		5	8/	2.....0.....0	0.....0.....5
do.		50	2/	5.....0.....0	0.....1.....0
DOWEL, Philip		186	4/6	41...17.....0	0.....8.....4 1/2
DAVIDSON, John		280	3/	42.....0.....0	0.....8.....5
DOAK, John		307	9/	138.....3.....0	1.....7.....7 1/2
DOAK, Robert		266	5/	66.....0.....0	0...13.....2 1/2
DOAK, David		300	9/	135.....0.....0	1.....7.....0

(page 9. contd. Augusta County Land Tax Return for 1782

Proprietors Names	Lotts	Lands	Value p Acre	Valuation	Tax
(?) DOWN William, Henry HALL Tenant a qtr. acre Lott				30.....0.....0	0.....6.....0
ESDALE, Rebecca		299	10/	149...10.....0	1.....9...10 3/4
EVINS, Griffeth (Trumble's Compa)		139	5/	34...15.....0	0.....6...11 1/2
EHART, Francis		400	5/	100.....0.....0	1.....0.....0
EDMISTON, Matthew		200	11/	110.....0.....0	1.....2.....0
do.		225	5/	56.....5.....0	0...11.....3
do.		90	2/	9.....0.....0	0.....1.....9 1/2
ERWIN, Edward (N. River)		200	6/	60.....0.....0	0...12.....0
EDWARDS, Arthur		100	5/.	25.....0.....0	0.....5.....0
EWING, James (Capt.)		252	9/	113.....8.....0	.1.....2.....8 1/4
do.		150	2/	15.....0.....0	0.....3.....0
EWING, James Junr.		145	2/	14...10.....0	0.....2...11
ELLIOTT, James		300	8/	120.....0.....0	1.....4.....0
ELLIOTT, John		219 1/2	5/	54.....7.....6	0...10...10 1/2
ESTROP, Robert	1			30.....0.....0	0.....6.....0
ERWIN, Francis		294	8/	117...12.....0	1.....3.....6 1/4
ERWIN, John		156	5/	39.....0.....0	0.....7.....9 1/2
ERWIN, Edward		208	8/	83.....4.....0	0...16.....7 3/4
do.		135	5/	33...15.....0	0.....6.....9
ERWIN, Edward Junr.		200	8/	80.....0.....0	0...16.....0
do.		67	3/	10.....1.....0	0.....2.....0
ERWIN, Andrew		150	6/	45.....0.....0	0.....9.....0
ERWIN, Jane (Widow)		240	6/	72.....0.....0	0...14.....5
ERWIN, Samuel (M. River)		167	7/	58.....9.....0	0...11.....8 1/2
do.		122	2/	12.....4.....0	0.....2.....5 1/2
FISHER, George		200	5/	50.....0.....0	0...10.....0
FINDLEY, John Senr.		300	6/	90.....0.....0	0...18.....0
do.		100	2/6	12...10.....0	0.....2.....6
do.		238	2/6	29...15.....0	0.....5...10 1/2
FLOYD, Charles		90	2/6	11.....5.....0	0.....2.....3
FERIS, John		136	6/	40...16.....0	0...18.....2
FRANCIS, John Senr.		400	9/	180.....0.....0	1...16.....0
do.		400	2/6	50.....0.....0	0...10.....0
do.		50	2/	5...12.....0	0.....1.....1 3/4
do. on M. River joining G. MOFFETT		200	6/	60.....0.....0	0...12.....0
FISHER, Frederick		60	3/	9.....0.....0	0.....1.....9 1/2
FLEMING, William (Copper Smith)	1			30.....0.....0	0.....6.....0
do.	1			5.....0.....0	0.....1.....0

(page 10. Augusta County Land Tax Return for 1782)

Proprietors Names	Lotts	Lands	Value p Acre	Valuation	Tax
FUDGE, John		242	9/	108...18.....0	1.....1.....9 1/2
do.		220	3/	33.....0.....0	0.....6.....7 1/4
FRAIZER, James (Long Meadow)		236	6/	70...16.....0	0...14.....2
FRAIZER, Samuel Junr.		236	6/	70...16.....0	0...14.....2
FRAIZER, Samuel Senr.		400	1/6	30.....0.....0	0.....6.....0
FULTON, William		200	10/	100.....0.....0	1.....0.....0
FRAIM, Thomas		288	8/	118...14.....0	1.....3.....9
FOSTER, Thomas		250	7/6	87...10.....0	0...17.....6

(page 10 contd. Augusta County Land Tax Return for 1782)

Proprietors Names	Lotts	Lands	Value p Acre	Valuation	Tax
FOSTER, William Junr.		250	7/6	87...10.....0	0...17.....6
FINDLEY, Robert Senr.		97	10/	48...10.....0	0.....9.....8 1/2
FINDLEY, Robert Junr.		328	10/	164.....0.....0	1...12.....9 1/2
do.		200	2/	20.....0.....0	0.....4.....0
FINDLEY, William Junr. (Capt.)		180	10/	90.....0.....0	0...18.....0
FINDLEY, John (S. River)		216	11/	118...16.....0	1.....3.....3
do.		49	2/	4...18.....0	0.....1.....0
FINDLEY, John (Wheelright)		100	7/	35.....0.....0	0.....7.....0
FOSTER, James		64	3/	9...12.....0	0.....1...11
FULWIDER, Ulrich		169 1/2	4/	32.....2.....0	0.....6.....5
do.		40	2/	4.....0.....0	0.....0 9 1/2
do.		30	2/	3.....0.....0	0.....0.....7 1/2
FERGUSON, William (Shoemaker)		170	5/6	46...15.....0	0.....9.....4 1/2
FULTON, Hugh		250	10/	125.....0.....0	1.....5.....0
FULTON, Mary (Widow)		387	9/	174.....3.....0	1...11.....9 3/4
FULTON, John		309	10/	154...10.....0	1...10...10 3/4
GARDNER, James		85	8/	34.....0.....0	0.....6.....9 1/2
GAMBLE, John		275	11/	151.....5.....0	1...10.....3
do.		132	8	52...16.....0	0...10.....6 3/4
do.		97	8/	38...16.....0	0.....7.....9
GAMBLE, Robert		247	7/	86.....9.....0	0...17.....3 1/2
do.		200	5/	50.....0.....0	0...10.....0
do.		30	10/	15.....0.....0	0.....3.....0
GILKISON, Archibald		200	12/	240.....0.....0	2.....8.....0
GILKISON, Hugh		220	9/	99.....0.....0	0...19.....9 1/2
GIBSON, Samuel		226	10/	113.....0.....0	1.....2.....7 1/4
GILMORE, James Senr.		204	9/	91...16.....0	0...18.....4 1/2
GILKISON, William		265	6/	79...10.....0	0...15...11
GARDNER, Ensign		183	5/	45...15.....0	0.....9.....2
do.		40	7/	14.....0.....0	0.....2.....9 1/2
GRAGG, Robert		307	8/	122...16.....0	1.....4.....6 1/2
do.		206	2/6	25...15.....0	0.....5.....2
do.		400	2/	40.....0.....0	0.....8.....0
do.		60	2/	6.....0.....0	0.....1.....2 1/2
GRAGG, Thomas		70	2/6	8...15.....0	0.....1.....9
do.		62	6/	18...12.....0	0.....3.....8 1/2
do.		45	2/6	5...12.....6	0.....1.....1 1/2

(page 11. Augusta County Land Tax Return for 1782)

Proprietors Names	Lotts	Lands	Value p Acre	Valuation	Tax
GRIFFETH, Able (DICKEY's Compa)		150	7/	40...12.....0	0.....8.....1
do.		86	3/	12...18.....0	0.....2.....7
do.		80	2/6	10.....0.....0	0.....2.....0
do.		200	9/	90.....0.....0	0...18.....0
do.		62	2/6	7...15.....0	0.....1.....1 1/2
do.		316	2/	31...12.....0	0.....6.....4 1/2
GIBSON, Robert		142	6/	42...12.....0	0.....8.....6
(?) GRUVIR) William		100	4/6	22...10.....0	0.....4.....6
GRASS, Peter		50	4/	10.....0.....0	0.....2.....0
GOOPASTURE, Abraham		80	3/	12.....0.....0	0.....2.....5

(page 11 contd. Augusta County Land Tax Return for 1782

Proprietors Names	Lotts	Land	Value p Acre	Valuation	Tax
GLEBE LAND given in by the Overseers of the Poor, Moses HAYES, Tenant		200	8/	80.....0.....0	0...16.....0
GIBSON, Alexander Senr.		220	9/	99.....0.....0	0...19.....9 1/2
do.		159	8/	63...12.....0	0...12.....8 1/2
do.		50	2/6	6.....4.....0	0.....1.....3
do.		205	5/	51.....5.....0	0...10.....3
do.		50	3/6	8...15.....0	0.....1.....9
do.		20	2/	2.....0.....0	0.....0.....5
do.		20	2/	2.....0.....0	0.....0.....5
GARDNER, Francis Junr.		199	6/	59...14.....0	0...11...11 1/2
do.		136	2/	13...12.....0	0.....2.....8 1/2
GARDNER, Samuel (Heir to Francis, deced., William & James BELL, Exrs)		250	4/	50.....0.....0	0...10.....0
GRONDER, David	1			12...10.....0	0.....2.....6
do.	1/2			25.....0.....0	0.....5.....0
GRASS, Peter		225	6/	67...10.....0	0...13.....6
GRASS, Jacob Senr.		10	5/	2...10.....0	0.....0.....6
do.	1/2			25.....0.....0	0.....5.....0
GRAHAM, Thomas		450	8/	180.....0.....0	1...16.....0
GLENN, George		100	6/	30.....0.....0	0.....6.....0
GARRISON, John		294	9/	134.....0.....0	1...6.....9 1/2
do.		63	2/	6.....6.....0	0.....1.....3
GIBSON, David		250	4/	50.....0.....0	0...10.....0
GREEN, Hugh		145	4/	29.....0.....0	0.....5.....9 1/2
GIVENS, John Senr.		360	17/	306.....0.....0	3...1.....2 1/2
GIVENS, James		311	176	272.....2.....6	2...14.....5
GIVENS, John (Capt.)		138	14/	96...12.....0	0...19.....4
do.		48 1/2	2/	4...17.....0	0.....0...11 3/4
GIVENS, George		138	14/	96...12.....0	0...19.....4
do.		48 1/2	2/	4...17.....0	0.....0...11 3/4
GILESPY, William		179	9/	80...11.....0	0...16.....1 1/4
do.		60	2/	6.....0.....0	0.....1.....2 1/2
do.		30	2/	3.....0.....0	0.....0.....7 1/2
do.		200	8/6	85.....0.....0	0...17.....0
GILESPY, James		180	7/	63.....0.....0	0...12.....7 1/2
do.		120	2/	12.....0.....0	0.....2.....5

(page 12. Augusta County Land Tax Return for 1782)

Proprietors Names	Lotts	Land	Value p Acre	Valuation	Tax
GREENWOOD, Margarett (Widow) and Heirs of Josiah GREENWOOD)		105	7/6	39.....7.....6	0.....7...10 1/2
GUTHRY, William		490	6/6	159.....5.....0	1...11...10
GROVE, Windle		114	8/	45...12.....0	0.....9.....1 1/2
GRAHAM, William		350	3/	52...10.....0	0...10.....6
HAMILTON, Archibald		151	10/	75...10.....0	0...15.....1 3/4
do.		8	10/	4.....0.....0	0.....0.....9 1/4
HAMILTON, Audley		151	10/	75...10.....0	0...15.....1 3/4
do.		121	3/	18.....3.....0	0.....3.....7 3/4
HINDS, Samuel		200	8/	80.....0.....0	0...16.....0
HOG, Capt.'s Widow		305	10/	152...10.....0	1...10.....6

(page 12 contd. Augusta County Land Tax Return for 1782)

Proprietors Names	Lotts	Land	Value p Acre	Valuation	Tax
HALL, John		137	8/	54...16.....0	0...10.....6
do.		42	3/	6.....6.....0	0.....1.....3
do.		27 1/2	5/	6...15.....0	0.....1.....4 1/4
HINSDALE, Philip		95	5/	23...15.....0	0.....4.....9
do.		170	6/	51.....0.....0	0...10.....2 1/2
HAKE, Henry		213	5/	53.....5.....0	0...10.....8
HEIZER, Samuel		110	5/	27...10.....0	0.....5.....6
HUSTON, George		183	7/6	68...12.....6	0...13.....8 3/4
HOGSHEAD, David		216	8/	86.....8.....0	0...17.....3 1/2
do.		30	2/6	3...15.....0	0.....0.....9 1/2
HOGSHEAD, John Senr.		217	7/	75...19.....0	0...15.....2 1/2
do.		100	7/	35.....0.....0	0.....7.....0
do.		200	4/	40.....0.....0	0.....8.....0
do.		40	3/	6.....0.....0	0.....1.....2 1/2
HOGSHEAD, Michael		237	8/	94...16.....0	0...18...11 1/2
do.		100	8/	40.....0.....0	0.....8.....0
HUFF, Francis		300	4/	60.....0.....0	0...12.....0
HOGSHEAD, John's Widow & Heirs		172	7/	60.....4.....0	0...12.....0 1/2
do.		45	10/	22...10.....0	0.....4.....6
do.		40	3/	6.....0.....0	0.....1.....2 1/2
HOGSHEAD, David Junr.		370	5/	92...10.....0	0...18.....6
do.		90	2/6	11.....5.....0	0.....2.....3
HOGSHEAD, James Junr.		299	8/	119...12.....0	1.....3...11
do.		80	2/6	10.....0.....0	0.....2.....0
HANKEY, Simon		50	2/6	6.....5.....0	0.....1.....3
HAIR, John Junr.		200	6/	60.....0.....0	0...12.....0
HENDERSON, Joseph (near Town)		520	4/	104.....0.....0	1.....0.....9 1/2
HANGER, Frederick		225	5/	56.....5.....0	0...11.....3
HANDLEY, John Junr.		230	5/	57...10.....0	0...11.....6
HAMILTON, Arthur		585	6/	175...10.....0	1...15.....1 1/4
HAGHTHORN, James		530	7/	185...10.....0	1...17.....2 1/2
do.		220	12/	132.....0.....0	1.....6.....5
do.		50	2/	5.....0.....0	0.....1.....0

(page 13. Augusta County Land Tax Return for 1782)

Proprietors Names	Lotts	Land	Value p Acre	Valuation	Tax
HANNAH, Robert		100	3/6	17...10.....0	0.....3.....6
do.		60	2/6	7...10.....0	0.....1.....6
HAISE, Moses		115	4/	23.....0.....0	0.....4.....7 1/2
do.		105	4/	21.....0.....0	0.....4.....2 1/2
do.		100	4/	20.....0.....0	0.....4.....0
HAISE, James (Son of Moses)		170	3/	25...10.....0	0.....5.....1 1/2
do.		50	10/	25.....0.....0	0.....5.....0
HILL, James		84	2/6	10...10.....0	0.....2.... 1 1/4
do.		33	2/6	4.....2.....6	0.....0.....9 3/4
do.		17	2/6	2.....2.....6	0.....0.....5
HANGER, Peter		280	6/	84.....0.....0	0...16.....9
do.		365	6/	109...10.....0	1.....1...10 1/2
do.		85	3/	10...15.....0	0.....2.....2
do.		187	7/	65.....9.....0	0...13.....1 1/4
do.		280	4/	56.....0.....0	0...11.....2 1/4

(page 13 contd. Augusta County Land Tax Return for 1782)

Proprietors Names	Lotts	Land	Price p Acre	Valuation	Tax
HANGER, Peter		124	3/	18...12.....0	0.....3.....8
HANDLEY, John Senr.		150	8/	60.....0.....0	0...12.....0
HUGHES, Euphemia		30	5/	7...10.....0	0.....1.....6
do.	1/2			27...10.....0	0.....5.....6
do.	1			12...10.....0	0.....2.....6
do.	1			12...10.....0	0.....2.....6
do.	1			12...10.....0	0.....2.....6
do.	1			12...10.....0	0.....2.....6
do.	1			12...10.....0	0.....2.....6
do.	1			12...10.....0	0.....2.....6
do.	1			12...10.....0	0.....2.....6
HAMILTON, William (C. Creek)		150	8/	60.....0.....0	0...12.....0
do.		65	2/6	8.....2.....6	0.....1.....7 1/2
HAMILTON, John (L. Meadow)		200	3/6	35.....0.....0	0.....7.....0
do.		100	2/	10.....0.....0	0.....2.....0
HUTCHISON, Sarah		100	3/	15.....0.....0	0.....3.....0
HUNTER, William		240	2/6	30.....0.....0	0.....6.....0
HINES, Thomas		120	3/	18.....0.....0	0.....3.....7 1/2
HULL, Francis		150	7/	52...10.....0	0...10.....6
do.		47	3	7.....1.....0	0.....2.....4 3/4
HARRIS, Robert		200	5/6	55.....0.....0	0...11.....0
do.		200	5/6	55.....0.....0	0...11.....0
HINDS, William (Admr. to the Estate of					
Jno. HINDS, deced.		280	12/	183.....0.....0	1...16.....7 1/4
do.		140	2/	14.....0.....0	0.....2.....9 1/2
HENDERSON, James Senr.		300	9/	135.....0.....0	1.....7.....0
HENEMAN, Andrew		50	5/	12...10.....0	0.....2.....6
HARPER, John		100	7/	35.....0.....0	0.....7.....0
do.		55	4/	11.....0.....0	0.....2.....2 1/2
HOOKE, John		200	8/	80.....0.....0	0...16.....0
do. in partnership with DONAHO		82	2/	8.....4.....0	0.....1.....7 1/2
HOGSHEAD, William (Rockingham)		380	5/	95.....0.....0	0...19.....0

(page 14. Augusta County Land Tax Return for 1782)

Proprietors Names	Lotts	Land	Price p Acre	Valuation	Tax
HENDERSON, Samuel Junr.		75	10/	39...10.....0	0.....7.....6
do.		66 1/2	4/	13...6.....0	0.....2.....8
HARLES, Emanuel		200	7/	70.....0.....0	0...14.....0
HENDERSON, Samuel Senr.		200	16/	160.....0.....0	1...16.....0
do.		154	18/	138...12.....0	1.....7.....8 1/2
do.		117	2/	11...14.....0	0.....2.....4 1/2
do.		130	5/	32...10.....0	0.....6.....6
do.		60	2/	5.....0.....0	0.....1.....2 1/2
HUGHES, Con: "At Neil"		317	6/	94.....2.....0	0...18.....9 3/4
HUNT. Charles (Doctr.)		100	3/	15.....0.....0	0.....3.....0
do.		20	10/	10.....0.....0	0.....2.....0
HARBURN, David		47	6/	14.....2.....0	0.....2.....9 1/2
do.		153	3/	22...19.....0	0.....4.....7 1/4
HENDERSON, William		390	8/	156.....0.....0	1...11.....2 1/2
HENDERSON, David Esqr.		278 1/2	9/	125.....6.....6	1.....5.....0 3/4

(page 14 contd. Augusta County Land Tax Return for 1782)

Proprietors Names	Lotts	Land	Price p Acre	Valuation	Tax
HALL, Edward		220	10/	110.....0.....0	1.....2.....0
do.		125	3/	18...15.....0	0.....3.....9
do.		100	3/	15.....0.....0	0.....3.....0
do.		20	2/	2.....0.....0	0.....0.....5
do.		38	2/	3...16.....0	0.....0.....9
HUTCHISON, George		150	4/6	33...15.....0	0.....6.....9
HENDERSON, David Senr.		200	7/	70.....0.....0	0...14.....0
HENRY, Samuel		360	4/6	81.....0.....0	0...16.....2 1/2
do.		50	2/6	6.....5.....0	0.....1.....3
do.		300	5/6	82...10.....0	0...16.....6
HAYS, Samuel		209	10/	104...10.....0	1.....0...10 3/4
HUMPHREY, David		300	8/	120.....0.....0	1.....4.....0
HENRY, James (Weaver)		100	8/	40.....0.....0	0.....8.....0
HALL, Patrick		200	8/	80.....0.....0	0...16.....0
HENRY, James (B. Smith)		340	8/	136.....0.....0	1.....7.....2 1/2
do.		250	5/	62...10.....0	0...12.....6
do.		250	8/	100.....0.....0	1.....0.....0
HAYS, Patrick		212	9/	95.....8.....0	0...19.....1
HAYS, Hugh		250	10/	125.....0.....0	1.....5.....0
HUFFMAN, Gasper		100	6/	30.....0.....0	0.....6.....0
HUNTER, Samuel		196	8/	78.....8.....0	0...15.....8
do.		255	9/6	121.....2.....6	1.....4.....2 1/2
HUNTER, John		240	6/6	78.....0.....0	0...15.....7 1/4
HATTON, Mark (for William BLACKWOOD's Heirs)		100	7/6	38...10.....0	0.....7.....7 1/4
HAMILTON, Robert (Doctor), (Jno. CAMPBELL Tenant)		160	4/6	35.....0.....0	0.....7.....2 1/2
HUGHES, Thomas		156	5/	44.....0.....0	0.....8.....9 1/2
do.	1			25.....0.....0	0.....5.....0
do.	1			25.....0.....0	0.....5.....0
JOHNSON, William (Brinkey Neck)		112	10/	56.....0.....0	0...11.....2 1/2
JOHNSON, John		115	10/	57...10.....0	0...11.....6

(page 15. Augusta County Land Tax Return for 1782)

JONES, Eniss		400	8/1	160.....0.....0	1...12.....0
do.		260	5/	65.....0.....0	0...13.....0
JAMES, Daniel		85	5/	21.....5.....0	0.....4.....3
JOSEPH, Daniel		365	3/	54...15.....0	0...10...11 1/2
do.		85	6/	25...10.....0	0.....5.....1 1/4
INGLEMAN, William		180	5/	45.....0.....0	0.....9.....0
JACKSON, John (Doctor) (to be paid by Thomas RANKIN, Tenant)		278	7/	97.....6.....0	0...19.....5 1/2
JOHNSON, Zachariah (Capt.)		150	8/6	63...15.....0	0...12.....9
do.		109	3/6	24.....1.....6	0.....4.....9 3/4
do.		213	7/6	78...17.....6	0...15.....9 1/4
JAMESON, George		336	4/	67.....4.....0	0...13.....5 1/2
do.		165	3/	24...15.....0	0.....4...11 1/2
JOHNSON, William (Stiller)		185	7/	64...15.....0	0...12...11 1/2

(page 15, contd. Augusta County Land Tax Return for 1782)

Proprietors Names	Lotts	Land	Price p Acre	Valuation	Tax
JASPER, John (Black Smith)		200	3/	30.....0.....0	0.....6.....0
do.		82	2/	8.....4.....0	0.....1.....7 1/2
INMAN, Sarah and Heirs of Lazarus INMAN					
deced.		200	2/	20.....0.....0	0.....4.....0
JONES, Gabriel (Jacob GABERT, Resident)		200	8/	80.....0.....0	0...16.....0
do.		902	1/	45.....2.....0	0.....9.....0 1/4
KENNY Robert		141	20/	141.....0.....0	1.....8.....2 1/2
KENNY, Matt:		142	20/	142.....0.....0	1.....8.....5 1/2
KERR, Gilbart		175	8/	70.....0.....0	0...14.....0
KERR, John		160	5/	41.10.....0	9.....8.....5 1/2
do.		29	5/	7.....5.....0	0.....1.....4 3/4
do.		300	3/	45.....0.....0	0.....9.....0
KENNERLY, James Junr.		367	12/6	229.....7...6	2.....5...10 1/2
do.		190	5/	47.10.....0	0.....9.....6
KENNERLY, James		911	15/	683.....5.....0	6...16.....8
do.		200	5/	50.....0.....0	0...10.....0
do.		227	2/	22.14.....0	0.....4.....6 1/2
KENNERLY, Samuel		350	10/	175.....0.....0	1...15.....0
KENNERLY, Thomas		399	10/	199.10.....0	1...19...10 3/4
KENNERLY, Reuben		303	12/6	189.....7...6	1...17...10 1/2
KENADY, William		244	10/	122.....0.....0	1.....4.....5
KING, John (M. River)		220	2/6	27.10.....0	0.....5.....6
KIRK. James		215	8/	86.....0.....0	0...17.....2 1/2
KIRK, John		76	8/	30.....8.....0	0.....6.....1
do.		150	4/	30.....0.....0	0.....6.....0
KENNY, Bryan		128	5/	32.....0.....0	0.....6.....5
KERR, John (Trimble's Compa)		360	2/	36.....0.....0	0.....7.....2 1/2
KING, William		236	3/	35.....8.....0	0.....7.....1
do.		63	2/6	7.17....6	0.....1.....7
KIRKPATRICK, John		210	6/	63.....0.....0	0...12.....7 1/2
do.		100	3/	15.....0.....0	0.....3.....0

(page 16. Augusta County Land Tax Return for 1782)

Proprietors Names	Lotts	Land	Price p Acre	Valuation	Tax
KILLER, George		100	5/6	27.10.....0	0.....5.....6
do.		90	2/	9.....0.....0	0.....1.....9 3/4
do.		32	3/	4.16.....0	0.....0...11 3/4
KIDD, Daniel		173	7/	60.11.....0	0...12.....1 1/4
do.		87	5/	21.15.....0	0.....4.....4 1/4
do.	1			35.....0.....0	0.....7.....0
do.	1			15.....0.....0	0.....3.....0
do.	1			10.....0.....0	0.....2.....0
KING, John Senr. (N. Creek)		400	9/	180.....0.....0	1...16.....0
do.		500	4/	100.....0.....0	1.....0.....0
KERR, James (B. Smith)		300	3/	45.....0.....0	0.....9.....0
do.		97	3/	14.11.....0	0.....2...11
do.		127	7/	44.....9.....0	0.....8...10 3/4
do.		160	7/	56.....0.....0	0...11.....2 1/2
do.		21	20/	21.....0.....0	0.....4.....2 1/2
do.		90	10/	45.....0.....0	0.....9.....0

(page 16 contd. Augusta County Land Tax Return for 1782)

Proprietors Names	Lotts	Land	Price p Acre	Valuation	Tax
KERR, James (for Joseph MARTIN)		750	9/	337...10.....0	3.....7.....6
KENADY. James (Rockbridge)		289	4/	57...16.....0	0...11.....6 1/2
KERR, William		188	7/	65...16.....0	0...13.....2
KING, John (B. Creek)		169	4/	33...16.....0	0.....6.....9
do.		190	2/6	23...15.....0	0.....4.....9
LINER, Henry		50	10/	25.....0.....0	0.....5.....0
do.		90	5/	22...10.....0	0.....4.....6
LEWIS, George		106	5/	26...10.....0	0.....5.....4 1/4
LASSLY, Sarah (Widow)		113	12/	67...16.....0	0...13.....6
LASSLY, Samuel		113	12/	67...16.....0	. 0...13.....6
LEWIS, Samuel (Colo.)		660	12/	396.....0.....0	3...19.....1 1/2
do.		740	10/	370.....0.....0	3...14.....0
do.		400	3/	60.....0.....0	0...12.....0
LEWIS, William		400	9/	180.....0.....0	1...16.....0
do.		120	6/	36.....0.....0	0.....7 2 1/2
LEWISTON, William		130	5/	32...10.....0	0.....6.....6
do.		20	10/	10.....0.....0	0.....2.....0
do.		15	4/	3.....0.....0	0.....0.....7 1/2
LAW, Robert		200	6/	60.....0.....0	0...12.....0
LEDGERWOOD, William		187	8/	74...16.....0	0...14...11 3/4
LOCKHART, James		130	3/	19...10.....0	0.....3...10 3/4
LEVRNGOOD, Harmon		210	7/	73...10.....0	0...14.....8 1/4
do.		210	3/	31...10.....0	0.....6 3 1/2
do.		50	3/	7...10.....0	0.....1.....6
do.		50	2/	10.....0.....0	0.....2.....0
LOCKHART, Sarah	1/2			20.....0.....0	0.....4.....0
LONG, William (Majr.)		310	4/	62.....0.....0	0...12.....5
do.	1			35.....0.....0	0.....7.....0
do.	1			35.....0.....0	0.....7.....0
do.	1			25.....0.....0	0.....5.....0
LACKEY, Andrew (Weaver)		143	3/	21.....9.....0	0.....4.....3 1/2

(page 17. Augusta County Land Tax Return for 1782)

Proprietors Names	Lotts	Land	Price p Acre	Valuation	Tax
LOWRY, John		118	8/	71.....4.....0	0...14.....3
LEMONIS, George		150	6/	45.....0.....0	0.....9.....0
ditto		80	4/	16.....0.....0	0.....3.....2 1/2
LINK, Matthias		330	6/6	109.....5.....0	1.....1.....5 1/2
LAIRD, David (Capt.)		136	10/	68.....0.....0	0...13.....7 1/4
ditto		120	4/	24.....0.....0	0.....4.....9 1/2
LAMME, James		181 1/2	17/	154.....5.....6	1...10...10
LAMME, Samuel		181 1/2	17/	154.....5.....6	1...10...10
LESTER, Robert		128	4/	25...12.....0	0.....5.....1 1/2
LOGAN, John & William		280	6/	66.....0.....0	0...13.....2 1/4
ditto ditto		50		10.....0.....0	0.....2.....0
LESSLEY, Thomas		144	2/6	18.....0.....0	0.....3.....7 1/4
LEDICK, George		108	7/6	40...10.....0	0.....8.....1 1/4
LEREW, Abraham		171	8/3	70...11.....0	0...14.....1 1/4
ditto		150	9/	67...10.....0	0...13.....6

Proprietors Names	Lotts	Land	Price p Acre	Valuation	Tax
LONG, Alexander		10	3/	1...10.....0	0.....0.....3 1/2
ditto		400	1/6	30.....0.....0	0....6.....0
LONG, Francis		100	10/	50.....0.....0	0...10.....0
LONG, James		145	10/	72...10.....0	0...14.....6
LONG, Samuel		145	10/	72...10.....0	0...14.....6
LONG, David		200	8/	80.....0.....0	0...16.....0
LONG, Joseph		200	8/	80.....0.....0	0...16.....0
LONG, William (Legatee of Wm. L., deced)		250	10/	125.....0.....0	1.....5.....0
LOCKHART, William		300	1/6	22...10.....0	0.....4.....6
McCLURE, Andrew		164	12/	98.....8.....0	0...19.....8 1/2
ditto		33	5/	8.....5.....0	0.....1.....8
McCLURE, William		150	15/	112...10.....0	1.....2.....6
ditto		48	5/	12.....0.....0	0.....2.....5
MOWRA, Lewis		550	7/	192...10.....0	1...18.....6
MATHEWS, George (Colo.)		572	10/	286.....0.....0	2...17.....2 1/2
ditto		150	3/	22...10.....0	0.....4.....6
ditto		560	4/	112.....0.....0	1.....2.....5
ditto		16	5/	4.....0.....0	0.....0...10
ditto on Least Land		86 1/2	7/	30.....5.....6	0.....6.....0 1/2
ditto	1/2			30.....0.....0	0.....6.....0
ditto	1/2			15.....0.....0	0.....3.....0

(page 18. Augusta County Land Tax Return for 1782)

MATHEWS, ( )		375	6/	112...10.....0	1.....2.....6
ditto		79 1/2	8/	31...16.....0	(blank)
ditto		400	3/	60.....0.....0	0...12.....0
ditto		390	3/	58...10.....0	0...11.....8 1/4
ditto		40	5/	10.....0.....0	0.....2.....0
ditto		30	3/	4...10.....0	0.....0...10 3/4
ditto		120	3/	18.....0.....0	0.....7.....3 3/4
MATHEWS, Richard		900	6/	270.....0.....0	2...14.....4 1/2
MOFFET, George (Colo)		604	9/	271...16.....0	2...14.....4 1/2
ditto		120	6/	36.....0.....0	0.....7.....2 1/2
do.		200	2/	20.....0.....0	0.....4.....0
MILLS, Robert		82 1/2	8/	33.....0.....0	0.....6.....7
MARSHAL, John		269	6/	80...14.....0	0...16.....1 3/4
McCLANACHAND, John deced. Heirs		310	8/	124.....0.....0	1.....4.....9 1/2
ditto		190	2/	19.....0.....0	0.....3.....9 1/2
(? MAURAH), Henry		120	6/	36.....0.....0	0.....7.....2 1/2
McFEETERS, Alexander		303	8/	121.....4.....0	1.....4.....3
McVEAR, Daniel		120	15/	90.....0.....0	0...18.....0
ditto		420	3/	63.....0.....0	0.....6.....7 1/4
McKETRICK, Robert		200	7/	70.....0.....0	0...14.....0
ditto		170	3/	25...10.....0	0.....5.....1 1/2
ditto		90	2/	9.....0.....0	0.....1.....9 1/2
ditto		100	7/	35.....0.....0	0.....7.....0
MARROW, Samuel's Heirs.					
Robert McKETRICK to pay		216	4/	43.....4.....0	0.....8.....8
McKENNY, William		107	8/	42...16.....0	0.....8.....6 3/4
ditto		140	2/6	17...10.....0	0.....3.....6
ditto		15	2/6	1...17.....6	0.....0.....5

(page 18 contd. Augusta County Land Tax Return for 1782)

Proprietors Names	Lotts	Land	Price p Acre	Valuation	Tax
McKENNY, William		110	7/	38...10.....0	0.....7.....8 1/2
do.		128	2/6	16.....0.....0	0.....3.....2 3/4
McKENNY, John Junr.		136 1/2	8/	54...12.....0	0...10...11 1/2
ditto		33	2/6	4.....2.....6	0.....0...10
McKENNY, James		136 1/2	8/	54...12.....0	0...10...11 1/2
ditto		140	2/6	17...10.....0	0.....3.....6
ditto		33	2/6	4.....2.....6	0.....0...10

(page 19. Augusta County Land Tax Return for 1782)

Proprietors Names	Lotts	Land	Price p Acre	Valuation	Tax
ditto		50	2/6	6.....5.....0	0.....1.....3
McVAY, John		100	5/	25.....0.....0	0.....5.....0
ditto		100	2/	10.....0.....0	0.....2.....0
MALCOM, John		170	7/	59...10.....0	0...11...11
MOFFET, James		200	7/	70.....0.....0	0...14.....0
McCUTCHEON, Samuel Elder		442	9/	198...18.....0	1...19.....9 1/2
ditto		300	9/	135.....0.....0	1.....7.....0
MENIS, Thomas		122	3/	18.....6.....0	0.....3.....8
ditto R. POAGE		200	2/	20.....0.....0	0.....4.....0
ditto		136	2/	13...12.....0	0.....2.....8 1/2
ditto		78	2/	7...16.....0	0.....1.....6 1/2
McCLUNG, James		200	10/	100.....0.....0	1.....0.....0
ditto POAGE		40	3/	6.....0.....0	0.....1.....2 1/4
McFEETERS, John		388	9/	174...12.....0	1...14...11 1/4
ditto		321	7/6	120.....7.....6	1.....4.....0 3/4
MOFFET, John Senr.		234	10/	117.....0.....0	1.....3.....4 3/4
McCLANACHAN, Alexander (Colo.)		560	7/6	210.....0.....0	2.....2.....0
ditto		200	2/	20.....0.....0	0.....4.....0
McCLANACHAN, Robert		340	3/6	59...10.....0	0...11...10
MILLER, John Senr.		276	6/6	89...14.....0	0...17...11
McKINNEY, Alexander		310	3/6	54...15.....0	0...10...10 1/2
McKEE, Alexander		355	6/	106.....0.....0	1.....1.....2 1/2
MIERS, Ludwick		200	3/	30.....0.....0	0.....6.....0
McFEETERS, William		367	11/	201...17.....0	2.....8.....4 1/2
MERTIN, Joseph Capt. Bill Wm.		160	2/	16.....0.....0	0.....3.....2 1/2
McCLINTUCK, William Senr.		172	5/	43.....0.....0	0.....8.....7 1/4
McCLINTUCK, William		100	4/6	22...10.....0	0.....4.....6
MATHEWS, Sampson (Colo.)		196 2/3	3/	29...10.....0	0.....5...10 3/4
ditto		196 2/3	3/	29...10.....0	0.....5...10 3/4
ditto		196 2/3	3/	29...10.....0	0.....5...10 3/4
ditto	1			60.....0.....0	0...12.....0
ditto	1			35.....0.....0	0.....7.....0
ditto	1			20.....0.....0	0.....4.....0
ditto	1			20.....0.....0	0.....4.....0
ditto	1			15.....0.....0	0.....3.....0
ditto	1			15.....0.....0	0.....3.....0

(page 20. Augusta County Land Tax Return for 1782)

Proprietors Names	Lotts	Land	Price p Acre	Valuation	Tax
MARRO, Francis		250	5/	62...10.....0	0...12.....6
ditto		15	4/	3.....0.....0	0.....0.....8 1/4

(page 20 contd. Augusta County Land Tax Return for 1782)

Proprietors Names	Lotts	Land	Price p Acre	Valuation	Tax
MARROW, Francis	1/2			15.....0.....0	0.....3.....0
McDAVID, Patrick		50	10/	25.....0.....0	0.....5.....0
ditto		25	5/	6....5.....0	0.....1.....3
ditto for 3/4 of 1/4 one Leased to					
Wm. MURPHY	1			25.....0.....0	0.....5.....0
McDAVID, William		25	5/	6....5.....0	0.....1.....3
ditto		27	5/	6...15.....0	0.....1.....4
ditto	1/2			30.....0.....0	0.....6.....0
McDOWEL, Hugh	1/2			15.....0.....0	0.....3.....0
McDONOUGH, John		95	7/	33.....5.....0	0.....6.....8
ditto	1			20.....0.....0	0.....4.....0
ditto	1/2			15.....0.....0	0.....3.....0
McCUNE, John		270	12/	162.....0.....0	1...12.....5
ditto		51	3/	7...13.....0	0.....1.....7
McCLURE, Andrew Senr.		260	8/6	110...10.....0	1.....2.....1 1/4
McCLURE, John Junr.		236	4/	47.....0.....0	0.....9.....5
ditto		71	2/	7.....2.....0	0.....1.....5
McCLURE, Samuel		230	8/6	97...15.....0	0...19.....6 1/2
ditto		270	9/	121...10.....0	1.....4.....3 1/2
ditto		170	3/	25...10.....0	0.....5.....1 1/4
ditto		100	2/	10.....0.....0	0.....2.....0
MOODY, Robert		472	9/	212.....8.....0	2.....2.....6
McCLURE, Elenore (Widow)		350	5/	87...10.....0	0...17.....6
ditto		350	2/	35.....0.....0	0.....7.....0
McCHESNEY, James		223	7/	78.....1.....0	0...15.....7 1/4
McCHESNEY, Robert		124	7/	43.....8.....0	0.....8.....8 1/4
McCUTCHEON. Samuel (Capt.)		150	7/	52...10.....0	0...10.....6
ditto		80	3/	12.....0.....0	0.....2.....5
ditto		390	2/	39.....0.....0	0.....7.....9 1/2
McCUTCHEON, John		150	5/	35.....0.....0	0.....7.....0
MINGS, Henry		127	7/	44.....9.....0	0.....8...10 3/4
McKINNEY, John Junr.		170	5/6	46...15.....0	0.....9.....4 3/4
McNEIL, Robert		258	6/6	83...17.....0	0...16.....9 1/4
McNEIL, James		161	7/6	60.....7.....6	0...12.....0 3/4
ditto		183	6/	54...18.....0	0...11.....0
McCOMB, Andrew		130	8/	52.....0.....0	0...10.....5
ditto		40	3/	6.....0.....0	0.....1.....2 1/2

(page 21. Augusta County Land Tax Return for 1782)

Proprietors Names	Lotts	Land	Price p Acre	Valuation	Tax
MILLER, Gasper		160	6/	48.....0.....0	0.....9.....7 1/4
McCUTCHEON, Jospeh		383	5/	95...15.....0	0...19.....2
McMACHAN, John		330	5/	82...10.....0	0...16.....6
McKEE, Samuel		230	6/	69.....0.....0	0...13.....9 1/2
McCLURE, Josiah		128	6/	38.....8.....8	0.....7.....8 1/4
McLARRY, Hugh		143	7/	50.....1.....0	0...10.....0
McCOLLOCK, Thomas		80	9/	36.....0.....0	0.....7.....2 1/2
ditto		60	2/	6.....0.....0	0.....1.....2 1/2
ditto		16	2/	1...12.....0	0.....0.....3 3/4
MILLER, Henry from Works		1150	3/	172...10.....0	1...14.....6
ditto		518	2/	51...16.....0	0...10.....4 1/4

(page 21 contd. Augusta County Land Tax Return for 1782)

Proprietors Names	Lotts	Land	Price p Acre	Valuation	Tax
MILLER, Henry		592	2/	59.....6.....0	0...11...10 1/2
ditto		490	2/	49.....0.....0	0.....9.....9 1/2
ditto		160	3/	24.....0.....0	0.....4.....9 1/2
ditto		400	2/	40.....0.....0	0.....8.....0
ditto		212	4/	42.....8.....0	0.....8.....6
ditto		134	4/	26...16.....0	0.....5.....4
ditto		170	10/	85.....0.....0	0...17.....0
MARSHAL, George		232	4/6	52.....4.....0	0...10.....5 1/2
McCLURE, John Senr.		155	8/	62.....0.....0	0...12.....5
McCLURE, James		370	6/	81.....0.....0	0...16.....2 1/4
McDOUGAL, John		400	8/	160.....0.....0	1...12.....0
ditto		200	7/	70.....0.....0	0...14.....0
ditto		277	4/	55.....8.....0	0...11.....1
ditto		200	2/	20.....0.....0	0.....4.....0
MITCHEL, James Senr.		234	10/	127.....0.....0	1.....5.....5
ditto		259	10/6	135...19.....6	1.....7.....2 1/2
ditto		370	2/	37.....0.....0	0.....7.....5
ditto		95	2/	9...10.....0	0.....1...10 3/4
MITCHEL, William		176	9/	79.....4.....0	0...15...10
McCUTCHON, William		172	7/6	42.....0.....0	0.....8.....5
ditto		100	4/	20.....0.....0	0.....4.....0
ditto		100	2/	10.....0.....0	0.....2.....0
MOORE, William		154	5/	38...10.....0	0.....7.....8 1/2
MATEER, James		200	7/	70.....0.....0	0...14.....0
ditto		36	4/	7.....4.....0	0.....1.....5 1/2
MITCHEL, James Junior		200	9/	90.....0.....0	0...18.....0
ditto		166	8/	(blank)	0...13.....3 1/4

(page 22. Augusta County Land Tax Return for 1792)

Proprietors Names	Lotts	Land	Price p Acre	Valuation	Tax
MITCHEL, Thomas		234	8/6	99.....9.....0	0...19...10 3/4
MITCHEL, Alexander		200	7/	70.....0.....0	0...14.....0
ditto		100	4/6	22...10.....0	0.....4.....6
McCUTCHON, William Senr.		231	2/6	28...17.....6	0.....5.....9 1/2
McCANTREE, Richard		150	3/	22...10.....0	0.....4.....8
NICKLE, John		250	8/	100.....0.....0	1.....0.....0
ditto		45	3/	6...15.....0	0.....1.....4 1/2
NELSON, Thomas		145	4/6	32...12.....6	0.....6.....6 1/4
ditto as Admr. to Thomas NELSON, deced.		84	4/6	18...18.....0	0.....3.....9 1/4
ditto for ditto		40	2/	4.....0.....0	0.....0.....9 3/4
NORTH, Phillip (Orphant) Owen OWENS Tenant	1			60.....0.....0	0...12.....0
ditto		50	6/	15.....0.....0	0.....3.....0
OLINGER, Phillip Senr.		180	8/	72.....0.....0	0...14.....5
OLINGER, Phillip Junr.		144	7/6	50.....8.....0	0...10.....1
OLIVER, John Senr.		150	9/	67...10.....0	0...13.....6
ditto		150	2/	15.....0.....0	0.....3.....0
OLIVER, James		150	9/	67...10.....0	0...13.....6
ditto		310	1/	15...10.....0	0.....3.....1 1/4

(page 22 contd. Augusta County Land Tax Return for 1782)

Proprietors Names	Lotts	Land	Price p Acre	Valuation	Tax
OTTS, John		155	3/	23.....5.....0	0.....4.....8
POAGE, Thomas		262	12/6	163...15.....0	1...12.....9
ditto		200	12/6	125.....0.....0	1.....5.....0
ditto		200	5/	50.....0.....0	0...10.....0
ditto		98	5/	24...10.....0	0.....4...11
ditto	1/2			5.....0.....0	0.....1.....0
PATTERSON, Deaf John		254		76.....4.....0	0...15.....3
PATTERSON, John (below Staunton)		190	12/6	118...15.....0	1.....3.....9
ditto		164	12/6	102...10.....0	1.....0.....6
PATTERSON, Thomas		167	17/6	146.....2.....6	1.....8.....3
ditto		178	6/	53.....8.....0	0...10.....8
PERREY, John		200	6/	60.....0.....0	0...12.....0
PATTERSON, James Senr.		230	8/	92.....0.....0	0...18.....5
PATTERSON, Joseph (Capt.)		114	8/	45...12.....0	0.....9.....1 1/4

(page 23. Augusta County Land Tax Return for 1782)

Proprietors Names	Lotts	Land	Price p Acre	Valuation	Tax
PATTERSON, William (Dumb)		70	6/	21.....0.....0	0.....5.....2 1/4
PATTERSON, Robert (N. Mountain)		202	9/	90...18.....0	0...18.....2 1/4
PHILLIPS, John		171	7/	62...13.....0	0...12.....6
ditto		86	2/	8...12.....0	0.....1.....8 1/2
ditto		50	2/	5.....0.....0	0.....1.....0
PARRISS, John (Taylor)		213	5/	53.....5.....0	0...10.....7 3/4
PERREY, John		210	6/	62.....0.....0	0...12.....7 1/2
PERREY, James		180	5/	45.....0.....0	0.....9.....0
PERREY, George		180	5/6	49...10.....0	0.....9...10 3/4
PERREY, Joshua	1			25.....0.....0	0.....5.....0
PECK, Jacob		188	3/	28.....7.....0	0.....5.....8 1/4
ditto		2	10/	1.....0.....0	0.....0.....2 1/2
PILSON, Samuel		148	9/	66...12.....0	0...13.....3 3/4
ditto		170	2/	17.....0.....0	0.....3.....5
PALMER, William		388	4/	77...12.....0	0...15.....6
PATTON, Hance		127	7/	44.....9.....0	0.....8...10 3/4
PATTERSON, William (S. River)		200	10/	100.....0.....0	1.....0.....0
PATTERSON, James (S. River)		111	12/	66...12.....0	0...13.....3 3/4
ditto		56	2/	5.....2.....0	0.....1.....1 1/2
PATRICK, John		437	15/	327...15.....0	3.....5.....6 1/4
ditto		280	7/	98.....0.....0	0...19.....7 1/2
ditto		235	2/	23...10.....0	0.....4.....8 1/2
PURVIS, William		184	5/	46.....0.....0	0.....9.....2 1/2
POAGE, William (at Pollock)		290	4/6	65.....5.....0	0...13.....0 1/2
PECK, Stephen		266	8/	106.....8.....0	1.....1.....3 1/4
ROBERTSON, Mathew		196	20/	196.....0.....0	1...19.....2
ditto		170	5/	42...10.....0	0.....8.....6
ditto		75	10/	39.....0.....0	0.....7.....9
RUTLEDGE, Edward		250	12/	150.....0.....0	1...10.....0
ditto		26	5/	6...10.....0	0.....1.....2
RUSSLE, Andrew		200	8/	80.....0.....0	0...16.....0
ditto		96	2/	9...12.....0	0.....1...10

(page 23 contd. Augusta County Land Tax Return for 1782

Proprietors Names	Lotts	Land	Price p Acre	Valuation	Tax
RICHEY, John (Black Smith)		200	12/6	125.....0.....0	1.....5.....0

(page 24. Augusta County Land Tax Return for 1782)

Proprietors Names	Lotts	Land	Price p Acre	Valuation	Tax
RANKIN, James		120	8/	48.....0.....0	0.....9.....7
ditto		380	3/	57.....0.....0	0...11.....5
RITCHEY, Hugh (Doctor)		60	6/	18.....0.....0	0.....3.....7
RUNKLE. Samuel		160	11/	88.....0.....0	0...17.....1 1/2
ditto		200	3/	30.....0.....0	0.....6.....0
ditto		127	2/6	15...12.....6	0.....3.....2 1/4
ROLSTON, John		300	3/	45.....0.....0	0.....9.....0
ROBERTSON, Mary (Widow) & Heirs to John ROBERTSON, deced.		200	9/	90.....0.....0	0...18.....0
ROLSTON, William		100	7/	38...10.....0	0.....7.....8 1/2
ditto		100	3/	15.....0.....0	0.....3.....0
ROLSTON, Samuel		113	7/	39...11.....0	0.....7...11
ditto		137	2/6	17.....2.....6	0.....3.....5
REID, Robert (Shoemaker)		81	7/	28.....7.....0	0.....5.....8
ditto		190	1/6	14.....5.....0	0.....2...10 1/2
REID, Alexander		142	7/	49...14.....0	0.....9...11 1/4
ditto		92	6/	27...12.....0	0.....5.....6
REID, Mathew (deced) (John POAGE, Esqr. Administrator)		200	3/	30.....0.....0	0.....6.....0
REDNOUR, Joseph		95	3/	14.....5.....0	0.....2...10
REID, Robert (Staunton)		300	10/	150.....0.....0	1...10.....0
ditto		400	3/	60.....0.....0	0...12.....0
ditto		50	5/	12...10.....0	0.....2.....6
ditto		25	5/	6.....5.....0	0.....1.....3
ditto	1/2			30.....0.....0	0.....6.....0
ditto	1/4			15.....0.....0	0.....3.....0
RUSSLE, Robert		196	7/	68...12.....0	0...13.....8 1/2
ditto		72	3/	10...16.....0	0.....2.....2
ditto		33	2/6	4.....2.....6	0.....0.....9 3/4
RUSSLE, Joshua		150	7/6	52...10.....0	0...10.....6
ditto		53	2/6	6...15.....0	0.....1.....4 1/4
RODGERS, Seth		135	10/	67...10.....0	0...13.....6
RODGERS, Thomas		298	6/	88.....8.....0	0...17.....8 1/4
RUSK, Margaret (Widow)		173	8/	69.....4.....0	0...12...10 1/
RUSK, William		107	5/6	29.....8.....6	0.....5...10 1/2
ditto of Robert BELL		190	3/	22...10.....0	0.....5.....8 1/2

(page 25. Augusta County Land Tax Return for 1782)

Proprietors Names	Lotts	Land	Price p Acre	Valuation	Tax
RUSK, David		176	4/	35.....4.....0	0.....7.....0 1/2
RUSK, Robert		160	8/	64.....0.....0	0...12.....9 1/2
RANKIN, Richard		1300	4/6	292...10.....0	2...18.....6
REBURN, John Senr.		320	6/	96.....0.....0	0...19.....2 1/2
RANKIN, Thomas (Capt.)		380	7/	133.....0.....0	1.....6.....7 1/4
ditto		109	15/	81...15.....0	0...15.....4 1/2
RANKIN, John		110	15/	82...10.....0	0...16.....6
RANKIN, William		109	15/	81...15.....0	0...15.....4 1/2

(page 25 contd. Augusta County Land Tax Return for year 1782)

Proprietors Names	Lotts	Land	Price p Acre	Valuation	Tax
RAMSEY, John Senr.		320	10/	160.....0.....0	1...16.....0
ditto		88	12/	52...16.....0	0...10.....6 3/4
ditto		97	2/	9...14.....0	0.....1...11 1/2
ditto		28	3/	4.....4.....0	0.....0...10
ditto		70	2/	7.....0.....0	0.....1.....5
RAMSEY, Andrew		165	12/6	103.....2...6	1.....0.....7 1/4
ditto		146	2/	14...12.....0	0.....2...11
RAMSEY, John Junr.		408	6/	122.....8.....0	1.....4.....6
ditto		100	2/	11.....0.....0	0.....2.....2 1/2
ditto		60	3/	9.....0.....0	0.....1.....9 1/2
ditto		75	2/	7...10.....0	.0.....1.....6
ROBERTSON, William Senr.		470	15/	354...15.....0	3...10...11 1/2
ditto		280	8/	112.....0.....0	1.....2.....5
ditto		100	15/	75.....0.....0	0...15.....0
ditto		96	2/	9...12.....0	0.....1...10 3/4
ditto		90	2/	9.....0.....0	0.....1.....9 1/4
ROBERTSON, James Junr.		350	10/	150.....0.....0	1...10.....0
ROGERS, Robert		478	4/6	107...11.....0	1.....1.....6
ditto		145	8/	58.....0.....0	0...11.....7 1/4
RUTLEDGE, Thomas Senr.		220	8/6	93...10.....0	0...18.....8 1/2
RIDDLE, Cornelius (Capt.)		317 3/4	9/	142...13.....0	1.....8.....6 1/4
RAY, Daniel		100	3/6	17...10.....0	0.....3.....6
RICE, William		120	6/	36.....0.....0	0.....7.....2 1/2
ROWAN, James (Tanner)		228	7/	79...16.....0	0...15...11 1/2
RICHARDSON, Phillamon		250	9/	112...10.....0	1.....2.....6
ditto		246	9/	110...14.....0	1.....2.....2

(page 26. Augusta County Land Tax Return for 1782)

Proprietors Names	Lotts	Land	Price p Acre	Valuation	Tax
STEWART, John		200	20/	200.....0.....0	2.....0.....0
ditto		40	8/	16.....0.....0	0.....3.....2 1/4
ditto		196	20/	196.....0.....0	1...19.....2
STORY, James		175	15/	131.....5.....0	1...16.....3
STORY, Thomas		100	17/7	87...10.....0	0...17.....6
STORY, Ann (Widow)		100	20/	100.....0.....0	1.....0.....0
SURSASS, John		150	5/	37...10.....0	0.....7.....6
SILLEN, Gasper		100	6/	30.....0.....0	0.....6.....0
ditto		78	3/	11...14.....0	0.....2.....4
SHIRES, John		200	5/	50.....0.....0	0...10.....0
SMITH, Lewis		923	6/	276...18.....0	2...15.....4 1/2
SCOTT, Andrew		200	5/6	55.....0.....0	0...10.....0
ditto		82	2/6	10.....5.....0	0.....2.....0 1/2
ditto		66	2/9	9.....1.....6	0.....1...10
SCOTT, Thomas		171	10/	85...10.....0	0...17.....1 1/4
ditto		68	2/3	7...13.....0	0.....1.....6 1/4
SWINK, Henry		109	5/	27.....5.....0	0.....5.....5 1/4
SWINK, Larance		125	5/	31.....5.....0	0.....6.....3
SWALLOW, Jacob		120	6/	36.....0.....0	0.....7.....2 1/4
SCOTT, Thomas Junr.		302	4/	60.....8.....0	0...12.....1
SAWYER, James Junr.		230	8/	92.....0.....0	0...18....( )
ditto		100	3/	15.....0.....0	0.....3.....0

(page 26 contd. Augusta County Land Tax Return for 1782)

Proprietors Name	Lotts	Land	Price p Acre	Valuation	Tax
SAWYER, James Junr.		115	3/	17.....5.....0	0.....3.....5 1/2
SUNKARD, John		230	8/	92.....0.....0	0...18.....5
SMITH John; Haires		200	9/	90.....0.....0	0...18.....0
STEVENSON, John		125	9/	26.....5.....0	0...11.....3
ditto		142	3/	21.....6.....0	0.....5.....3
STEVENSON, Adam		125	9/	26.....5.....0	0...11.....3
ditto		142	3/	21.....6.....0	0.....5.....3
SHAUNDS, Leonard		330	4/	66.....0.....0	0...13.....2 1/2
SCOTT, Archibald (Revd.)		150	6/	45.....0.....0	0.....9.....0
SLUSHER, Conrod		320	5/	80.....0.....0	0...16.....0
STEEL, Samuel (Black Smith)		113	7/	39...11.....0	0.....7...11

(page 27. Augusta County Land Tax Return for 1782)

Proprietors Name	Lotts	Land	Price p Acre	Valuation	Tax
STEEL, David Senr.		186	7/	54.....2.....0	0...13.....0
SHIELDS, William Senr.		100	3/6	17...10.....0	0.....3.....6
SHIELDS, William Junr.		84	3/	12...12.....0	0.....2.....6
SHARP, John Senr.		470	5/	117...10.....0	1.....3.....6
SHARP, John Junr.		73	3/	10...19.....0	0.....2.....2 1/4
STEWART, Elizabeth (Widow)		100	10/	50.....0.....0	0...10.....0
SCOTT, John		452	3/	67...16.....0	0...13.....6 3/4
SYLOR, Jacob		334	6/	100.....0.....0	1.....0.....0
STARRET, William		343	4/6	77.....3.....0	0...15.....5
SUMMERS, John		200	4/6	45.....0.....0	0.....9.....0
SPOTS, George		30	4/	6.....0.....0	0.....1.....2 1/2
ditto	1			25.....0.....0	0.....5.....0
SMITH, John (see Mr.		80	5/	20.....0.....0	0.....4.....0
ditto	1			40.....0.....0	0.....8.....0
SINKLER, Alexander (Marcht.)		80	15/	60.....0.....0	0...12.....0
ditto		50	5/	12...10.....0	0.....2.....6
ditto		80	3/	12.....0.....0	0.....2.....4 1/2
ditto	1			35.....0.....0	0.....7.....0
ditto	1/2			35.....0.....0	0.....7.....0
ditto	1/2			30.....0.....0	0.....6.....0
SMITH, Zachariah		160	5/	40.....0.....0	0.....8.....0
SPROUL, William		490	9/	180.....0.....0	1...16.....0
SPROUL, Alexander		300	7/	105.....0.....0	1.....1.....0
SPROUL, James		300	7/6	112...10.....0	1.....2.....6
SEAWRIGHT, John Senr.		400	9/	180.....0.....0	1...16.....0
ditto		200	2/	20.....0.....0	0.....4.....0
SMITH, Abraham (Rockingham)		540	7/0	189.....0.....0	1...19.....7 1/2
SHEETS, Jacob (Black Smith)		415	6/	124...10.....0	1.....4...10 3/4
ditto		280	4/	56.....0.....0	0...11.....2 1/2
STEEL, Frederick		419	3/	62...17.....0	0...12.....6 3/4
ditto		77	2/	7...14.....0	0.....1.....6 1/2
STEVEN, Robert		180	2/	18.....0.....0	0.....3.....7 1/4

(page 28. Augusta County Land Tax Return for 1782)

Proprietors Name	Lotts	Land	Price p Acre	Valuation	Tax
STEEL, Andrew		300	10/	150.....0.....0	1...10.....0
STEEL, Samuel Senr.		200	10/	100.....0.....0	1.....0.....0
ditto		175	2/	17...10.....0	0.....3.....6

(page 28 contd. Augusta County Land Tax Return for 1782)

Proprietors Names	Lotts	Land	Price p Acre	Valuation	Tax
STEEL, Samuel Senr.		233	2/	23.....6.....0	0.....4.....7 1/2
STEWART. Alexander (Majr.)		100	12/	60.....0.....0	0...12.....0
ditto		320	2/	32.....0.....0	0.....6.....5
ditto		180	4/	36.....0.....0	0.....7.....2 1/2
John RIDDLE Tenant					1.....5.....7 1/2
STEWART, Benjamin		497	7/6	179...12.....6	1...15...11
STEEL, James Esqr.		200	10/	100.....0.....0	1.....0.....0
ditto		187 1/2	5/	46...17.....6	0.....9.....4 1/2
ditto		187 1/2	3/	28.....2.....6	0.....5.....7 1/2
SUMMERS, John (Black Smith)		250	5/	62.....0.....0	0...12.....6
SEAWRIGHT, Alexander		252	6/	75...12.....0	0...15.....1 1/2
STEVENSON, Thomas		180	4/	36.....0.....0	0.....7.....2 1/2
STEEL, David		244	6/	73.....4.....0	0...14.....7 1/2
ditto		50	8/	20.....0.....0	0.....4.....0
STEEL, Samuel (Taylor)		150	5/	37...10.....0	0.....7.....6
SINK, John		100	2/	10.....0.....0	0.....2.....0
STEEL, Robert Senr.		160	7/	56.....0.....0	0...11.....2 1/2
STEEL, Samuel (Holster)		260	8/	104.....0.....0	1.....0 9 1/2
STEEL, James		230	7/	80...10.....0	0...16.....1 1/4
SHOLTS. George		154	6/	46.....4.....0	0.....9.....3
STEEL, Nathaniel		484	10/	242.....0.....0	2.....8.....3
SHIELDS, William (Miller)		70	8/	28.....0.....0	0.....5.....7 1/4
SHIELDS, Thomas		200	8/6	85.....0.....0	0...17.....0
STIRLING, John		231	7/6	86...12.....6	0...17.....4
SHIELDS, John (Pine Run)		129	2/6	16.....2.....6	0.....3.....2 1/2
SHIELDS, Margaret (Widow) & Heirs of Thomas SHIELDS, deced)		225	6/6	73.....2.....6	0...14.....7 1/2
ditto		43	2/	4.....6.....0	0.....0...10 1/2
SHIELDS, William (Ch. Creek)		200	6/6	65.....0.....0	0...13.....0
STARRET, Robert (Back Creek)		128	3/	18...18.....0	0.....3.....9 1/4
SCOTT, William (Sadler)		224		56.....0.....0	0...11.....2 1/2
ditto		100		10.....0.....0	0.....2.....0
ditto for Robert STARRET (Back Creek)		50	1/6	3...15.....0	0.....0.....9

(page 29, Augusta County Land Tax Return for 1782)

Proprietors Names	Lotts	Land	Price p Acre	Valuation	Tax
STEWART, Thomas (S. River)		352	9/	138.....8.....0	1...11.....8 1/4
ditto		120	4/	34.....0.....0	0.....4.....9 1/2
ditto		128	2/	22...16.....0	0.....4.....6 1/2
ditto one half acre	1/2			40.....0.....0	0.....8.....0
TROTHER, William (Mid. R.)		190	20/	190.....0.....0	1...18.....0
ditto		70	5/	17...10.....0	0.....3.....6
TURK, Thomas Senr.		218 1/2	17/6	185...14.....9	1...17.....1 3/4
ditto		150	5/	37...10.....0	0.....7.....6
ditto		400	3/	60.....0.....0	0...12.....0
ditto		190	8/	76.....0.....0	0...15.....2 1/2
TURK, Thomas Junr.		218 1/2	17/6	185...14.....9	1...17.....1 3/4
ditto		150	5/	37...10.....0	0.....7.....6
TEAS, Charles		150	9/	72.....0.....0	0...14.....5
ditto		98	2/	9...16.....0	0.....1...11 1/2

(page 29 contd. Augusta County Land Tax Return for 1782)

Propriertors Names	Lotts	Land	Price p Acre	Valuation	Tax
TRIMBLE, David		160	8/	64.....0.....0	0...12.....9 1/2
ditto		140	2/6	17...10...0	0.....3.....6
ditto		110	2/6	13...15...0	0.....2.....9
TANDY, Smith		300	6/	98.....0.....0	0...18.....0
TRIMBLE, John (Son to David)		48	5/	12.....0.....0	0.....2.....5
ditto		160	3/	24.....0.....0	0....4.....9 1/2
TRIMBLE, James (Capt.)		300	8/	120.....0.....0	1.....4.....0
ditto		200	3/	37...10...0	0.....7.....6
TALMON, Benjamin		145	8/	58.....0.....0	0...11.....8 1/2
ditto		154	6/	46.....4.....0	0.....9....3
ditto		136	4/	27.....4.....0	0.....5.....5
ditto		290	2/6	36.....5.....0	0.....7.....2 1/2
THOMPSON, Andrew		270	5/	67...10.....0	0...13.....6
ditto		122	4/	24...8.....0	0.....4...10
TROTTER, James Esqr.		192	7/	67.....4.....0	0...13....3 1/2
ditto		45	2/6	5...12...6	0.....1.....1 1/4
TROTTER, James Junr.		130	9/	58...10.....0	0...11....3 1/2
TROTTER, David		170	9/	76...10.....0	0...15....3 1/2
TRIMBLE, Walter		188	10/	94.....0.....0	0...18.....9 1/2
ditto		62	4/	12.....8.....0	0.....2.....6

(page 30. Augusta County Land Tax Return for 1782)

Propriertors Names	Lotts	Land	Price p Acre	Valuation	Tax
TRIMBLE, Robert		167	12/	100.....4.....0	1.....0.....9 1/2
ditto		34	2/	3.....8.....0	0.....0....8 1/4
TRIMBLE, John Senr.		343	12/	205...16.....0	2.....1....2
TROTTER, Joseph		150	6/	45.....0.....0	0.....9.....0
ditto		82	2/	8.....0.....0	0.....1....7 1/2
TRIMBLE, James		317	5/	79.....5.....0	0...13...10
TEAFORD, Jacob		200	4/	40.....0.....0	0.....8.....0
THOMPSON, Margaret		236	2/6	29...10.....0	0.....5...10 1/4
THOMPSON, Robert (Capt.)		200	9/	90.....0.....0	0...18.....0
ditto		140	2/	14.....0.....0	0.....2.....9 1/2
THOMPSON, Alexander (Colo.)		302	9/	135.....0.....0	1.....7.....2 1/4
ditto		130	2/	13.....0.....0	0.....2....8 1/2
THOMPSON, William (W. Creek)		100	4/	20.....0.....0	0.....4.....0
TAYLOR, Joseph		200	4/	40.....0.....0	0.....8.....0
TEAS, Mary (Widow)		400	15/	300.....0.....0	3.....0.....0
TATE, Robert		186	8/	74...10.....0	0...14...10
ditto		146	5/	36...10.....0	0.....5.....3 1/2
ditto	23	8/		9.....0.....0	0.....1...10
THOMPSON, Joseph		155	5/	32...15.....0	0.....7....9
TATE, Sarah (Widow)		200	7/	70.....0.....0	0...14.....0
ditto		27	7/	9.....9.....0	0.....1...10 3/4
TEAT. Thomas		200	7/6	75.....0.....0	0...15.....0
TEAT, John Senr.		244	8/6	103...14.....0	1.....0.....0
ditto		400	1/6	30.....0.....0	0.....6.....0
TEAT, William (Capt.)		160	5/	40.....0.....0	0.....8.....0
THOMPSON, William		306	7/	107.....2.....0	1.....1....5
TORBIT, Hugh		314	8/6	133.....9.....0	1.....6....8 1/4

(page 30 contd. Augusta County Land Tax Return for 1782)

Proprietors Names	Lotts	Land	Price p Acre	Valuation	Tax
THOMPSON, Mathew		202	7/	70...14.....0	0...14.....2
ditto		110	3/6	19.....5.....0	0.....3...10
ditto to Patrick BUCHANAN		60	2/	6.....0.....0	0.....1.....2
THOMPSON, John		255	5/	62...15.....0	0...12.....9
ditto		110	3/6	19.....5.....0	0.....3...10
THOMPSON, Alexander		150	6/6	48...15.....0	0.....9.....9
USHER, William		130	3/	19...10.....0	0.....3...10 3/4
UTT, John Senr.		180	3/	27.....0.....0	0.....5.....5
ditto		50	2/	5.....0.....0	0.....1.....0

(page 31, Augusta County Land Tax Return for 1782)

Proprietors Names	Lotts	Land	Price p Acre	Valuation	Tax
VANCE, John deced., Heirs					
John MOFFETT, Executor		385	6/	91...10.....0	0...18.....3 1/2
VERNER, Henry		107	5/	26...15.....0	0.....5.....2
VANLEAR, Jacob		490	4/6	110.....5.....0	1.....2.....0 1/2
do. Executor for the Estate of George					
ROBERTSON, deced, JOHN SHIELDS					
Tennant		141	6/	42...16.....0	0.....8.....0 1/4
WHITE, David		265	15/	198...15.....0	1...19.....9
ditto		150	3/	22...10.....0	0.....4.....6
ditto		92	5.	23.....0.....0	0.....4.....7 1/4
WHITE, Isaac Junr.		243	11/	133...13.....0	1.....6.....9
ditto		94	1/6	7.....1.....0	0.....1.....5
WALLACE, Jean (Widow)		200	12/6	125.....0.....0	1.....5.....0
ditto		200	5/	50.....0.....0	0...10.....0
WOODS, Mary (Widow)		110	5/	27...10.....0	0.....4.....6
WALLACE, John		250	4/	50.....0.....0	0...10.....0
WILSON, William		301	10/	150...10.....0	1...10.....1 1/4
WILSON, Robert Junr.		290	10/	145.....0.....0	1.....9.....0
WILLIAMS, Moses		300	5/	75.....0.....0	0...15.....0
WILSON, James		115	12/6	71...17.....6	0...14.....4 1/2
ditto		190	2/	19.....0.....0	0.....3.....9 1/2
WILLIAMS, David		200	6/	60.....0.....0	0...12.....0
WADDLE, Joseph Junr.		152	6/	45...12.....0	0.....9.....1 1/2
WADDLE, Thomas Senr.		263	9/	118.....7.....0	1.....3.....8
ditto		66	2/6	8.....5.....0	0.....1.....8
WADDLE, James		130	9/	58...10.....0	0...11.....6
WOODS, Steven		140	4/6	31...10.....0	0.....6.....3 1/2
WILSON, Mathew		343	9/	136.....2.....0	1...11.....2 1/2
ditto		299	5/	74...15.....0	0...14...11 1/2
WALLACE Robert		160	10/	80.....0.....0	0...16.....0
WALLACE, Jennett & Rachel					
James NELSON, Tennant		100	10/	50.....0.....0	0...10.....0
WILLIAMS, John		150	2/6	18...15.....0	0.....3.....9
WIDEMAN, Peter		200	3/6	35.....0.....0	0.....7.....0
WALTER, Henry (see Danl. KIDD)	1			10.....0.....0	0.....2.....0
WILSON, Marth (Widow)	1/4 of 1/3			10.....0.....0	0.....2.....0
WRIGHT, Samuel		155	9/	74...15.....0	0...14...11 1/2

(page 32. Augusta County Land Tax Return for 1782)

Proprietors Names	Lotts	Land	Price p Acre	Valuation	Tax
WILLIAMS, Richard					
Hugh DANIEL Tennant to pay		120	3/6	21.....0.....0	0.....4.....2 1/2
WALKER, Alexander Junr. deced. Heirs					
Thomas BLEAKLY, Tennant		287	7/	100.....9.....0	1.....0.....1 1/2
Said Heirs in Partnership with					
Thomas CONOLY		79 1/2	2/	7...19.....0	0.....1.....7 1/4
WALKER, Alexander Senr., deced. Capt. John					
CAMP & ARTHER CONOLY, Executors		424	6/	127.....4.....0	1.....5.....5 1/2
The said Heirs for a Tract of Land Left Andrew					
WALKER, deced. in nonage, the same					
Executors		90	3/	13.....0.....0	0.....2.....8 1/4
WILSON, William (Reverend)		430	12/	258.....0.....0	2...11.....7 1/4
WILLIAMS, John		327	7/	114.....9.....0	1.....2...10 3/4
WADDLE, John		100	6/	30.....0.....0	0.....6.....0
WEAVER, George		150	4/	19.....0.....0	0.....3.....9 1/2
ditto		44	2/	4.....8.....0	0.....0.....9 1/2
WILEY, John		95	4/	19.....0.....0	0.....3.....9 1/2
WASON, Robert		150	4/	30.....0.....0	0.....6.....0
WILSON, David		461	8/6	195...18.....6	1...19.....2 3/4
WRIGHT, James		260	9/	117.....0.....0	1.....3.....5
WILSON, Robert Senr.		360	5/	90.....0.....0	0...18.....0
WARDER, Jeremiah (Robert GRAY, Tenant)	1/2			15.....0.....0	0.....3.....0
WILSON, Andrew		180	3/	27.....0.....0	0.....5.....5
WADDLE, James (Minister)		1400	6/	420.....0.....0	4.....4.....0
YEARACIT, Charles		80	7	28.....0.....0	0.....5.....7 1/4
ditto		123	6/	37.....4.....0	0...11.....5
YOUNG, John (Lieut.)		228	12/	136...16.....0	1.....7.....4 1/4
ditto		23	12/	13...16.....0	0.....2.....9
YOUNG, William (Black Smith		187	12/	112.....4.....0	1.....2.....5 1/4
ditto		53	3/	7...19.....0	0.....1.....7 1/4
YOUNG, James Junr.		335	8/	134.....0.....0	1.....6.....9 1/2
ditto		104	3/	15...12.....0	0.....3.....1 1/2
YOUNG, William Senr.		200	8/	80.....0.....0	0...16.....0
YOUNG John (Capt.)		536	7/	187...12.....0	1...17.....6
ditto		190	5/6	52.....5.....0	0...10.....5 3/4
YOUNG, James Senr.		50	6/	15.....0.....0	0.....3.....0
YOUNG, William		50	6/	15.....0.....0	0.....3.....0
YOUNG, Robert		100	6/	30.....0.....0	0.....6.....0
ditto		100	3/	15.....0.....0	0.....3.....0

(page 33.)

Agreeable to an Order of the Court of Augusta County to me directed, to value and ascertain and value the Land of the Commissioners of the Land for the First Battalion of said County, for the year 1782, do value the same as follow -

Proprietors Names	Quantity of Land in Tract	Average Price p. Acre	Valuation on Land	Tax on Land
Joseph BELL	300	7/	105.....0.....0	1.....1.....0
do.	274	6/	82.....4.....0	0...16.....5 1/4
do.	196	4/	39.....4.....0	0.....7...10
	770		226.....8.....0	2.....5.....3 1/4
Elijah McCLENACHAN	390	5/	97...10.....0	0...19.....6
John POAGE	476	4/	95.....4.....0	0...19.....0 1/2

WILLIAM McPHEETERS   )
WILLIAM TATE   ) Commrs.

A Copy   RD. MADISON, Cl, A. Ct.

(page 34)

(There is a single page at the beginning of a Report titled "Alterations for 1784", somewhat faded especially the upper half, the numbers being more readable than the names. but only a few names that can be taken down with any accuracy. The Report is signed by JOSEPH BELL and JOHN WILSON, Commrs. and continues

(page 35)

A List of new Pattent Lands received from the Register's Office from the first day of January 1782 untill the thirty first day of August 1784. assest in Augusta County and delivered with the other List to the Sheriff to be collected for the year 1784 by the Commissioners of the Land Tax in said County as followeth
1st Battalion of Augusta County

	Quantity of Land	Price p Acre	Value	Tax
ARMAGAST, Michael	118	2/0	11...16.....0	0.....3.....4 1/2
ADARE, John (N. Mountain)	100	2/0	10.....0.....0	0.....3.....0
BELL, John and James	92	1/0	4...12.....0	0.....1.....4 1/2
ditto	150	1/0	7...10.....0	0.....2.....3 1/4
COOK, John	225	2/0	25...10.....0	0.....7.....6
CRAIGG, Robert	98	2/0	9...16.....0	0.....2...11
COCKRAN, Robert (Sadler)	149	13/0	96...17.....0	1.....9.....0 3/4
ditto	267	7/0	93.....9.....0	1.....8.....0 3/4
DONOHO. Hugh	98	1/8	8.....3.....4	0.....1.....8
DORAN, Jacob	127	1/8	10...11.....0	0.....3.....1
DIXON, Archibald	50	3/0	7...10.....0	0.....2.....3

(page 35 contd. Augusta County Land Tax Alterations Returned for 1784)

	Quantity of Land	Price p Acre	Value	Tax
HOGSHEAD, David	53	2/0	5.....6.....0	0.....1.....6 1/2
HENDERSON, David (S. River)	100	1/0	5.....0.....0	0.....1.....6
KING, John (N. Creek)	178	1/8	14.....6.....8	0....4.....6
KEILLER, Michael	150	1/8	12.....9.....0	0.....3...10
KING, Henry & SUSANNAH his Wife	75	13/0	48...15.....0	0...14...10
ditto	103	7/0	46...11.....0	0...14.....1 1/2
LAIRD, David	58	2/0	6...16.....0	0.....2.....1
McFEETERS, William &				
Robert TRIMBLE	121	3/0	18.....3.....0	0.....5...11 1/2
McCUTCHAN, John	330	1/8	27...10.....0	0....4...10 3/4
MILLER, Henry	85	1/9	7.....8.....9	0.....2.....4 1/2
OLIVER, John (N. Creek)	125	1/6	9....7.....0	0.....2...10 1/2
ditto	186	1/6	13...19.....0	0....4.....1 1/2
PHILLIPS, John	164	1/6	12.....6.....0	0....3.....6 1/2
RISK, Robert	120	2/0	12.....0.....0	0....3.....5
STEWART, John (M. River)	30	3/0	4...10.....0	0.....1.....4 1/2
SEAWRIGHT. George	210	1/6	15...15.....0	0.....4.....7 1/2
TALLMAN, Benjamin	589	1/0	29.....9.....0	0.....8...10 1/2
THOMPSON, William (Elder)	93	1/9	8.....2.....9	0.....2.....4 3/4
TATE, John Senr.	400	1/5	28.....6.....8	0....8.....6

Second Battalion of Augusta

BENSTON, George	263	1/6	19...14.....6	0.....5.....9 1/2
BLACK, Allexander	34	2/0	3.....8.....0	0.....1.....0
BODKIN, John	140	1/3	8...15.....0	0.....2.....8 1/2
ditto	140	1/3	8...15.....0	0.....2.....8 1/2
BAXTER, John	50	1/3	3.....2.....6	0.....1.....0
BERRY, John	142	2/0	14.....4.....0	0.....4.....2
CAROL, Samuel & Jacob (?)	71	3/0	10...13.....0	0.....5...10 1/4

(Three more names on this page but the surnames are torn off)

(page 36. Augusta County Land Tax Alterations, 2nd Battalion of Augusta for 1784)

DENISON, John	205	1/0	10.....5.....0	0....3.....0 3/4
ditto	100	1/0	5.....0.....0	0.....1.....6
ECCORD, Abraham	150	2/6	18...15.....0	0.....5.....6 3/4
ECCORD, Phillip	58	2/0	5...16.....0	0.....1.....6 1/2
ELLIOTT, John (L. River)	43	1/6	3.....4.....6	0.....1.....0
FLETCHER, Robert	22	2/0	2.....4.....0	0.....9.....8

(page 36 contd. Augusta County Land Tax Alterations, 2nd Battalion of Augusta, for 1784)

	Quantity of Land	Price p Acre	Value	Tax
FEMSLER, Thomas	185	2/0	18...10.....0	0.....5.....6 1/2
FENTLEYROY, Moore	128	1/6	9...12.....0	0.....2...11
GUM, John	220	1/9	19.....5.....0	0.....5.....9 3/4
GROIN, Joseph	100	1/9	8...15.....0	0.....2.....7 1/2
GAMBLE, William (Son of Widow)	150	1/6	11.....5.....0	0.....3.....4 1/2
GRAHAM, Elizabeth	53	2/0	5.....6.....0	0.....1.....7
GRAHAM, John	91	2/0	9.....2.....0	0.....2...10 3/4
HUMPHREYS, Jonathan	76	1/6	5...14.....0	0.....1.....7 1/4
ditto	54	1/6	4.....1.....0	0.....1.....4 1/2
HICKLAND, Thomas (Capt.)	150	1/9	12...12.....2	0.....2.....9 1/2
HARPER, Nicholas	227	1/6	17.....0.....6	0.....5.....1 1/2
HULL, Peter (Capt.)	341	1/6	25...11.....6	0.....7...9
HEMPINSTALL, Abraham	32	2/0	3.....4.....0	0.....1.....0
JORDAN, John	87	2/0	8...14.....0	0.....2...8
IRWIN, Charles	119	1/6	3...13.....6	0.....1...1
IRWIN, James	140	1/3	8...15.....0	0.....2.....7 1/2
JONES, Gabriel	100	5/0	25.....0.....0	0.....7...6
KILLPATRICK, William	121	1/3	7...11.....3	0.....2.....9 1/2
KILLINGSWORTH, Richard	95	1/3	5...18.....9	0.....1.....6 3/4
LEWIS, John	26	2/0	2...12.....0	0.....0.....10
LOUGHRIDGE, John	143	1/6	10...14.....6	0.....3.....2
LOWREY, Allexander	160	1/0	8.....0.....0	0.....2.....3 1/2
MILLER, John	58	1/6	4.....7.....0	0.....1...3
ditto	232	1/6	17.....8.....0	0.....5.....2 1/2
McCLUNG, John	81	2/0	8.....2.....0	0.....2...3
ditto	148	1/9	13.....0.....9	0.....3.....8 1/2
ditto	92	1/9	8.....1.....0	0.....2...3
McCASTLAND, John	40	2/0	4.....0.....0	0.....1.....1 3/4
McFARLAND, Duncan	119	1/3	7.....8.....9	0.....2...2
MULLONIX, John Senr.	60	2/0	6.....0.....0	0.....1...10 1/2
McCUTCHAN, Robert	101	2/0	10.....2.....0	0.....3.....0 1/2
McCUTCHAN, John	31	2/0	3.....2.....0	0.....1...0
McCOY, John	118	2/0	11...16.....0	0.....3.....5 1/2
ditto	117	1/9	10.....4.....6	0.....3.....0 3/4
McCREREY, Robert	30	2/0	3.....0.....0	0.....0...10 1/2
NICHOLAS, George	123	1/6	(faded)	0.....2...10
PENN, Mathew	250	2/2	27.....1.....8	0.....8.....1 1/2
POAGE, George (Capt.)	382	1/0	19.....2.....0	0.....5...1
POAGE, John (Gent.)	240	1/6	18.....0.....0	0.....5.....6 1/2
PULLIN, Lofty	400	1/3	25.....0.....0	0.....7...6
PENINGER, Henry	98	2/0	9...16.....0	0.....2...11
PEEBLES, John	193	1/3	11...( ).....6	(torn)

(page 36 contd. Augusta County Land Tax Alterations, 2nd Battalion of Augusta, for 1784)

	Quantity of Land	Price p Acre	Value	Tax
REAGH, William	112	1/6	8.....8...( )	(torn)

(page 37. Augusta Land Tax Alterations, 2nd Battalion of Augusta, for 1784)

	Quantity of Land	Price p Acre	Value	Tax
RUCKER, James Senr.	345	1/6	25...17.....6	0.....7.....9 1/2
RISK, Robert	358	1/3	22.....7.....6	0.....5.....7 1/2
SOMMERS, Paul	50	1/3	3.....2.....6	0.....0...10 1/2
SIDLINGTON, Andrew	157	1/6	12...10.....6	0.....3.....9 1/2
SLATEREY, Patrick	300	1/3	18...15.....0	0.....5.....6 3/4
SEIMONS, Leonard	86	1/3	5.....7.....6	0.....1.....7
ditto	30	1/3	1...17.....6	0.....0.....6 1/2
ditto	27	1/3	1...13.....9	0.....0.....5 1/4
SEIMONS, Leonard Junr.	26	1/6	1...19.....0	0.....0.....6 3/4
STOUT, George	50	1/3	3.....2.....6	0.....0...10 1/2
TACKET, Christopher	375	1/9	32...16.....3	0.....9...10 1/2
VERNER, Adam Senr.	17	1/9	1.....9.....9	0.....0.....6 1/2
WILLSON, Ralph	62	1/3	3...17.....6	0.....1.....2
WORMSLEY, John	384	1/3	24.....0.....0	0.....5...10 1/2
WILSON, William	400	1/3	25.....0.....0	0.....7.....6
WHITEMAN, Henry	146	1/6	10...19.....0	0.....3.....2 1/2
WYMER, Jacob	154	1/3	9...12.....6	0.....2...11
WARRICK, John	200	1/9	17...10.....0	0.....5.....3
WYMER, Phillip	146	1/3	9.....2.....6	0.....2...10 1/2

Peter HANGER Credit for 52 acres of land at 5/3 p acre rong charged, L. 0...14.....0
Thomas HINGE Credit for 150 acres rong charged at 1/9 per acre which is deducted in our Return
      to the Sheriff for 1784   L. 0.....3...11 1/2

Some further mistakes corrected as followeth.
    1st Battalion from the Return of the Equalizers.

Mathew ROBERTSON	196	17/6	73...10.....0	1.....2.....0 1/2
thus Corrected	196	17/6	171...10.....0	2...11.....5 1/2
Benjamin TALLMON	290	2/2	31.....8.....4	1...10.....5
thus Corrected	290	2/2	31.....8.....4	0.....9.....9 1/2
2nd Battalion.				
Robert CARLILE, Senr. (old Entry)	150	9/7	58.....2.....6	0...17.....5 1/4
thus Corrected	150	9/7	71...17.....6	1.....1.....6 3/4

    NB. The Lands here valued to Robert COCKRAN and Henry KING & Wife was returned to the Sheriff to collect for 1783, which you will please to charge to his Acct. for that year
                COCKRAN Tax   L.   2...17.....1 1/2
                KING & Wife   1.....8...11 1/2
    The Commonwealth of Virginia   To Jos. BELL and Jno. WILSON Dr.
1784   To our Service in Valuing 15954 acres of Land as Commrs. for Augusta @ 25/ p thousand
                L. 19...18.....8   JOS: BELL   JOHN WILSON

(page 38)
A List of Lands not before valued in Augusta County & return'd the Sheriff for 1785 Collection

Proprietors Names	No. of Acres	Value p Acre	Amount of Valuation	Tax
Joseph GWINN	18	6/1	5.....9.....6	0.....1.....8
David SHULTS	30	3/6	3...10.....0	0.....1.....0 1/2
James RANKIN	30	7/	10...10.....0	0.....3....1 3/4
Henry MILLER	52	5/0	13.....0.....0	0.....4.....0
John ERWIN	78	1/9	4.....0.....6	0.....1....3 1/2
do.	46	1/9	6...16.....6	0.....2.....0 1/2
Robert LISTER	80	3/6	14.....0.....0	0.....4.....2
Christifer BUMGARDNER & Lewis CHILMORE	82	5/3	21...10.....6	0.....6.....5
Thomas SCOTT, Junr.	98	3/6	17.....2.....0	0.....5.....2
Robert KINNEY	10	8/8	4.....6.....8	0.....1.....4 3/4
John ASKIN	49	3/11	9...11...11	0.....2...10
Ozburn HAMILTON	21	8/8	9.....2.....0	0.....2.....9
William RANDOLPH	55 1/2	5/8	15...11.....8	0.....4.....7 1/2
Jacob PECK	140	1/9	12.....5.....0	0.....3.....8 1/2
James CRAWFORD, Junr.	75	6/	22...10.....0	0.....6.....9
John McKEMY	32	2/8	4.....5.....4	0.....1.....4 1/2
William YOUNG	72	10/6	37...16.....0	0...11.....3
	958			3.....3.....7 1/2

The above is lands formerly granted but not before valued chiefly discovered by the Titles made them from the former Owners for the quantities charged more than was given in in the former Returns.

The following is Tract formerly granted but not valued nor before return'd for Collection

Proprietors Names	No. of Acres	Value p Acre	Amount of Valuation	Tax
Jacob LESLIA	194	2/8	25...17.....4	0.....7.....8
Richard RANKIN, Junr.	400	3/0	60.....0.....0	0...18.....0
Adam STEVENSON	100	2/6	12...10.....0	0.....3.....9
William BEARD	240	2/2	26.....0.....0	0.....7.....9
Thomas PATTERSON	87	5/	21...15.....0	0.....6.....7
Samuel FRAZOR, Jr.	236	5/3	61...19.....0	0...18.....7
Andrew McCOMB	200	7/	70.....0.....0	1.....1.....0
Andrew LAWELLS, deced., Hairs	188	4/4	40...14...10	0...12.....2 3/4
William McDOWELL one 1/2 acre Lot			25.....0.....0	0.....7.....6

New Grants not before valued for 1785.

Proprietors Names	No. of Acres	Value p Acre	Amount of Valuation	Tax
David LAIRD	77	1/6	5...15.....6	0.....1.....9
Hugh McDAWILL	200	5/	50.....0.....0	0...15.....0
Josiah McCLURE	110	2/	11.....0.....0	0.....3.....3 1/2
Abraham BURNER	400	1/6	30.....0.....0	0.....9.....0
John BAXTER	124	2/	12.....8.....0	0.....3.....9
John BENNETT	48	1/6	3...12.....0	0.....1.....1
Robert McCREA	110	1/	5...10.....0	0.....1.....7 1/2
Robert McCUTCHAN	50	1/6	3...15.....0	0.....1.....1 1/2
Moses MOORE	124	2/0	12.....8.....0	0.....3.....9
William STEWART	122	1/6	9.....3.....0	0.....2...10 1/2

The remainder of the Grants lye in other Counties, they having taken place since the Survays was made.

(page 39).
New Grants. Not in Augusta County.

George HARNESS   220 acres dated 1 Oct. 1784,   Harrison County
Robert MAXWELL 300 acres   do.   do.
William NEWILL   32 acres cannot be ascertained where it lies
William CUNNINGHAM 200 acres. Oct. 1, 1794   Harrison County
Nicholas WOLF   100 acres Decr. 16.   ditto
Nicholas SMITH   270 acres   do   ditto
Abraham SPRINGSTON   118 acres. Feby. 23   ditto 1785
Benjamin HORNBACK 277 acres   do   do.
Abraham KITTLE   288 Acres   do.   do.
        same   210 acres   Feby. 22   do.
George BREADON   200 acres   do.   do.
George REED   180 acres   Aprl. 25.   d0.
William TIPTON   cannot be ascertained 43 acres March 20

Credit the following persons being overcharged in quantity.

6/3   John VANCE 80 acres, part of 385 at 5/3 proved he holds by 305.
5/   James CUNNINGHAM, Sadler, 95 part of 320 at 3/6 he hold by 228. he having given
               Testimony that he holds this much less that are charged in the former Returns
1..11..2   John McCUNE, on 270 acres Error in carrying out the Tax.   L. 1...10.....0
2..18   Moses MOORE on 1005 acres error in carrying out the Tax   L. 2...18.....0
2..11   Alexander BARRET on 66 acres   do   do.   L. 0.....2.....11 1/2

Charge the following persons being under charged in carrying out the Tax
Henry MILLER on 160 acres   L   0.....3.....0
John CUNNINGHAM, Admr. of Alexander, deced., on 150 acres   L   0.....4.....0

The foregoing being thus stated & corrected, added into the List return'd the Sheriff for 1785
to collect.
                         JOSEPH BELL
                              &   Commrs.
                         JOHN WILSON

To the Auditors of Public Accts., Richmond City

Gentleman. You will please to grant us a Certificate for our Service in this List with much
difficulty we have ascertained the Land.

(page 40.)

Augusta County Land Book Alterations for 1785 has no other description

Thomas STEVENSON	James HENRY	100	180	0.....3.....6
Hugh BROWN	Samuel CARTMELL	306	306	0.....3.....6
The same	Joseph TROTTER	22	22	0.....5.....3
William BURKE	Andrew SCOTT	5: 20 rod	268 3/4	0.....3...11
James COWSEY	Jacob PECK	196	196	0.....6.....1
John DAVIS	Osburn HAMILTON	130	130	0.....8.....8
dirto	ditto	35	35	0.....0...10
Arthur EDWARDS	John KILHENNY	100	100	0.....4.....4
Emanuel HARLIS	William BEARD	200	200	0.....6.....1
Moses HAYS	Henry MILLAR (I. Works)	115	115	0.....3.....6
ditto	ditto	105	105	0.....5.....6
James HUGHART	Nathaniel CRAWFORD	100	100	0.....4.....4
Thomas KENNERLY	Frederick MIRES	399	399	0.....8.....8
John MILLAR	William RANDOLPH	267	267	0.....5.....8
Jacob PECK	John HUPMAN	188	188	0.....2.....8
Valentine CLUNINGER	Nicholas SPRING	320	320	0.....1.....9
Nicholas SPRING	Jacob PECK	320	320	0.....1.....9
Nicholas SYBERT	George EOVICK	317	1380	0.....3.....0

(page 41)

Stephen PECK	Peter TRINGAR	266	266	0.....7.....0

We do certify the aove to be a true list of the Alterations & Partitions as returned to the Sheriff for 1785

JOSEPH BELL
&   Commrs.
JOHN WILSON

(page 42)

A List of the Alienations and Partitions that have taken place in Augusta County for 1785

From whom Alienated	To whom Alienated	No. of Acres Alienated	Acres in the Original Tract	Rate p Acre so alienated
Nicholas SYBERT	Joseph BELL	294	1380	0.....1.....9
Andrew SCOTT	Anguish McDONALD	40	66	0.....2.....4
Janet & Rachel WALLACE	Benjamin BROWN	100	100	0.....8.....8
William TROTTER	David STEVENSON	190	190	0...17.....6
the same -	the same	70	70	0.....4.....4
Charles TEAS	Robert CRAIG	160	160	0.....7.....9
William McCUTCHAN	Sampson & George MATHEWS	112	112	0.....6.....6
James GIVENS	James CRAWFORD	311	311	0...15.....3
Alexander BROWNLEE	Alexander McCLANACHAN	222	222	0.....7.....9
Alexander STEWART	John STEWARD	246	246	0.....5.....3
Daniel JOSEPH	George HAMMER	365	365	0.....2.....8
Steven PECK	Peter TRENGER	266	266	0.....7.....0

(page 42 contd. Augusta County Land Alterations for 1785).

From whom alienated	To whom Alienated	No. of Acres Alienated	Acres in the Original Tract	Rate p Acre so alienated
John FUDGE	Joseph BELL	65	220	0.....2.....0
Joseph McCUTCHAN	James BLAIR	136	383	0.....4.....4
ditto	do	118	383	0.....4.....4
ditto	John BLAIR	136	383	0.....4.....4
Robert TAIT	Phillip (? PATTON)	23	23	0.....7.....0
Florance BELL	William BELL	240	400	0.....7.....3 1/2
the same	the same	91 1/2	183	0.....4.....4
the same	David BELL	160	400	0...10...11
the same	the same	91 1/2	183	0.....4.....4
James McCLEREY	John JAMESON	200	200	0.....8.....8
do	do	40	40	0.....0.....8
Robert RODGERS	Palzer TAVENBOUGH	200	478	0.....3...11
Margaret THOMPSON	Zacharia JOHNSTON	236	236	0.....2.....2
Thomas EDWARDS	James GRIFFITH & John GARDNER	250	250	0.....4.....4
Mathew GLAVIS	Robert PORTERFIELD	250	250	0.....6.....6
James HUGHART	Nathaniel CRAWFORD	12	490	0.....4.....4
John YOUNG (Lieut.)	William YOUNG (B. Smith)	228	228	0...10.....6
do	do	23	23	0...10.....6
Daniel JAMES	William RICHARDS	85	85	0.....5.....6 1/2
Alexander MITCHEL	Randolph (? HAUPE)	200	200	0.....6.....1
do.	do.	100	100	0.....3...11
James SPROWL	James McCHESNEY	300	300	0.....6.....6
Elizabeth BLACK (Widow)	Phillip ANGLEMAN	120	120	0.....3.....6
William ANDERSON	Enoss JONES	65	200	0.....2.....2
Ralph WILSON	Joseph BELL	62	62	0.....1.....3
Frederick BIRKETT	Samuel McKEE	75	75	0.....3.....6
Samuel McKEE	Frederick BIRKETT	15	230	0.....5.....3
Frederick BIRKETT	Jacob GABERT	27	213	0.....3.....6
Thomas NELSON, Admr. of Robert EAGER	John FULWATER	42	84	0.....3...11

(page 43. Augusta County Land Alterations for 1785)

From whom alienated	To whom Alienated	No. of Acres Alienated	Acres in the Original Tract	Rate p Acre so alienated
Joseph REDNOUR	John CRAWFORD	95	95	0.....2.....8
Stephen WOODS	Archibald SCOTT (Revd.)	95	140	0.....3...11
the same	James CAMPBELL	27	140	0.....3...11
ditto	Alexander McPHEETERS	28	140	0.....3...11
Edmund BURTON	Frederick BIRKETT	213	213	0.....3.....6
Robert RODGERS	Daniel JOSEPH	145	145	0.....7.....0
Robert HALL	William ALLEN	100	1350	0...10.....6
Adam DUNLAP	Thomas GARVIN	185	185	0...2...8
ditto	ditto	100	100	0.....6.....1
William FOSTER	Mathew GLEAVES	250	250	0.....6.....6
Bryan KENNY	John McGLAMERY	80	80	0.....4.....4
Benjamin TALMAN	George FAULL	145	145	0.....7.....0
ditto	ditto	154	154	0.....5.....3
ditto	ditto	136	136	0.....3.....6
ditto	ditto	290	290	0.....2.....2
John RITCHEY	John PATTERSON	50	200	0...14.....0
William USHER	Thomas DORSETT	130	130	0.....2.....8

(page 43 contd. Augusta County Land Alterations for 1785).

From whom Alienated	To whom Alienated	No. of Acres Alienated	Acres in the Original Tract	Rate p Acre so Alienated
John COULTER	David COULTER	50	200	0.....5.....3
Samuel McCUTCHAN	John McCUTCHAN	215	300	0.....7.....9
the same	William (blank)	290	444	0.....7.....9
Joseph TAYLOR	John McKEAMY	200	200	0.....3.....6
Hugh HAYS	James HENRY	250	250	0.....8.....8
Moses HAYS	Hugh RICHEY	100	100	0.....3.....6
Samuel HIND	Gilbert KERR	200	200	0.....7.....0
Edward ERWIN	Henry MILLER (I Works)	208	208	0.....7.....0
the same	the same	135	135	0.....4.....4
William ALLEN	Augustine ARGNBRIGHT	121	121	0.....6.....1
John OTT	John McKEMEY	155	155	·0.....2.....8
William DUNLAP	Robert KENNY	150	150	0.....6.....6
John RICHEY	Teeter FISHBURN	150	200	0.....9.....0
Daniel JOSEPH	John BANCE	145	145	0.....7.....0
Robert McCUTCHAN	William McCUTCHAN	100	100	0.....8.....8
Robert GWINN	James FULTON	240	240	0.....8.....8
James TROTTER, Esqr.	George MILLER	192	192	0.....6.....1
Francis MARA	Thomas EDWARDS	250	250	0.....4.....4
Robert FINLEY, Senr.	Robert FINLEY, Junr.	88	88	0.....8.....8
John CLARK	George EAGLE	100	100	0.....5.....3
Mathew (? KIRTKEN)	Joseph GIVEN	336	336	0.....6.....1
John ALEXANDER	John LAMB	90	90	0.....7.....0
Mathew PENN	Isaac JOHNS	250	250	0.....2.....2
Robert CLARK	James SCOTT	380	380	0.....6.....6
the same	the same	86	86	0.....2.....8
David FRAIM	John BROWN	215	215	0.....9.....7
William ALLEN	William HANDLEY	100	100	0...10.....6
Edward RUTLEDGE	James RUTLEDGE	117	250	0...10.....6
ditto	ditto	26	26	0.....4.....4
Jacob DORAN	Henry MILLER (I., Works)	238	238	0.....4.....4
the same	the same	209	209	(torn)

(Nothing further recorded for Augusta County Land Alterations for 1785.)

(page 44.)

A List of the Alienations and Partitions that have taken place in Augusta County for 1786.

From whom Alienated	To whom Alienated	No. of Acres Alienated	No. of Acres in Original Tract from whence Taken	Rate p Acre of Land so Alienated
Samuel ANDERSON	Allexander St. CLAIR	200		0.....7.....9
Robert ALLEN	Mounticue ALLEN	400		0.....8.....8
James BLAIR	Hugh DONAGUE	106 1/2		0.....4.....4
William BLAIR	Jacob SHEETS	107		0.....2.....8
John BROCK	John GRAHAM	100		0.....2.....8
John COWMAN	Rhandolp HORYNE	200		0.....6.....1
John CUNINGHAM, Capt.	James EWING	150		0.....4.....4
Tully DEVITT	Thomas SMITH	303		0.....5.....3
Walter DAVIS	James DAVIS	327 1/2		0.....7.....0

(page 44 contd. Augusta County Land Alterations for 1786)

From who Alienated	To whom Alienated	No. of Acres Alienated	No. of Acres in Original Tract from wjemce talem	Rate p Acres of Land so Alienated
John FULTON	James CRAIG	200		0.....5.....3
Robert GWIN	Joseph GWIN	220	260	0.....8.....8
James ELLIS	Peter HULL	140		0.....7.....0
John KINKEAD	Allexander THOMPSON	88		0.....5.....1
Reuben KENNERLY	Archibald BOLLING`	303		0...10...11
William KENNERLY	William ANDERSON	224		0.....8.....8
Frederick LIPEN	George MATHEWS	half acre lot @ L. 25		0.....7.....6
Henry MOUROW	John HEIZER	120		0.....5.....3
Allexander McNUTT	Thomas SMITH	half acre lot		(blurred)
George MATHEWS	William McDOWELL	half acre lot @ L. 25		0.....7.....6
ditto	Allexander NELSON	572		0.....8.....8
Thomas MURRY	John ALLISON, Junr.	216		0.....3.....6
John McDOUGHAL	Henery MILLER	277		0.....3.....6
ditto	Edward ERWIN	209		0.....6.....1
Andrew McCLURE	John DICKSON	180		0...10.....6
Lewis MYRES	Samuel RUNCKLE	200		0.....2.....8
John SMITH deced. of morgage	Henery MILLER	80		0.....4.....4
ditto	ditto	half acre lott L. 40		0...12.....0
Mathew PATTON	James STEVENSON	286	880	0.....3.....6
ditto	Henery BUZZARD	82	880	0.....3.....6
William PATTERSON, Senr.	William PATTERSON, Junr.	200		0.....8.....8
Thomas SMITH (Major)	Peter HYSKILL	13		0.....4.....4
ditto	ditto	quarter acre lott 27.10		0.....8.....3
Allexander STEWART	Archibald STEWART	100		0...10.....6
ditto	ditto	340		0.....1.....9
John STUNKARD	William STUNKARD	230		0.....7.....0
Abraham GOODPASTURE	William SCOTT	2 1/2	80	0.....2.....8
ditto	William BRUBANK	77 1/2	80	0.....2.....8
David TROTTER	William SCOTT	190		0.....7.....9
John TAITE	Thomas STEVENSON	200	400	0.....1.....5
Samuel WRIGHT	Zachariah JOHNSTON	155		0.....7.....9
John WRIGHT	William YOOL	205		0.....6.....1
Thomas MINER	Arthur HIGANS	35	136	0.....1.....9

JOSEPH BELL
JOHN WILSON   Commrs.

(page 45)
(On part of this page, there is a small list apparently of persons who received Grants)

BUFFINBURY, Jonathan (Harrison)	390	October 17, 1785
MATHEWS, Adonijah (supp'd Greenbriar)	480	October 24, 1785
(the following unknown)		
CIREL, Samuel	300	November 2, 1785
LAWYERS, Alexander	86	November 23, 1785
DEAN, Adam	290	do.
MONTGOMERY, John	110	do.
BAKER, Humphrey	430	do,

(page 45 contd. Additional Grants.

SMITH, Robert	25	November 15, 1785
HITRIGHT, John	200	April 10, 1786
BOMAN, Jacob	145	April 1, 1786
SHOEMAKER, Henry	150	December 2, 1785
MILLAR, Jacob	150	December 2, 1785

JOSEPH BELL
JOHN WILSON   Commrs.

A List of New Grants & other Land not before valued in Augusta County as return'd the Sheriff for Collection for the year 1786.

Proprietors Names	No. of Acres	Average Price p Acre	Amount of Valuation	Tax at 1 1/2 p cent
COBB, William	87	2/6	10...17.....6	0.....3.....3 1/4
CRAIG, George (S. River)	97	2/0	9...14.....0	0.....2...11
CRAIG, James	390	2/	39.....0.....0	0...11.....8 1/2
SHEETS, Jacob	27	3/	4.....1.....0	0.....1.....2 1/2
TARBET, Hugh	317	1/6	23...15.....6	0.....7.....1 1/2
DOUGHERTY, Michael (part of his Grant given in before remains)	150	4/4	32...10.....0	0.....9.....9
HOG, James (the same)	104	4/0	20...16.....0	0.....6.....3
HORRIS, Hugh	95	3/0	14.....5.....0	0.....4.....3 1/4
HOUGHT, Hezekiah	92	1/6	6...18.....0	0.....2.....0 3/4
SIMMONS, George	85	3/9	12...15.....0	0.....3.....9 3/4
McCUTCHAN, John	330	1/	16...10.....0	0.....7...10 1/2
BRADSHA, John (Lands not before valued other then Grants)	333	1/6	24...19.....6	0.....7.....6
McCHESNEY, James	280	3/9	52...10.....0	0...15.....9
BEVERLEY, Robert Esqr.	200	3/9	37...10.....0	0...11.....3
ditto	120	1/6	9.....0.....0	0.....2.....9
LIONS, Henry	350	2/6	43...15.....0	0...13.....1 1/2
ASH, Charles	81	2/6	10.....2.....6	0.....3.....0 1/4
MORTAN, Edward	125	2/6	15...12.....6	0.....4.....8 1/4
RODMAN, Samuel (in Beverlys Mannor ascertained from Titles made in said year not before valued)	44	2/6	5...10.....0	0.....1.....8
NELSON, Alexander	155	5/	38...15.....0	0...11.....7
LOVINGOOD, Hermon	70	2/5	3...15.....0	0.....2.....7
WADDLE, James (Revd.)	17	5/	4.....5.....0	0.....1.....3
HALL, Edward	32	5/0	8.....0.....0	0.....2.....5
SHIELDS, John	43	5/0	10...15.....0	0.....3.....2 3/4
JOHNSTON, Zachariah	70	3/0	10...10.....0	0.....3.....1 3/4
HANGER, Peter	438	2/6	54...12.....6	0...16.....4 3/4
	4132			8.....0.....7 1/4

The following Grants do not appear to be in this County. The County Surveyor gives in as follows:

LEWIS, Andrew	(Rockingham)	46	issued June 1, 1785
TEETER, Abraham	do.	36	" September 27, 1785
JOHNSTON, Andrew	do.	30	" October 12, 1785
HOPKINS, John	do.	93	" June 24, 1785

(the sheet noted "continued" but nothing more is included.)

(page 46.)

List of the Land Tax within the District of CHARLES CAMERON, Commissioner in the County of Augusta, for the year 1787.

Persons Name Owning Land	No. of Lotts	Yearly Rent	Quantity of Land	Rate of Land per Acre	Total Amt. of Value of Land excl. of Lots	Amt. of Tax at 1 1/2 p cent
Thomas ADAMS, (Colo).			995	6/1	302...12...11	4...18.....9 1/2
ditto unpatented Land			211	/10	8...15...10	0.....2.....7 3/4
Richard ADAMS			525	7/0	183...15.....0	2...15....1
Archibald ARMSTRONG			213	7/0	74...11.....0	1.....2.....4 1/4
Thomas ANDERSON			520	1/9	45...10.....0	0...13.....7 1/2
Michael ARMAGAST			630	3/6	110.....5.....0	1...13.....0 3/4
ditto			118	2/0	11...16.....0	0.....3.....6 1/2
Charles ASH			81	2/6	10.....2.....6	0.....3.....0 1/4
John BROWN (Capt.)			210	9/7	105.....0.....5	1...10...11
Robert BRATTON (deced., Estate)			425	8/8	184.....3.....4	2...15.....3
William BLACK			125	8/8	54.....3.....4	0...16.....3
Alexander BLACK			125	8/8	54.....3.....4	0...16.....3
ditto			34	2/0	3.....8.....0	0.....1.....0
George BENSTON			342	6/1	104.....0.....6	1...11.....2 1/2
ditto			263	1/6	19...14.....0	0.....5...11 3/4
Mathias BENSTON, SENR.			216	4/4	46...16.....0	0...14.....0 1/2
James BOTKIN			105	5/3	27...11.....3	0.....8.....8
John BOTKIN			114	3/6	19...19.....0	0.....5...11 3/4
ditto			140	1/3	8...10.....0	0.....2.....8 1/2
Charles BOTKIN			140	1/3	8...10.....0	0.....2.....8 1/2
Joseph (? BEACH)			114	3/6	19...19.....0	0.....5...11 3/4
John BRADSHAW			160	7/0	35.....0.....0	0...10.....6
ditto			333	1/6	24...19.....6	0.....7.....6
Theophilas BLAKE			47	2/7	6.....1.....5	0.....1.....9 3/4
John BLAKE			47	2/8	6.....5.....4	0.....1...10 1/2
Leonard BELL			200	4/4	43.....6.....8	0...13.....0
ditto			60	/10	2...10.....0	0.....0.....9
John BELL			271	4/4	58...14.....4	0...17.....7 1/4
Rebecca BLACK			230	4/4	49...16.....8	0...14...11 3/4
James BERRY			307	7/0	107.....9.....0	1...12.....2 1/4
Joseph BENNET, SENR.			70	8/8	30.....6.....8	0.....9.....1
John BENNET			351	2/8	46...16.....0	0...14.....0 1/2
ditto			48	6/6	3...12.....0	0.....1...11 1/4
Jacob BENNETT			62	7/0	21...14.....0	0.....6.....6
David BELL's Estate			150	2/8	20.....0.....0	0.....6.....0
Joseph BELl (Capt.)			97	2/8	12...18.....8	0.....3...10 1/2
ditto			294	1/9	15...16.....6	0.....4.....8
ditto			62	1/3	3...17.....6	0.....1.....2
George BUFFINBERGER			100	5/3	26.....5.....0	0.....7...10 1/2
William BARNETT			400	2/8	53.....6.....8	0...16.....0
John BEVERAGE			93	2/8	12.....8.....0	0.....3.....8 1/2
Hugh BOTKIN			287	4/4	62.....3.....8	0...18.....7 3/4
George BRATTON			285	8/8	123...10.....0	1...17.....0 1/2
John BIRD			125	10/6	65...12.....6	0...19.....8 1/2
Andrew BOURLAND			327	8/8	141...14.....0	2.....2.....6
John BAXTER			300	3/6	52...10.....0	0...15.....9

(page 47. Augusta County Land Tax Return of Charles Cameron for 1787)

Persons Names Owning Land	No. of Lotts	Yearly Rent	Quantity of Land	Rate of Land per Acre	Total Amt. of Value of Land excl. of Lotts	Amt. of Tax at 1 1/2 p cent
John BAXTER			50	1/3	3.....2.....6	0.....1.....0
ditto			124	2/0	12.....8.....0	0.....3.....9
Ephraim BAITES			172	3/6	30.....2.....0	0.....9.....0 1/2
Thomas BLAKE			115	3/6	20.....2.....0	0.....6.....0 1/2
Joseph BROWN			50	1/9	4.....7.....0	0.....1.....3 3/4
Abraham BURNER			400	1/6	30.....0.....0	0.....9.....0
John BERRY			142	2/0	14.....4.....0	0.....4.....2
James BRATTON (Capt.)			400	8/8	173.....6.....8	2...12.....0
ditto			325	4/4	70.....8.....4	1.....1.....1 1/2
Hugh BROWN			215	6/1	65.....7...11	0...19.....7 1/2
Henry BUZZARD			82	3/6	12.....6.....0	0.....3.....8
Robert BEVERLEY Esqr.			200)			
ditto			166)	9/7	132.....5.....6	1...19.....8
Nathan CRAWFORD			112	4/4	24.....5.....4	0.....7.....4
John CARLILE (C. Pasture)			250	6/1	76.....0...10	1.....2.....9 1/2
John CHESNUTT			232	2/8	30...18.....8	0.....9.....3 1/4
John CARLILE (B. Pasture)			150	9/7	71...17.....6	1.....1.....6 3/4
ditto			50	/10	2.....1.....8	0.....0.....7 1/2
Robert CARLILE, SENR.			150	9/7	71...17.....6	1.....1.....6 3/4
Robert CARLILE, (Son to John)			300	7/9	116.....5.....0	1...14...10 1/2
James CARLILE			130	9/7	65.....3.....4	0...19.....6 1/2
John CARTMILL			140	5/3	36...15.....0	0...11.....0 1/4
John COWARDINE			200	3/6	36.....1.....0	0...10.....9 3/4
ditto			359	1/9	31.....8.....3	0.....9.....2
ditto part sold Wm. GARRIX			58	1/9	5.....1.....6	0.....1.....6 1/4
Olery CONROD, SENR.			476	6/1	144...15.....8	2.....3.....4
Olery CONROD, JUNR.			206	2/8	27.....9.....4	0.....8.....2 3/4
Christopher CRUMMET			40	2/8	5.....6.....8	0.....1.....7
Robert CUNINGHAM (Hampshire)			300	7/0	105.....0.....0	1...11.....6
James CLARK			240	4/4	52.....0.....0	0...15.....7
Thomas CARTMILL			581	2/8	77.....9.....4	1.....3.....2 3/4
James CARSON			100	1/9	8...15.....0	0.....2.....7 1/2
Alexander CRAWFORD's Estate			240	11/5	137.....0.....0	2.....1.....1
Samuel CRAIGE			200	5/3	52...10.....0	0...15.....9
John COWGAR			170	4/1	34...14.....2	0...10.....5
John DICKENSON (Colo.)			570	18/	370...10.....0	5...11.....1 3/4
Thomas DAVIS			135	4/4	29.....5.....0	0.....8.....9 1/4
Thomas DOUGLASS			168	2/8	22.....8.....0	0.....6.....8 1/2
Charles DONNALLY			484	6/1	147.....4.....4	2.....4.....2
Charles DAVIS			105	/10	4.....7.....6	0.....1.....3 3/4
Hugh DIVER (Rockingham)			150	2/8	20.....0.....0	0.....6.....0
Robert DUFFILL			330	8/6	57...15.....0	0...16...11 1/2
James DYER (Rockingham)			174	3/6	30.....8.....0	0.....9.....1 1/2
Robert DINWIDDIE			210	5/3	55.....2.....6	0...16.....6 1/2
James DINWIDDIE & William			180	1/9	15...15.....0	0.....4.....8 1/2
Michael DOUGHERTY			200	2/8	26...13.....4	0.....8.....0

(page 48. Augusta County Land Tax Return of Charles Cameron for 1787)

Persons Names Owning Land	No. of Lotts	Yearly Rent	Quantity of Land	Rate of Land per Acre	Total Amt. of Value of Land excl. of Lotts	Amt. of Tax at 1 1/2 p cent
Michael DOUGHERTY			150	4/4	32...10.....0	0.....9.....9
John DEAN			90	/10	3...15.....0	0.....1..... 1/2
Laurance DRINNEN			300	2/8	40.....0.....0	0...12.....0
Jacob DRINNEN			500	5/3	131.....5.....0	1...19.....4
Thomas DRINNEN			333	1/9	29.....2.....9	0.....8.....9
William DICKEY			100	8/8	43.....6.....8	0...13.....0
John DENISON			400	/10	16...13.....4	0.....4.....9 1/2
ditto			205	1/0	10.....5.....0	0.....3.....0 3/4
Alexander DUNLAP			400	2/4	46...13.....0	0...14.....1 1/2
William ERWIN			204	5/3	53...11.....3	0...16.....0 3/4
Charles ERWIN			130	6/1	39...10...10	0...11...10 3/4
Janett ERWIN			100	8/8	43.....6.....8	0...13.....0
John ELLIOTT			340	7/9	119.....0.....0	1...15.....8 1/4
ditto			43	1/6	3.....4.....6	0.....1.....0
Stuffell EVE			100	2/8	13.....6.....8	0.....4.....0
Phillip ECORD			95	4/4	20...11.....8	0.....6.....2
ditto			50	2/0	5...16.....0	0.....1.....6 1/2
Abraham ECORD			150	2/6	18...15.....0	0.....5.....6 3/4
George EVACK			317	3/0	47...10.....0	0...14.....3
James ERWIN			140	1/3	8...15.....0	0.....2.....7 1/2
Charles ERWIN			49	1/6	3...13.....6	0.....1.....1
James FULTON			241	8/8	104.....8.....8	1...11.....2 1/2
Thomas FEMSTER			290	13/0	188...10.....0	2...16...10 1/2
ditto			185	2/0	18...10.....0	0.....5.....6 1/2
David FRAIM			270	/10	11...10.....0	0.....3.....4 1/2
Moore FENTSLEROY			235	3/6	41.....2.....6	0...12.....4
Peter FLESHER			200	5/3	52...10.....0	0...15.....9
Robert FLETCHER (R. Bridge)			50	3/6	8...15.....0	0.....2.....7 1/2
ditto			22	2/0	2.....4.....0	0.....0.....8
Conrod FLESHER			200	3/6	35.....0.....0	0...10.....6
William GARRIX			139	1/9	11...13.....3	0.....3.....5 1/2
David GIVIN			967	4/4	209...12.....0	3.....2...10 1/2
Joseph GIVIN			216	6/1	65...14.....0	0...19.....8 1/2
ditto			100	1/9	8...15.....0	0.....2.....7 1/2
ditto			18	6/1	5.....9.....6	0.....1.....7 1/2
ditto			260	8/8	112...13.....4	1...13.....9 1/2
ditto			318	6/1	96...14.....6	1.....9.....0 1/4
Christopher GREHAM			289	10/6	151...14.....6	2.....5.....6 1/4
Thomas GILLASPY			300	4/4	65.....0.....0	0...19.....6
John GILLASPY			190	5/3	49...17.....6	0...14...11 1/2
ditto			108	4/4	23.....8.....0	0.....7.....0 1/2
Hugh GILLASPY's Estate			90	2/8	10...13.....4	0.....3.....2 1/4
James GAY			200	7/0	70.....0.....0	1.....1.....0
Elizabeth GREHAM			312	8/8	135.....4.....0	2.....0.....6 1/2
ditto			53	2/0	5.....6.....0	0.....1.....7 1/2
John GREHAM			128	8/8	55.....9.....4	0...16.....7 1/4
ditto			91	2/0	9.....2.....0	0.....2...10 3/4
John GREHAM (B. Pasture			137	2/8	18.....5.....4	0.....5.....5 3/4

(page 48 contd. Augusta County Land Tax Return of Charles Cameron for 1787)

Persons Names Owning Land	No of Lotts	Yearly Rent	Quantity of Land	Rate of Land per Acre	Total Amt. of Value of excl. of Lotts	Amt. of Tax at 1 1/2 p cent
Isabella GAMBLE (Widow)			300	4/4	65.....0.....0	0...19.....6

(page 49. Augusta County Land Tax Return of Charles Cameron for 1787)

Persons Names Owning Land	No of Lotts	Yearly Rent	Quantity of Land	Rate of Land per Acre	Total Amt. of Value of excl. of Lotts	Amt. of Tax at 1 1/2 p cent
Isabella GAMBLE (for Son, William)			150	1/6	11.....5.....0	0.....3.....4 1/2
William GEENS			100	2/8	13.....6.....8	0.....4.....0
ditto			143	7/9	12.....10.....3	0.....3.....9
John GUM			216	3/6	37...16.....0	0...11.....4
ditto			220	1/9	19.....5.....0	0.....5.....9 3/4
Isaac GUM			193	2/8	25...14.....8	0.....7.....8 1/4
John GUM, JUNR.			390	1/9	34.....2.....6	0...10.....2 1/2
Abraham GUM			220	1/9	19.....5.....0	0.....5.....9 3/4
William GIVINS			354	7/9	137.....3.....6	2.....1.....1 3/4
Mary GRAGORY			220	5/3	57...15.....0	0...17.....3 3/4
Samuel GRAGORY			148	5/3	38...17.....0	0...11.....73/4
Jacob GILLASPY			400	1/9	35.....0.....0	0...10.....6
James GRIFFETH			155	5/3	40...13.....9	0...12.....2 1/2
John GREGORY			100	2/8	13.....6.....8	0.....4.....0
Thomas GALFORD			90	/10	3...17.....6	0.....1.....1 3/4
Robert GREHAM's Estate			128	8/8	35.....9.....4	0...16.....7 1/2
John GEENS			90	1/9	7...17.....6	0.....2.....4 1/2
John HICKLEN			350	(nothing else recorded)		
John HICKLEN			589	7/9	228.....4.....9	3.....8.....5 3/4
Robert HALL			1250	10/6	656.....5.....0	9...16...10 1/2
Thomas HUGHART (Colo.)			395	10/11	215...12.....1	3.....4.....8
ditto			95	2/8	12...13.....4	0.....3.....9 1/2
Thomas HICKLEN			200	10/6	105.....0.....0	1...11.....6
ditto			150	1/9	12...12.....2	0.....3.....9 1/2
Edward HINDS's Estate			150	4/4	32...10.....0	0.....9.....9
Hugh HICKLEN			200	7/0	70.....0.....0	1.....1.....0
James HUGHART			370	4/4	81...18.....0	1.....4.....7 1/2
John HODGE			350	6/1	106.....9.....2	1...11...11 1/4
Andrew HAMILTON			185	7/0	64...15.....0	0...19.....5
ditto			200	/10	8.....6.....8	0.....2.....6
Jones HENDERSON			314	6/1	95...10.....2	1.....8.....7 3/4
ditto			100	/10	4.....3.....4	0.....1.....3
Paul HINKLE			97	2/8	12...18.....8	0.....3...10 1/2
Henry HEATH (Fort Pitt)			1000	4/4	216...13.....4	3.....5.....0
Nicholas HARPER			200	5/3	52...10.....0	0...15.....9
ditto			227	1/6	17.....0.....6	0.....5.....1 1/2
Jacob HOOVER			375	6/1	114.....1.....3	1...14.....2 1/2
Michael HOOVER			50	4/4	10...16.....8	0.....3.....3
Bostian HOOVER's Estate			150	2/8	20.....0.....0	0.....6.....0
Adam HARPER (Hampshire)			100	3/6	17...10.....0	0.....5.....9 3/4
John HYNES			140	2/8	18...13.....4	0.....5.....7
ditto			58	1/9	5.....1.....6	0.....1.....6 1/4
Roger HICKMAN			140	7/9	49.....0.....0	0...14.....8 1/4
Peter HALL (Capt.)			628	5/3	164...17.....0	2.....9.....5
ditto			341	1/6	25...11.....6	0.....7.....9
ditto (from ELLIS)			140	7/0	49.....0.....0	0...14.....8 1/2
George HALL			242	5/3	63...10.....6	0...19.....0 3/4

(page 49 contd. Augusta County Land Tax Return of Charles Cameron for 1787)

Persons Names Owning Land	No. of Lotts	Yearly Rent	Quantity of Land	Rate of Land per Acre	Total Amt. of Value of Land excl. of Lotts	Amt. of Tax at 1 1/2 p cent
Jonathan HUMPHREY			300	3/6	52...10.....0	0...15.....9
ditto			76	1/6	5...14.....0	0.....1.....7 1/2

(page 50. Augusta County Land Tax Return of Charles Cameron for 1787)

Persons Names Owning Land	No. of Lotts	Yearly Rent	Quantity of Land	Rate of Land per Acre	Total Amt. of Value of Land excl. of Lotts	Amt. of Tax at 1 1/2 p cent
Jonathan HUMPHREY			54	1/6	4.....1.....0	0.....1.....4 1/2
William HUTCHISON			240	6/1	73.....0.....0	1.....1...10 3/4
John HENSHAW			361	1/9	31...11...9	0.....9.....5 3/4
Ozburn HAMILTON			94	7/0	32...18.....0	0.....9.....9 1/4
ditto			130	8/8	56.....6....8	0...16...10 1/2
ditto			21	8/8	9.....2.....0	0.....2.....9
ditto			35	/10	1.....9.....2	0.....0 5 1/4
Alexander HAMILTON			170	6/1	51...14.....2	0...15.....6
Charles HAMILTON			100	6/1	30.....8....4	0.....9.....1 1/2
Thomas HICKMAN, JUNR.			100	2/8	13.....6....8	0.....4.....0
Abraham HEMPENSTALL			32	2/0	3.....4.....0	0.....1.....0
William HANDLEY (from HALL)			100	10/6	52...10.....0	0...15.....9
Isaac JOHNS			250	2/2	27.....1....8	0.....8.....1 3/4
Anthony JOHNSTON			198	2/8	26.....8....0	0.....7...11
John JOURDEN			90	5/3	23...12...6	0.....7.....1
ditto			87	1/6	8...14.....0	0.....2.....8
Abraham INGREHAM			150	2/8	20.....0.....0	0.....6.....0
Abraham INGREHAM, JUNR.			205	2/8	27.....6....8	0.....8.....2 1/4
Thomas JERVIS			400	1/9	35.....0.....0	0...10.....6
Gabriel JONES			100	5/0	25.....0.....0	0.....7.....6
John KINKEAD Esqr.			286	4/4	61...19.....4	0..18.....6 3/4
William KINKEAD (Capt.)			350	6/1	106.....9....2	1...11...11 1/2
William KILPATRICK			200	/10	8.....6....8	0.....2.....6
Thomas KINKEAD			300	6/1	91.....5.....0	1.....7.....4 1/2
William KINKEAD (Stiller)			250	5/3	65...12...6	0...19.....8 1/2
James KILPATRICK			50	5/3	13.....2....6	0.....3...11 1/4
Andrew KILPATRICK			40	5/3	10...10.....0	0.....3.....1 3/4
John KINKEAD (S. River)			163	1/3	7...11.....3	0.....2.....3 1/4
Richard KILLINGSWORTH			95	1/3	5...18...9	0.....1.....6 3/4
John KELLY			295	5/3	67...19...9	1.....0.....8 1/2
John LAMBERT			33	1/9	2...17.....9	0.....0...10 1/4
Charles LEWIS, deced. Estate			1130	12/2	687.....8....4	10.....6.....2 1/2
Ralph LAUFFERTY			40	7/	14.....0.....0	0.....4.....2
Rebecca LAUFFERTY (of Ralph)			300	7/0	105.....0.....0	1...11.....6
William LOCKRIDGE			250	7/0	87...10.....0	1.....6.....3
Andrew LOCKRIDGE			565	8/8	244...16.....8	3...13.....5 1/2
ditto (of John HICKLEN)			196	(nothing else recorded)		
John LOCKRIDGE			200	5/8	52...10.....0	0...15.....9
ditto			143	1/6	10...14...6	0.....3.....2
Joseph LEEZER			44	3/6	7...14.....0	0.....2.....3 3/4
Barnard LANCE			1211	4/4	262.....7....8	3...18....8 1/2
William LEWIS			250	5/3	61...12...6	0...19.....8 1/4
ditto			400	6/4	126...13....4	1...18.....1 1/2

(page 50 contd. Augusta County Land Tax Return of Charles Cameron for 1787)

Persons Names Owning Land	No. of of Lotts	Yearly Rent	Quantity of Land	Rate of Land per Acre	Total Amt. of Value of Land Excl. of Lotts	Amt. of Tax at 1 1/2 p cent
Thomas LEWIS			1350	5/3	354.....7.....6	5.....6.....3 1/2
Alexander LOWERY			50	1/9	4.....7.....6	0.....1.....3 3/4
ditto			160	1/0	8.....0.....0	0.....2.....3 1/2
William LANDSDALE			66	1/9	7...15.....6	0.....2.....6
John LEWIS (Capt.)			580	17/6	507...10.....0	7...12.....3
ditto			70	1/9	6.....2.....6	0.....1...10
ditto			26	2/0	2...12.....0	0.....0...10

(page 51. Augusta County Land Tax Return of Charles Cameron for 1787)

Persons Names Owning Land	No. of of Lotts	Yearly Rent	Quantity of Land	Rate of Land per Acre	Total Amt. of Value of Land Excl. of Lotts	Amt. of Tax at 1 1/2 p cent
John McDONALD			277	7/0	91...19.....0	1.....7.....6 3/4
Patrick MILLER`			193	9/7	92.....9.....7	1.....7.....8 3/4
Lewis MARTIN			65	1/9	5...13.....9	0.....1.....8 1/4
Adam MARTIN			66	1/9	5...15.....6	0.....1.....8 3/4
Joseph MALCOM			280	7/9	108...10.....0	1...12.....6 1/2
Robert McMULLIN			310	/10	12...18.....4	0.....3...10
William MOORE			94	5/3	24...13.....6	0.....7.....4 3/4
John MILLER			290	4/4	52...16.....8	0...18...10
ditto			282	1/6	17.....8.....0	0.....5.....2
ditto			58	1/6	4.....7.....0	0.....1.....3
Robert McCREERY (Capt.)			260	9/7	124...11.....8	1...17.....4 1/2
ditto			30	2/0	3.....0.....0	0.....0...10 1/2
John MONTGOMERY			108	11/2	60.....6.....0	0...18.....1
Joseph MAY's Estate			182	7/9	70...10.....6	1.....1.....1 3/4
ditto			80	/10	3.....6.....8	0.....1.....0
John McCLUNG			209	5/3	54...17.....3	0...16.....5 1/2
ditto			81	2/0	8.....2.....0	0.....2.....3
ditto			148	1/9	13.....8.....9	0.....3.....8 1/2
ditto			92	1/9	8.....1.....0	0.....2.....3
Andrew MOODY			80	3/6	14.....0.....0	0.....4.....2 1/4
John McCASTLAND			174	6/1	52...18.....6	0...15...10 1/2
ditto			40	2/0	4.....0.....0	0.....1.....1 3/4
Sampson MATHEWS (Colo.)			2150	6/1	653...19.....2	9...16.....2 1/4
John McCUTCHEN			342	7/0	132...10.....6	1...19.....9
ditto			31	2/0	3.....2.....0	0.....1.....0
Thomas MEEK			310	7/9	115.....2.....6	1...14.....6 1/2
Samuel McCHESNEY			500	4/4	108.....6.....8	1...12.....6
Daniel MEEK			250	6/1	76.....0...10	1.....2.....9 1/2
John MEEK			566	4/4	122...12.....8	1...16.....9 1/2
William MATEER			520	6/1	158.....3.....4	2.....7.....5 1/4
George MATHEWS (Genl.)			200	1/9	17...10.....0	0.....5.....9
John McCOLLOM			150	1/9	12...14.....2	0.....3...11 1/4
John McCOY (Capt.)			146	10/6	76...13.....0	1.....2...11 1/4
ditto			117	1/9	10.....4.....6	0.....3.....0 3/4
ditto			118	2/0	11...16.....0	0.....3.....5 1/2
Duncan McFARLAND			100	7/9	38...15.....0	0...11.....7 1/2
ditto			119	1/3	7.....8.....9	0.....2.....2
Moses MOORE			1105	3/6	198.....7.....6	2...18.....0
ditto			124	2/0	12.....8.....0	0.....3.....9
Levi MOORE			500	2/8	66...13.....4	1.....0.....0
James McCARTY			215	2/8	28...13.....4	0.....8.....7

(page 51 contd. Augusta County Land Tax Return of Charles Cameron for 1787)

Persons Names Owning Land	No. of Lotts	Yearly Rent	Quantity of Land	Rate of Land per Acre	Total Amt. of Value of Land excl. of Lotts	Amt. of Tax at 1 1/2 p cent
John MAULENAX JUNR.			50	2/8	6...13.....4	0.....2.....0
ditto			60	2/8	6.....0.....0	0.....1...10 1/2
Samuel McDANNALD			300	5/9	78...15.....0	1.....3.....7 1/2
Samuel MOSSES			100	/10	4.....3.....4	0.....1.....3
Robert McCRAY			110	1/0	5...10.....0	0.....1.....7 1/2
William McCOY			70	3/6	12.....5.....0	0.....3.....8
James McCLOUGHLIN			163	1/9	14.....5.....3	0.....4.....3 1/4
Mary MOORE (Widow)			220	4/4	47...13.....4	0...14.....2 1/2
William McCUTCHEN			100	8/8	43.....6.....8	0...13.....1 1/2
Robert McCUTCHEN			258	8/8	111...16.....0	1...13.....4 1/2
ditto			50	1/6	3...15.....0	0.....1.....1 1/2

(page 52. Augusta County Land Tax Return of Charles Cameron for 1787)

Persons Names Owning Land	No. of Lotts	Yearly Rent	Quantity of Land	Rate of Land per Acre	Total Amt. of Value of Land excl. of Lotts	Amt. of Tax at 1 1/2 p cent
Robert McCUTCHEN			101	2/0	10.....2.....0	0.....3.....0 3/4
Edward MORTON			125	2/6	15...12.....6	0.....4.....8 1/4
Hugh MORRISON			95	3/0	14.....5.....0	0.....4.....3 1/4
William NUTINGHAM			323	1/9	28.....5.....8	0...10.....8
ditto			123	1/6	9.....4.....6	0.....2...10
George NEAGLE			100	1/9	8...15.....0	0.....2.....7 1/2
Henry NULL			100	2/8	13.....6.....8	0.....4.....0
John POAGE			1039	3/6	181...16.....6	2...14.....6 1/2
ditto			240	1/6	18.....0.....0	0.....5.....6 1/2
ditto			400	4/4	86...13.....4	1.....6.....0
George POAGE (Capt.)			200	4/4	43.....6.....8	0...13.....0
ditto			382	1/0	19.....2.....0	0.....5...11
Lofty PULLIN			321	8/8	139.....2.....0	2.....1.....8 1/4
ditto			400	1/3	25.....0.....0	0.....7.....6
John PEEBLES			209	10/6	109...14.....6	1...12...10 3/4
ditto			198	1/3	11...11.....6	0.....3.....6
John PLUNKET			160	3/6	17...10.....0	0.....5.....3
Christian PICKLE			100	4/4	21...13.....4	0.....6.....6
Henry PENNINGER			180	10/6	94...10.....0	1.....8.....4
ditto			98	2/0	9...16.....0	0.....2...11
Garrit PECK			53	2/8	7.....1.....4	0.....2.....1 1/4
John PAINTER			45	3/6	7...17.....6	0.....2.....4 1/2
Mathew PATTON			512	3/6	89...10.....0	1.....7.....6 1/4
James RAMSEY (of John)			240	7/0	84.....0.....0	1.....5.....2 1/4
ditto (of do.)			316	7/0	110...12.....0	1...13.....2
William RHEA			257	6/1	78.....3.....5	1.....3.....5 1/2
ditto			150	/10	6.....5.....0	0.....1...10 1/2
ditto			112	1/6	8.....8.....0	0.....2.....7 1/2
John RADMAN			124	4/4	26...17.....4	0.....8.....0 3/4
Henry ROCKEY			568	3/6	99.....8.....0	1.....9.....9 3/4
John RHEA			110	6/1	33.....9.....2	0...10.....3 1/2
ditto			50	/10	2.....1.....8	0.....0.....7 1/2
William RAMSEY			72	2/8	9...12.....0	0.....2...10 1/2
ditto			50	2/0	6.....0.....0	0.....1.....9 1/2
William ROBERTSON			80	2/8	10...13.....4	0.....3.....2 1/4

(page 52 contd. Augusta County Land Tax Return of Charles Cameron for 1787)

Persons Names Owning Land	No. of Lotts	Yearly Rent	Quantity of Land	Rate of Land per Acre	Total Amt. of Value of Land excl. of Lotts	Amt. of Tax at 1 1/2 p cent
Joseph RAY			100	2/8	13.....6.....8	0.....4.....0
Robert RUSK			500	3/6	87...10.....0	1.....6.....3
ditto			385	1/9	22.....7.....6	0.....6.....7 1/2
James RUCKER, SENR.			360	2/8	48.....0.....0	0...14.....4 3/4
ditto			145	1/9	12...13.....9	0.....3.....9 3/4
ditto			345	1/6	25...17.....6	0.....7.....9 1/4
James RUCKER, JUNR.			285	2/8	38.....0.....0	0...11.....4 3/4
William RIDER			176	/10	7.....6.....8	0.....2.....2 1/4
John RICE's Estate			50	2/8	6...13.....4	0.....2.....0
Samuel RADMAN			200	3/6	35.....0.....0	0...10.....6
ditto (from FLECK)			44	2/6	5...10.....0	0.....1.....8
Nicholas SYBERT			769	1/6	57...13.....6	0...17.....2 1/2
William SMITH's Estate			180	5/8	47.....5.....0	0...14.....2
Zachariah STOUT			92	2/6	6...18.....0	0.....2.....0 3/4
Robert ST. CLAIR (for McCLANAHAN)			500	7/9	195.....0.....0	2...12.....6

(page 53. Augusta County Land Tax Return of Charles Cameron for 1787)

Persons Names Owning Land	No. of Lotts	Yearly Rent	Quantity of Land	Rate of Land per Acre	Total Amt. of Value of Land excl. of Lotts	Amt. of Tax at 1 1/2 p cent
William STEWART			437	4/4	94...13.....8	1.....8.....4 3/4
ditto			122	1/3	7...12.....0	0.....1...10 1/2
Peter SICKAFORIS			200	7/9	77...10.....0	1.....3.....3
ditto			250	3/6	43...15.....0	0...13.....1 1/2
Van SWARINGIN			116	2/8	15.....9.....4	0.....4.....7 1/2
ditto			100	/10	4.....3.....4	0.....1.....3
Robert STEWART			300	5/3	78...15.....0	1.....3.....7 1/2
Andrew SUTTELINGTON			310	13/1	202...15...10	3.....0...10
ditto			337	3/6	58...19.....6	0...17.....8 1/4
ditto			167	1/6	12...10.....6	0.....3.....9 1/2
John SUTTELINGTON			224	10/6	117...12.....0	1...15.....3 1/4
James STONE			69	2/8	9.....4.....0	0.....2.....9
Robert SHIELDS			150	3/6	26.....5.....0	0.....7...10 1/2
John STEWART			246	5/3	67...11.....6	0...19.....7 1/2
Robert SMITH			300	4/4	65.....0.....0	0...19.....6
Leonard SEEMAN			200	5/3	52...10.....0	0...15.....9
ditto			86	1/9	5.....7.....6	0.....1.....7
ditto			30	1/3	1...17.....6	0.....0.....6 1/2
ditto			27	1/3	1...13.....9	0.....0.....5 1/2
Leonard SEEMAN, JUNR.			26	1/6	1...19.....0	0.....0.....6 3/4
John SUMWALT			150	5/3	39.....7.....6	0...11.....9 3/4
George SUMWALT			150	2/8	20.....0.....0	0.....6.....0
Michael SNARE (Hampshire)			50	3/6	8...15.....0	0.....2.....7 1/2
John SNIDER			50	2/8	6...13.....4	0.....2.....0
Michael SEIMAN			40	3/6	7.....0.....0	0.....2.....1
John SEIMAN			100	4/4	21...13.....1	0.....6.....6
Leonard SEIMON (S. Fork)			50	1/9	4.....7.....6	0.....1.....3 3/4
George SEIMON			139	4/4	29...18.....4	0.....8...11 1/2
ditto			85	3/0	12...15.....0	0.....3.....9 3/4
Peter SMITH			100	5/3	26.....5.....0	0.....7...10 1/2
Paul SUMMERS			225	4/4	48...15.....0	0...14.....7 1/2
ditto .			50	1/3	3.....2.....6	0.....0...10 1/2
Patrick SLATERY			300	1/3	18...15.....0	0.....5.....6 3/4

(page 53 contd. Augusta County Land Tax Return of Charles Camron for 1787)

Persons Names Owning Land	No. of Lotts	Yearly Rent	Quantity of Land	Rate of Land per Acre	Total Amt. of Value of Land excl. of Lotts	Amt. of Tax at 1 1/2 p cent
Patrick SLATORY			300	/10	12...10.....0	0.....3.....9
Henry STONE			180	2/8	24.....0.....0	0.....7.....2 1/4
Jonis SUCK (Hampshire)			200	3/6	35.....0.....0	0...10.....6
Henry SYBERT			100	2/8	13.....6.....8	0.....4.....0
Pastian STONE			95	7/0	33.....5.....0	0.....9...11 1/2
John SLAVENS			380	1/9	33.....5.....0	0.....9...11 1/2
William SHARP			300	4/4	65.....0.....0	0...19.....6
Henry SWADLEY			100	3/6	17...10.....0	0.....5.....3
Stuffell SUMWALT			200	/10	8.....6.....8	0.....2.....6
George SHEITZE			50	2/8	6...13.....4	0.....2.....0
Daniel SMITH, JUNR.			160	1/9	13.....2.....6	0.....3...11 1/4
Ralph STEWART			100	2/8	13.....6.....8	0.....4.....0
Joseph SUTTON			100	1/9	8...15.....0	0.....2.....7 1/2
Daniel STOUT			100	1/9	8...15.....0	0.....2.....7 1/2
George STOUT			131	5/3	34.....7.....9	0...10.....4
ditto			50	1/3	3.....2.....6	0.....0...10 1/2
James STEPHENSON			286	3/6	50.....1.....0	0...15.....0
Thomas SMITH (Major)			303	5/3	79...10.....9	1.....3...10 1/2
William THOMPSON			325	7/0	113...15.....0	1...14.....1 1/2

(page 54. Augusta County Land ax Return of Charles Cameron for 1787)

Persons Names Owning Land	No. of Lotts	Yearly Rent	Quantity of Land	Rate of Land per Acre	Total Amt. of Value of Land excl. of Lotts	Amt. of Tax at 1 1/2 p cent
Edward THOMPSON			50	5/3	13.....2.....6	0.....3...11 1/2
Lewis TACKET			797	1/9	69...14.....9	1.....0...11
Ezekiel TOWNDSEND			40	2/8	5.....6.....8	0.....1.....7
James TANNER			387	1/9	38...17.....3	0...11.....7 3/4
James TOWNDSEND			80	2/8	10...13.....4	0.....3.....2 1/4
Christopher TACKET			375	1/9	32...16.....3	0.....9...10 1/2
Alexander THOMPSON			84	6/1	25...11.....0	0.....7.....8
John VANCE's Estate			187	7/0	65.....9.....0	0...19.....7 1/2
Samuel VANCE (Colo.)			577	4/4	125.....0.....4	1...17.....6
Adam VERNER			117	1/9	10.....4.....9	0.....3.....2
John VACHUB			307	7/0	107.....9.....0	1...12.....2 3/4
ditto			16	/10	0...13.....0	0.....0.....2 1/2
Robert VACHUB			300	5/3	78...15.....0	1.....3.....7 1/2
Joseph VACHUB			78	8/8	33...16.....0	0...10.....1 1/2
William WILSON			304	8/8	131...14.....8	1...19.....6
ditto			262	2/8	34...18.....8	0...10.....5 3/4
ditto			400	1/3	25.....0.....0	0.....7.....6
Stephen WILSON			300	8/8	130.....0.....0	1...19.....0
John WILSON			304	8/8	131...14.....9	1...19.....6
James WOODS			305	2/8	40.....3.....4	0...12.....2 1/2
Elizabeth WILSON			175	10/6	91...17.....6	1.....7.....6 3/4
ditto			86	1/9	7.....6.....6	0.....2.....3
William WRIGHT			106	5/3	27...16.....6	0.....8.....4 1/2
Robert WALLACE			240	8/8	104.....0.....0	1...11.....2 1/2
Jacob WARRICK			1745	3/6	305.....7.....6	4...11.....7 1/4

(page 54 contd. Augusta County Land Tax Return of Charles Cameron for 1787)

Persons Names Owning Land	No. of Lotts	Yearly Rent	Quantity of Land	Rate of Land per Acre	Total Amt. of Value of Land excl. of Lotts	Amt. of Tax at 1 1/2 p cent
John WORMSLEY			150	3/6	26.....5.....0	0.....7...10
ditto			384	1/3	24.....0.....0	0.....5...10 1/2
William WARD			135	1/9	11...16.....3	0.....3.....6 1/2
Michael WILFONG			120	3/6	21.....0.....0	0.....6.....3 1/2
Christopher WAGONER			90	2/8	12.....0.....0	0.....3.....7
Alexander WILEY			200	1/9	17...13.....0	0.....5.....3
ditto			91	/10	3...15...10	0.....1.....1 1/2
Joseph WRIGHT's Estate			200	2/8	26...13.....4	0.....8.....0
William WARRICK			800	2/8	106...13.....4	1...12.....0
William WILSON (B. Pasture)			172	6/1	52.....6.....4	0...15.....8 1/4
Thomas WORMSLEY			45	2/8	6.....0.....0	0.....1.....9 1/2
Phillip WIMOUR			100	1/9	8...15.....0	0.....2.....7 1/2
ditto			146	1/3	9.....2.....6	0.....2...10 1/2
Abijah WARREN			288	/10	12.....0.....0	0.....3.....7
John WAIDE			100	/10	4.....3.....4	0.....1.....3
John WARRICK			200	1/9	17...10.....0	0.....5.....3
Jacob WIMERT			154	1/3	9...12.....6	0.....2...11
Henry WHITEMAN			146	1/6	10...19.....0	0.....3.....2
Andrew YEAGER			98	2/8	13.....1.....4	0.....3...11
William YOOL (from WRIGHT)			205	6/1	62.....7.....1	0...18.....8

(page 55)

List of the Land Tax within the District of JAMES RAMSAY, Commissioner in the County of Augusta for the year 1787.

Persons Names Owning Land	No. of Lots	Yearly Rent	Quantity of Land	Rate of Land pr. Acre	Total Amt. of Value of Land excl. of Lots	Amt. of Tax at 1 1/2 p cent
ASKINS, John (Shoemaker			200	3/6	35.....0.....6	0...10.....6
ASKINS, John			127	3/11	24...19.....5	0.....7.....5 3/4
do.			49	3/11	9...11...11	0.....2...10
ARMSTRONG, William			200	6/1	60...16.....8	0...18.....3
do.			328	6/1	99...15.....4	1.....9...11 1/2
ARGABRIGHT. John			150	3/11	29.....7.....6	0.....8.....9 3/4
ARGABRIGHT, Augustine			121	5/3	31...15.....3	0.....9.....7
ALLEN, William			130	6/1	39...10...10	0...11...10 1/2
AFREEL. Jeremiah			260	7/9	100...15.....0	1...10.....2
AFREEL, Daniel			220	6/1	66...10.....0	1.....0.....0 3/4
do.			77	1/9	6...15.....7	0.....2.....0 1/4
do (for Son)			188	2/8	24...13.....4	0.....7.....4 3/4
ABNEY, John	2	36	230	5/3	60.....7.....6	0...18.....1 1/4
do. (Exr. for McDONOUGH)	1/2	15		(nothing else recorded)		
ABNEY, John			120	2/8	16.....0.....0	0.....2.....9 1/2

(page 55 contd. Augusta County Land Tax Return of James Ramsay for 1787)

Persons Names Owning Land	No. of Lots	Yearly Rent	Quantity of Land	Rate of Land pr. Acre	Total Amt. of Value of Land excl. of Lots	Amt. of Tax at 1 1/2 p cent
ABNEY, John			6	5/3	1...11.....6	0.....0.....5 1/2
do.			1	8/8	0.....8.....9	0.....0.....1 1/2
(New Grant) do.			275	1/9	24.....1.....0	0.....7.....2
ADAIR, Neal			200	3/6	30.....0.....0	0...10.....6
do.			150	1/5	10...12.....6	0.....3.....2 1/2
ALLEN, Monticu			400	8/8	173.....6.....8	2...12.....0
do.			80	8/8	34...13.....4	0...10.....3
ALLEN, Robert Junr.			80	15/3	61.....0.....0	0...18.....3 1/2
do.			100	2/8	13.....6.....8	0.....4.....0
ALEXANDER, Andrew			204	6/6	66.....6.....0	0...19...10
ALLEN, Elizabeth			147	6/1	44...14.....3	0...13.....5
ALEXANDER, Hugh			314	8/8	136.....1.....4	2.....9.....0
do.			50	7/0	17...10.....0	0.....5.....2
ARMSTRONG, William			200	7/	70.....0.....0	1.....1.....0
do.			170	1/9	14...17.....6	0.....4.....5 1/2

(page 56. Augusta County Land Tax Return of James Ramsay for 1787)

Persons Names Owning Land	No. of Lots	Yearly Rent	Quantity of Land	Rate of Land pr. Acre	Total Amt. of Value of Land excl. of Lots	Amt. of Tax at 1 1/2 p cent
ARMSTRONG, Robert			224	7/	78.....8.....0	1.....3.....6 1/2
ALEXANDER, Gabriel			360	7/	127.....1.....0	1...18.....1 1/2
do.			130	1/5	9.....4.....2	0.....2.....9 1/4
ALEXANDER, John			260	3/6	45...10.....0	0...13.....7 3/4
ALEXANDER, Andrew			194	2/8	25...17.....4	0.....7.....9
do.			90	1/5	6.....7.....6	0.....2.....3
ADAIR, John			100	2/	10.....0.....0	0.....3.....0
BEVERLEY, Robert	1	5				
BURNS, Elizabeth	2	45				
BLAIR, Elizabeth	1/2	16				
BRAND, James (Dr.)			200	6/1	60...16.....8	0...18.....3
BUCHANAN, Patrick (Capt.)			200	3/6	35.....0.....0	0...10.....6
BUCHANAN, John Senr.			125	7/9	48.....8.....9	0...14.....6 3/4
BLAIR, William			150	3/11	29.....7.....6	0.....8.....9 1/4
BRAWFORD, Rebecca			200	7/	70.....0.....0	1.....1.....0
BLAIR, Joseph			300	4/4	65.....0.....0	0...19.....6
BERRY, George			249	7/9	96...11.....9	1.....8...11 1/2
BERRY, William Junr.			98	7/	34.....6.....0	0...10.....3 1/2
do.			50	2/2	5.....8.....4	0.....1.....7 1/2
BURGESS, William			240	1/9	21.....0.....0	0.....6.....3 1/2
BROWN, Benjamin			100	8/8	43.....6.....8	0...13.....0
do.			30	7/	10...10.....0	0.....3.....1 3/4
do.			55	2/2	5...19.....2	0.....1.....9 1/2
do.			100	8/8	43.....6.....8	0...13.....0
BROWN, Thomas			300	7/9	116.....5.....0	1...14...10 1/4
do.			70	5/3	18...17.....6	0.....5.....6
BROWN, James			295	6/6	95...17.....6	1.....8.....9
BURK, William			268	3/11	32...12..7 1/2	0...19.....9 1/4
BELL, William Senr.			200	2/8	26...13.....4	0.....8.....0
do.			217	1/5	15...17.....5	0.....4.....9
BELL, James Senr.			300	6/1	91.....5.....0	1.....7...10 1/2
do.			113	2/8	14...11.....4	0.....4.....3

(page 56 contd. Augusta County Land Tax Return of James Ramsay for 1787)

Persons Names Owning Land	No. of Lots	Yearly Rent	Quantity of Land	Rate of of Land p Acre	Total Value of Land excl. of Lots	Amt. of Amt. of Tax at 1 1/2 p cent
BELL, William Junr.			206	7/5	76.....7...10	1.....2...11

(page 57. Augusta County Land Tax Return of James Ramsay for 1787)

Persons Names Owning Land	No. of Lots	Yearly Rent	Quantity of Land	Rate of of Land p Acre	Total Value of Land excl. of Lots	Amt. of Amt. of Tax at 1 1/2 p cent
BELL, James (Capt.)			240	6/1	73.....0.....0	1...11...10 3/4
do.			80	1/9	7.....0.....0	0.....2.....1
do.			100	1/6	7...10.....0	0.....2.....3
BROWN, John			155	6/1	47.....2...11	0...14.....1 3/4
BAILER, Jacob			235	4/9	55...16.....3	0...16.....9
BRADY, James			300	1/5	21.....5.....0	0.....6.....4 1/2
BOWYER, William (Colo.)	1	35	50	8/8	21...13.....4	·0.....6.....6
do.			146	4/4	31...12.....8	0.....9.....5 3/4
do.			54	3/6	9.....9.....0	0.....2.....9 1/2
do.			15 1/2 (carried to the last page)			
BOWYER, Michael	1	18	23	3/6	4.....0.....6	0.....1.....2
do.			33	3/6	5...15.....6	0.....1.....8
BUCKHANAN, David			415	3/3	67.....8.....9	1.....0.....2 3/4
BUCKHANAN, Sarah			150	3/	22...10.....0	0.....6.....9
BELL, Robert			190	2/8	25.....6.....8	0.....7.....7
BUCKHANAN, William			370	3/6	64...15.....0	0...19.....4 1/2
BROWN, John			252	5/3	66.....3.....0	0...19...10
BERRY, Charles			426	7/	149.....2.....0	2.....4.....8 1/2
BEARD, Thomas			318	4/9	75...10.....6	1.....2.....7 1/2
BEARD, William Senr.			400	9/7	191...13.....4	2...17.....6
BROOKS, John Senr.			364	8/3	150.....3.....0	2.....5.....0 1/2
BEST, James			275	2/2	29...15...10	0.....8.....1 1/4
BRATTON, Elizabeth			200	3/6	32...10.....0	0.....9.....9
do.			120	1/5	8...10.....0	0.....2.....6 1/2
BRATTON, John			120	4/4	26.....0.....0	0.....7.....9 1/2
BELL, James			247	8/8	107.....0.....8	1...12.....1 1/4
BUMGARDNER, Christopher			120	5/3	31...10.....0	0.....9.....5 1/4
BURNS, Richard			280	1/5	19...16.....8	0.....5.....6 1/4
BELEW, Abraham			20	3/6	3...10.....0	0.....1.....0 3/4

(page 58. Augusta County Land Tax Return by James Ramsay for 1787)

Persons Names Owning Land	No. of Lots	Yearly Rent	Quantity of Land	Rate of of Land p Acre	Total Value of Land excl. of Lots	Amt. of Amt. of Tax at 1 1/2 p cent
BOYD, Thomas			240	7/	84.....0.....0	1.....5.....2 1/4
do.			80	1/9	7.....0.....0	0.....2.....1
BOYD, John			115	7/	40.....5.....0	0...12.....0 3/4
do.			20	3/6	3...10.....0	0.....1.....0 1/2
BROWNLEE, John Senr.			222	8/3	91...11.....6	1.....7.....2
do.			62	3/6	10...17.....0	0.....3.....3
BROWNLEE, William			100	8/3	41.....5.....0	0...12.....4 1/2
do.			83	2/8	11.....1.....4	0.....3.....3 3/4
BROWNLEE, John			232	7/9	51.....3.....0	0...15.....4
do.			18	3/6	3.....3.....0	0.....0...11 1/4
BRIGHT, George			170	7/	59...10.....0	0...17...10
do.			300	1/5	21.....5.....0	0.....6.....4 1/2
BLACK, Cutlive			160	4/	32.....0.....0	0.....9.....7
BRAWFORD, Samuel			400	8/3	169.....2.....6	2...10.....9
BURK, John			212	7/5	78...12.....4	1.....3.....7

(page 58 contd. Augusta County Land Tax Return of James Ramsay for 1787)

Persons Names Owning Land	No. of Lotts	Yearly Rent	Quantity of Land	Rate of of Land p Acre	Total Amt. of Value of Land excl. of Lots	Amt. of Tax at 1 1/2 p cent
BLACK, John			121	5/3	31...15.....3	0.....9.....6 1/4
do.			134	8/8	58.....1.....4	0...17.....5
BLACKWOOD, Samuel			105	4/4	22...15.....0	0.....6.....9 3/4
BROWN, William			225	5/8	63...15.....0	0...19.....1 1/2
do.			148	5/3	38...17.....0	0...11.....7 3/4
do.			80	1/9	7.....0.....0	0.....2.....1
BELL, James (S. R.)			300	7/9	116.....5.....0	1...14...10 1/2
BELL, John (S. R.)			300	7/9	116.....5.....0	1...14...10 1/2
do.			130	1/5	9.....4.....2	0.....2.....9 1/4
BLACK, William			316	7/5	117.....3.....8	1...15.....1 3/4
BLACK, Samuel			369	7/5	136...16.....9	2.....1.....0 1/2
do.			200	6/1	61.....5.....0	0...18.....4 1/2
do.			200	1/5	14.....3.....4	0.....4.....3
BERRY, John (B. Creek)			389	2/2	43.....2.....4	0...12...11

(page 60. Augusta County Land Tax Return of James Ramsay for 1787)

Persons Names Owning Land	No. of Lotts	Yearly Rent	Quantity of Land	Rate of of Land p Acre	Total Amt. of Value of Land excl. of Lots	Amt. of Tax at 1 1/2 p cent
BRENT, James			200	4/4	43.....6.....8	0...13.....0
do.			90	1/9	7...17.....6	0.....2.....4
do.			400	1/5	28.....6.....8	0.....8.....6
BROBACK, Philip			80	2/8	18...13.....4	0.....3.....2 1/4
BOFANG, John	1	40				
CALDWELL, John			300	7/9	116.....5.....0	1...14...10 1/2
CHAPMAN, John			100	4/4	23...16.....8	0.....7.....1 3/4
COOK, John			30	5/3	7...17.....6	0.....2.....4 1/4
COCKS, Jacob			100	2/2	10...16.....8	0.....3.....3
CROW, Benjamin			200	5/3	52...10.....0	0...15.....9
CAMPBELL, James			200	4/4	43.....6.....8	0...13.....0
do.			27	3/11	7.....5.....9	0.....1.....7 1/2
CALLISON, James			266	5/8	75.....7.....4	1.....2.....7 1/4
CAIL, Peter			214	5/3	55.....3.....6	0...16.....6 1/2
do.			122	2/8	16.....5.....4	0.....4...10 1/2
CUNINGHAM, David			226	7/	79.....2.....0	1.....3.....8 3/4
CUNINGHAM, John (Capt.)			173	6/6	56.....4.....6	0...16...10 3/4
CAIL, David Senr.			30	4/4	6...10.....0	0.....1...11 1/4
CAIL, Jacob			198	5/8	56.....2.....0	0...16...10
COULTER, Michael			436	7/9	168...19.....0	2...10.....8 1/4
do.			100	6/	30.....0.....0	0.....8.....9
CRAWFORD, William	1	45	800	4/4	173.....6.....8	2...12.....0
do.			90	2/8	12.....0.....0	0.....3.....7
do.			130	2/2	14.....1.....8	0.....4.....2 3/4
do.			133	1/9	11...12.....9	0.....3.....5 3/4
CRAWFORD, John			390	5/3	102.....7.....6	1...10.....8 1/2
do.			201	4/4	43...11.....0	0...13.....0 3/4
do.			95	2/8	12...13.....4	0.....3.....9 1/2
CUNINGHAM, James Senr.			90	7/	31...10.....0	0.....9.....5 1/4
do.			26	1/9	2.....5.....6	0.....9.....8
CUMMINS, Robert Senr.			164	6/6	53.....6.....0	0...15...11 3/4
do. (New Grant)			135	1/6	10.....9.....6	0.....3.....1

(page 61. Augusta County Land Tax Return of James Ramsay for 1787)

Persons Names Owning Land	No. of Lotts	Yearly Rent	Quantity of Land	Rate of Land p Acre	Total Amt. of Value of Land excl. of Lots	Amt. of Tax at 1 1/2 p cent
CLUNIGER, Valentine			16	4/4	3.....4.....4	0.....1.....0 3/4
CALDWELL, William (T. S.)			130	7/5	48.....4.....2	0...14.....5 1/2
do.			186	6/1	56...11.....6	0...16.....8
CAMPBELL, Sarah			390	7/5	174...12.....6	2...12.....4 1/2
CUNINGHAM, John			210	4/4	45...10.....0	0...13.....7 3/4
CLARK, James Junr.			212	5/5	54.....5.....6	0...16.....8 1/4
CALDWELL, John (T. S.)			275	7/5	101...19.....7	1...10.....7
CARRUTHERS, James			113	3/6	19...15.....6	0.....5...11 1/4
CARRUTHERS, David			200	2/8	26...13.....4	0.....8.....0
COULTER, John Senr.			150	5/3	40.....4.....3	0...12.....0
do.			106	2/6	13.....5.....0	0.....3...11 1/2
COULTER, David			114	3/6	19...19.....0	0.....5...11 3/4
do.			50	5/3	13.....2.....6	0.....4.....0
CHESNUT, William			300	2/8	42...13.....4	0...12.....9 1/2
CAMPBELL, Andrew			30	2/8	4.....0.....0	0.....1.....2 1/4
COULTER, James			300	4/4	32...10.....0	0.....9.....9
CAMPBELL, James & John (S.R.)			247	5/3	64...16.....9	0...19.....5 1/2
do.			130	1/9	11.....7.....6	0.....3.....4 3/4
CARRUTHERS, Thomas			100	3/6	17...10.....0	0.....5.....3
COOPER, James			150	3/6	26.....5.....0	0.....7...10 1/2
CUNINGHAM, James			225	3/6	39.....7.....6	0...11...10
CARSON, Samuel			175	8/3	72.....3.....9	1.....1.....7 1/2
CAMPBELL, Mary			100	2/8	13.....6.....8	0.....4.....0
CAMPBELL, Robert			100	2/8	13.....6.....8	0.....4.....0
do.			150	1/9	13.....2.....6	0.....3...11 1/4
CAMPBELL, George			140	1/9	12.....5.....0	0.....3.....8
do.			50	1/9	4.....7.....6	0.....1.....3 3/4
CHRISTIAN, John Senr.			208 1/2	7/9	80...15...10 1/2	1...4....2 3/4
CHRISTIAN, Robert Junr.			208 1/2	7/9	80...15...10 1/2	1...4....2 3/4
CHRISTIAN, Gilbert			269	8/8	116...11.....4	1...14...11 1/2
CHRISTIAN, Patrick			269	8/8	116...11.....4	1...14...11 1/2
CHRISTIAN, William			200	8/8	86...13.....4	1.....6.....0

(page 62. Augusta County Land Tax Return of James Ramsay for 1787)

CHRISTIAN, John, Gilbert & Robert, Legatees of John, deced.			338	8/8	146.....9.....4	2.....3...11 1/4
COAL, James			400	1/5	28.....6.....9	0.....8.....6
COFFEY, William			186	2/8	24...16.....0	0.....7.....5 1/4
COALTER, John Junr.			100	2/8	13.....6.....8	0.....4.....0
COALTER, Joseph			253	3/6	44.....5.....6	0...13.....3 1/4
COMER, Margaret			116	1/9	10.....3.....0	0.....3.....0 1/2
CARTMELL, Samuel			306	3/6	53...11.....0	0...16.....0 3/4
COOK, John			225	2/	25...10.....0	0.....7.....8
CLARK, James Senr.			200	5/3	52...10.....0	0...15.....9
COBB, William			87	2/6	10...17.....6	0.....3.....3 1/4
CHILMORE, Lewis			101	5/3	26...10.....3	0.....7...11 1/2
DONALDSON, Robert			238	5/3	61...13.....9	0...18.....6
DOWNY, Martha			700	5/8	198.....6.....8	2...19.....6
DAILEY, John			150	6/6	48...15.....0	0...14.....7 1/2

(page 62 contd. Augusta County Land Tax Return of James Ramsay for 1787)

Persons Names Owning Land	No of Lotts	Yearly Rent	Quantity of Land	Rate of of Land p Acre	Total Amt. of Value of Land excl. of Lots	Amt. of Tax at 1 1/2 p cent
DAUGHERTY, Hugh			200	3/11	39.....3.....4	0...11.....3
DAVIS, Walter			160	7/9	62.....0.....0	0...18.....7
do.			50	1/9	4.....7.....6	0.....1.....3 3/4
DAVIS, James			322	7/	112...14.....0	1...13.....9 3/4
do.			5	7/	1...15.....0	0.....0.....6 1/4
DOWEL, Philip			186	3/11	36.....8.....6	0...10...11
DAVISON, John			280	2/8	37.....6.....8	0...11.....2 1/4
DOAKE, John			307	7/9	118...19.....3	1...15.....8 1/2
DOAKE, Robert			266	4/4	57...12.....8	1...17.....3 1/2
DOAKE, David			300	7/9	116.....5.....0	1...14...10 1/4
DORSET, Thomas			160	2/8	17.....6.....8	0.....5.....2 1/4
DAVIS, William / HALL, Henry	1	14				

(page 63. Augusta County Land Tax Return of James Ramsay for 1787)

Persons Names Owning Land	No of Lotts	Yearly Rent	Quantity of Land	Rate of of Land p Acre	Total Amt. of Value of Land excl. of Lots	Amt. of Tax at 1 1/2 p cent
EMMITT, John			60	7/	21.....0.....0	0.....6.....0
ESTILL, Rebecca			299	8/8	129...11.....4	1...18...10 1/4
ERWIN, James (Capt.)			252	7/9	79...13.....0	1...9.....3 1/2
do.			150	1/9	13.....2.....6	0...3...11 1/2
ERWIN, James Junr.			145	1/9	12...13.....9	0...3.....9 3/4
do.			150	4/4	32...10.....0	0.....9.....9
ELLIOTT, John			219 1/2	4/4	47...11.....2	0...14.....3
ELLIOTT, James			300	7/	105.....0.....0	1...11.....6
ESTRAP, Robert	1/2	12				
EAGLE, George			100	5/3	26.....5.....0	0.....7...10 3/4
ERWIN, James			156	4/4	33...16.....0	0...10.....1 1/2
do.			190	7/9	73.....2.....6	1.....3.....5
do.			2 1/2	7/9	0...19.....3	0.....0.....3 1/4
FULTON, Andrew			260	5/3	68...15.....6	1.....0.....7 1/2
FISHER, George			200	4/4	43.....6.....8	0...13.....0
FLOYD, Charles deced., (William McKENNY, Admr.)			90	2/2	9...15.....0	0.....2...11
FISHER, Frederick			60	2/8	8.....0.....0	0.....2.....4 3/4
FULTON, William			200	8/8	86...13.....4	1.....6.....0
FULLWIDER, Ulbrick			160 1/2	3/6	28.....1.....9	0.....8.....5
do.			40	1/9	3...10.....0	0.....1.....1
do.			30	1/9	2...12.....6	0.....0.....9 1/2
FERGUSON, William			170	4/9	40.....7.....6	0...12.....1 1/2
FULTON, Hugh			250	8/8	108.....6.....8	1...12.....6
FULTON, Mary			387	7/9	149...19.....3	2.....4...11
FULTON, John			309	8/8	133...18.....0	2.....0.....8
FAUL, George			195	7/	50...15.....0	0...15.....2 1/2
do.			154	5/3	40.....8.....6	0...12.....1 1/2
do.			136	3/5	23...16.....0	0.....7.....1 1/2
do.			290	2/2	31.....8.....4	0.....9.....5 1/4
FULLWIDER, John			42	3/11	8.....4.....6	0.....2.....5 1/2
FRINGER, Peter			266	7/	93.....2.....0	1.....9.....7 1/2

(page 64. Augusta County Land Tax Return of James Ramsay for 1787)

Persons Names Owning Land	No. of Lots	Yearly Rent	Quantity of Land of Land	Rate of Value of Land p Acre	Total Amt. of Value of Land excl. of Lots	Amt. of Tax at 1 1/2 p cent
GAMBLE, ROBERT (Colo.)	1/2	55				
GRINER, David	1	25				
do.	1	12				
GILKISON, Hugh			220	7/9	85.....5.....0	1.....5.....6 3/4
GIBSON, Samuel			226	8/8	97...18.....8	1.....9.....4 1/2
GILMER, James Senr.			204	7/9	79.....1.....0	1.....3.....8 1/2
GILKISON, William			265	5/3	69...11.....6	1.....0...10 1/4
GIBSON, Robert			142	5/3	37.....5.....6	0...11...2
GREAVES, William			100	3/11	19...11.....8	0.....5...10 1/2
GLEBE LAND, Moses HAYES, Tenant			200	7/	70.....0.....0	1.....1.....0
GIBSON, Alexander			220	7/9	85.....5.....0	1.....5.....6 3/4
do.			159	7/	55...13.....0	0...16.....8 1/2
do.			50	2/2	5.....8.....4	0.....1.....7 1/2
do.			205	4/4	44.....8.....4	0...13...4
do.			50	3/1	7...10.....2	0.....2.....3 3/4
do.			20	1/9	1...15.....0	0.....0.....6 1/4
do.			20	1/9	1...15.....0	0.....0.....6 1/4
GARDNER, Francis			199	5/3	52.....4.....9	0...15...8
do.			136	1/9	11...18.....0	0.....3.....6 3/4
GARDNER, Samuel			250	3/6	43...15.....0	0...13.....1 1/2
GREENWOOD, Margaret (Heir to Jennet, deced.)			105	6/6	33.....1.....6	0.....9...11
GUTHERY, William			490	5/8	138...16.....8	2.....1.....7 3/4
GROVE, Windle			114	7/	39...18.....0	0...11...11 1/2
GRAHAM, William			350	2/8	46...13.....4	0...14.....0
GRASS, Jacob Senr.			10	4/4	2.....3.....4	0.....0.....7 3/4
GABBERT, Jacob			210	5/3	55.....2.....6	0...16.....6 1/2
GRIFFIN, John	1/3	15				
HYSKEL, Peter	1	38	13	4/4	2...16.....4	0.....0...10
HUGHES, Euphemia	1	20	30	4/4	6...10.....0	0.....1...11 1/2
HANDREL, Philip			170	5/3	45.....8.....6	0...10.....7 1/2
HANDREL, Lawrence & George			95	4/4	20...11.....8	0.....6.....2

(page 65. Augusta County Land Tax Return of James Ramsay for 1787)

Persons Names Owning Land	No. of Lots	Yearly Rent	Quantity of Land	Rate of Value p Acre	Total Amt. of Value of Land	Amt. of Tax
HAWK, Henry			213	4/4	45.....3.....0	0...13...10
HEIZER, Samuel			110	4/4	23...16.....8	0.....7.....1 3/4
HUTSON, George			183	6/6	59.....9.....6	0...17...10 3/4
HANKEY, Simon			50	2/2	5.....8.....4	0.....1.....7 1/2
HENDERSON, Joseph			520	3/6	91.....7.....3	1.....7.....3 1/2
HANGER, Frederick			225	4/4	48...15.....0	0...14.....7 1/2
HAMILTON, Arthur			232	5/3	60...18.....0	0...18.....8 3/4
HAMILTON, James			153	5/3	40.....3.....1	0...10.....8
HAMILTON, John			200	5/3	60.....0.....0	0...16.....8
HAWTHORN, James			530	6/1	161.....4.....2	2.....8.....4 1/4
do.			220	10/6	115...10.....0	1.....14.....7 3/4
do.			50	1/9	4.....7.....6	0.....1.....3 1/4
HANNA. Robert			100	3/1	15.....8.....4	0.....4.....7 1/2
do.			60	2/2	6...10.....0	0.....1...11 1/4

(page 65 contd. Augusta County Land Tax Return of James Ramsay for 1787)

Persons Names Owning Land	No. of Lots	Yearly Rent	Quantity of Land	Rate of Land p Acre	Total Amt. of Value of Land excl. of Lots	Amt. of Tax at 1 1/2 p cent
HAYS, James			170	2/8	22...13.....4	0.....6.....9 1/2
do.			50	8/8	17...10.....0	0.....5.....3
HILL, James			84	2/2	9.....2.....0	0.....2.....8 3/4
do.			33	2/2	3...11.....6	0.....1.....0 3/4
do.			17	2/3	1...16...10	0.....0.....6 1/2
HANGER, Peter			280	5/3	73...10.....0	1.....2.....0 1/2
do.			313	5/3	93...16.....6	1.....8.....8
do.			85	2/8	11.....6.....8	0.....3.....4 3/4
do.			187	6/1	56...17.....6	0...17.....0 3/4
do.			280	3/6	49.....0.....0	0...14.....8 3/4
do.			124	2/8	16...10.....8	0.....4...11 1/2
do.			438	2/6	54...12.....6	0...16.....4 3/4
HANDLEY, John Senr.			150	7/	52...10.....0	0...15.....9
HUNTER, William			240	2/2	26.....0.....0	0.....7.....9 1/2
HINDS, Thomas			120	2/8	16.....0.....0	0.....4.....9 1/2
HULL, Francis			150	6/1	45...12.....6	0...13.....8 1/2
do.			47	2/8	6.....5.....4	0.....1...10 1/2
HARRIS, Robert			400	4/9	45.....0.....0	0.....8.....6

(page 66. Augusta County Land Tax Return of James Ramsay for 1787)

Persons Names Owning Land	No. of Lots	Yearly Rent	Quantity of Land	Rate of Land p Acre	Total Amt. of Value of Land excl. of Lots	Amt. of Tax at 1 1/2 p cent
HUNT, Charles			100	2/8	13.....6.....8	0.....4.....0
do.			20	8/8	8...13.....4	0.....2.....7
HARRISON, David			47	5/3	12.....6.....9	0.....3.....8 1/2
do.			153	2/8	20.....8.....0	0.....6.....1 1/4
HENDERSON, William			390	7/	136...10.....0	2.....0...11 1/2
HENDERSON, David			278 1/2	7/9	107...18.....4	1...12.....4 1/2
HALL, Edward			220	8/8	95.....6.....8	1.....8.....7
do.			125	2/8	16...13.....4	0.....5.....0
do.			100	2/8	13.....6.....8	0.....4.....0
do.			20	1/9	1...15.....0	0.....0.....6
do.			38	1/9	3.....6.....6	0.....1.....0
do.			32	5/	8.....0.....0	0.....2.....5
HUTCHISON, George			150	3/7	29.....7.....6	0.....9.....4 1/2
HENDERSON, David Senr.			100	1/	5.....0.....0	0.....1.....6
HENRY, Samuel			360	3/11	70...10.....0	1.....1.....1 3/4
do.			50	2/2	5.....8.....4	0.....1.....7 1/2
do.			300	4/9	71.....3.....0	1.....1.....4 1/2
HAYS, Samuel			209	8/8	90...11.....4	1.....7.....2
HUMPHREY, David			300	7/	105.....0.....0	1...11.....6
HENRY, James (Weaver)			100	7/	35.....0.....0	0...10.....6
HALL, Patrick			200	7/	70.....0.....0	1.....1.....0
do.			2	7/	0...14.....0	0.....0.....2 1/2
HENRY, James (B. S.)			334	7/	119.....0.....0	1...15.....8 1/2
do.			250	4/4	50.....3.....4	0...15.....1 3/4
do.			250	7/	87...10.....0	1.....6.....3
do.			250	8/8	108.....6.....8	1...12.....6
do.			100	3/6	17...10.....0	0.....5.....3
HAY, Patrick			212	7/9	62.....3.....0	0...18.....4
HOOFMAN, Gasper			100	5/3	26.....5.....0	0.....7...10 1/2

(page 66. contd. Augusta County Land Tax Return of James Ramsay for 1787)

Persons Names Owning Land	No. of Lots	Yearly Rent	Quantity of Land	Rate of Land p. Acre	Total Amt. of Value of Land excl. Lots	Amt. of Tax at 1 1/2 p cent
HUNTER, Samuel			196	7/	68...12.....0	1.....0.....6 3/4
do.			255	8/3	105.....3.....9	1...11.....6 1/2
do.			200	6/1	60...18.....8	0...18.....3

(page 67. Augusta Xounty Land Tax Return of James Ramsay for 1787)

HUNTER, John			240	5/8	68.....0.....0	1....0.....4 1/2
HAMILTON, Robert			160	3/11	31.....6.....8	0.....9.....4 3/4
HUGHS, Thomas			150	4/4	33...16.....0	0...10.....1 1/2
HOOFMAN, John			188	2/8	25.....0.....8	0.....7.....6
HANDLEY, William			100	10/6	52...10.....0	0...15.....9
HAUPH, Randolph			200	6/1	60...16.....8	0...18.....3
do.			100	3/11	19...11.....8	0.....5...10 1/2
do.			200	6/1	60...16.....8	0...18.....3
HEIZER, John			120	5/3	31...10.....0	0.....9.....5 1/2
HATTON, Mark (for Samuel BLACKWOOD's Heirs)			100	6/6	32...10.....0	0.....9.....9
HAGAN, Arthur			35	1/9	2...11.....3	0.....0.....9
INGLEMAN, William			180	4/4	39.....0.....0	0...11.....8 1/4
INGLEMAN, Peter			230	4/4	49...16.....8	0...14.....9
INNMAN, William			200	1/9	17...10.....0	0.....5.....3
JACKSON, John (Doctr:)			278	6/1	84...12.....2	1.....5.....4 1/2
JAMESON, George			366	3/6	54...12.....0	0...16.....4 1/2
do.			165	2/8	22.....0.....0	0.....6.....9
JONES, Gabriel			200	7/	70.....0.....0	1.....1.....0
do.			902	/10	37...11.....8	0...11.....3 1/4
JAMESON, John			200	8/8	86...13.....4	1.....4.....7
do.			40	2/8	5.....6.....8	0.....1.....7
KIRK. James			250	7/	75.....5.....0	1.....2.....6 3/4
KIRK, John			150	3/6	26...12.....0	0.....7...11 3/4
do.			76	7/	26.....6.....0	0.....7...10 1/2
KIRKPATRICK, John			110	5/3	55.....2.....6	0...16.....6 1/4
do.			100	2/8	13.....6.....8	0.....4.....0
KILLER, George			100	4/9	23...15.....0	0.....7.....1 1/4
do.			90	1/9	7...17.....6	0.....2.....4 1/4
do.			32	2/8	4.....5.....4	0.....1.....3 1/4

(page 68. Augusta County Land Tax Return of James Ramsay for 1787)

KIDD, Daniel	1	25	173	6/1	52...12.....5	0...15.....9 1/2
do.			87	4/4	18...17.....0	0.....5.....7 3/4
KERR, James for Joseph MARTIN			750	7/9	290...12.....6	4.....7.....2 1/4
KENNEDY, James (Rockbridge)			26	3/6	4...11.....0	0.....1.....4 1/4
KERR, William			188	6/1	57.....3.....8	0...17.....1 3/4
KING, John			169	3/6	27.....9.....3	0.....8.....2 3/4
do.			190	2/2	20.....4.....8	0.....6.....2
KILLER, Michael			150	1/8	19.....9.....0	0.....3...10

(page 68 contd. Augusta County Land Tax Return of James Ramsay for 1787)

Persons Names Owning Land	No. of Lots	Yearly Rent	Quantity of Land	Rate of land p Acre	Total Amt. of Value of Land excl. of Lots	Amt. of Tax at 1 1/2 p cent
KENEDY, William			370	1/8	25...16.....8	0.....7.....8 1/2
LIVINGSTON, William			130	4/4	38.....3.....4	0.....8.....5 1/4
do.			20	8/8	8...13.....4	0.....2....7
do.			15	3/6	2...12.....6	0.....0....9 1/2
LEDGERWOOD, William			187	7/	65.....9.....0	0...19....7
LOCKHART, James			130	2/8	17.....6.....8	0.....5....2 1/4
LOVINGOOD, Herman			210	6/1	63...17.....6	0...19.....2
do.			210	2/8	28.....0.....0	0.....8.....4 3/4
do.			50	1/9	4.....7.....6	0.....1.....3 3/4
do.			50	2/8	6...13.....4	.0.....2.....0
do.			70	2/6	8...15.....0	0.....2....7 1/2
LOGAN, William			140	5/3	36...15.....0	0...11....0 1/4
do.			25	3/6	4.....7.....6	0.....1.....3 3/4
LASSLEY, Thomas			144	2/2	15...12.....0	0.....4.....8
LODOWICK, George			108	6/6	35.....2.....0	0...10.....6 1/2
LEREW, Abraham			171	7/2	61.....5.....6	0...18.....4 1/2
do.			150	7/9	38.....2.....6	0...17.....5 1/4
LONG, Alexander			10	2/8	1.....6.....8	0.....0.....4 3/4
do.			400	1/5	28.....6.....8	0.....8.....6
LONG, Francis			100	8/8	43.....6.....8	0...13.....0
LONG, James			145	8/8	62...16.....8	0...18...10
LONG, Samuel			145	8/8	62...16.....8	0...18...10

(page 69. Augusta County Land Tax Return of James Ramsay for 1787)

Persons Names Owning Land	No. of Lots	Yearly Rent	Quantity of Land	Rate of land p Acre	Total Amt. of Value of Land excl. of Lots	Amt. of Tax at 1 1/2 p cent
LONG, David			200	7/	70.....0.....0	1.....1.....0
LONG, Joseph			200	7/	70.....0.....0	1.....1.....0
LOCKHART, William			300	1/5	21.....5.....0	0.....6.....4 1/2
LAIDCHEY, George			100	4/	20.....0.....0	0.....6.....0
do.			8	10/	4.....0.....0	0.....1.....2 1/2
LYONS, Henry			350	2/6	43...15.....0	0...13.....1 1/2
MATHEWS, George (Gl)			150	2/8	20.....0.....0	0.....6.....0
do.			560	3/6	98.....0.....0	1...9.....4 1/2
do.			16	4/4	3.....9.....6	0.....1.....0 1/2
do.			86 1/2	6/1	26.....6.....2	0.....7...10 3/4
MILLER, George			192	6/1	58.....8.....0	0...17.....6 1/4
do.			45	2/2	5.....5.....0	0.....1.....6 3/4
MARSHAL, John			269 1/2	5/3	70...14...10	1.....1.....2 1/2
McCLANAHAN's Heirs			310	7/	103...10.....0	1...11.....0 1/2
do.			190	1/9	16...12.....6	0.....4...11 3/4
McCORCLE, Samuel			321	3/1	49.....9.....9	0...14...10 3/4
McPHEETERS, Alexander			303	7/	106.....1.....0	1...11.....9
do.			28	3/11	5.....9.....0	0.....1.....9 3/4
McPHEETERS, John			388	7/9	150.....7.....0	2.....5.....1 1/4
do.			321	6/6	102.....7.....0	1...10.....8 1/2
McKITRICK, Robert			200	6/1	60...16.....8	0...18.....3
do.			170	2/8	22...13.....4	0.....6.....9 1/2
do.			90	1/9	7...17.....6	0.....2.....4 1/2
do.			100	6/1	30.....8.....4	0.....9.....1 1/2

(page 69 contd. Augusta County Land Tax Return of James Ramsay for 1787)

Persons Names Owning Land	No. of Lots	Yearly Rent	Quantity of Land	Rate of Land p Acre	Total Amt. of Value of Land excl. Lots	Amt. of Tax at 1 1/2 p cent
MOFFET, James			200	6/1	60...16.....8	0...18.....3
McCUTHEN, Samuel			237	7/9	91...16.....0	1.....7.....5 1/2
MINER, Thomas			122	2/8	16.....5.....4	0.....4...10 1/2
do.			50	1/9	4.....7.....6	0.....1.....4 3/4
do.			100	1/9	8...16.....9	0.....2.....6 3/4
do.			78	1/9	6...16.....6	0.....2.....0 1/2
McCROSKEY, David			181	3/6	31...13...10	0.....9.....4 1/2
MOFFETT, John Senr.			234	8/8	101.....8.....0	1...10.....5 1/2

(page 70. Augusta County Land Tax Return of James Ramsay for 1787)

Persons Names Owning Land	No. of Lots	Yearly Rent	Quantity of Land	Rate of Land p Acre	Total Amt. of Value of Land excl. Lots	Amt. of Tax at 1 1/2 p cent
McCLANAHAN, Alexander (Colo.)			560	6/6	182.....0.....0	2...14.....7
do.			200	1/9	17...10.....0	0.....5.....3
do.			222	7/9	86.....0.....6	1.....5.....9 1/4
McCLANAHAN, Robert			340	3/1	55.....5.....0	0...16.....6 3/4
McKINNEY, Alexander			310	3/1	47...15...10	0...14.....2
McKEE, Alexander			355	5/3	93.....3.....9	1.....7...11 1/2
McPHEETERS, William			367	9/7	175...17.....1	2...12.....9
MARTIN, Joseph			160	1/9	14.....0.....0	0.....4.....2 1/4
McCLINTOCK, William Senr.			172	4/4	38.....7.....0	0...11.....6
McCLINTOCK, William Junr.			100	3/1	19...11.....8	0.....5...10 1/2
McPHEETERS, William and Robert TRIMBLE			121	3/	18.....3.....0	0.....5.....4 1/2
McCUTCHIN, John			215	7/9	83.....6.....3	1.....5.....0
McCUTCHIN, William			290	7/9	112.....7.....6	1...13.....9 1/2
MARROW, Francis	1	24	15	3/6	2...12.....6	0.....0.....9 1/2
McDAVID, Patrick			50	8/8	21...13.....4	0.....6.....6
do.			25	4/4	5.....8.....4	0.....1.....7 1/2
MATHEWS, Sampson (Colo.)	1	5	196 1/2	2/8	26.....4.....5	0.....7...10 1/4
do.	1	1	196 1/2	2/8	26.....4.....5	0.....7...10 1/4
do. for NORTH	1	40				
do.			196 1/2	2/8	26.....4.....5	0.....7...10 1/4
do for McCUTCHIN			112	6/6	36.....8.....0	0...10...10
McDOWEL, William	1/2	35	25	4/4	5.....8.....4	0.....1.....7 1/2
do.	1	6	27	4/4	5...17.....0	0.....1.....9
do. from SHOWN			254	3/6	43...19.....0	0...13.....9
McDOWEL, Hugh	1/2	35	204	5/	51.....0.....0	0...15.....3 3/4
dp/	1	26				
McGIBBINS, John	1	14				
McGIBBINS, John & James			109 1/4	4/4	23...11.....7	0.....7.....1 1/4
McGONIGLE, James	1	18				
MERRIT, Samuel	1	25				
do.	1	10...10				
MUSTER, Anthony	1/2	16				
do. & William CHAMBERS			275	3/6	48.....2.....6	0...14.....6 1/2

(page 71. Augusta County Land Tax Return of James Ramsay for 1787)

Persons Names Owning Land	No. of Lots	Yearly Rent	Quantity of Land	Rate of Land p Acre	Total Amt. of Value of Land excl. Lots	Amt. of Tax at 1 1/2 p cent
McCHESNEY, James			223	6/1	67...16.....7	1.....0.....4 1/3
do.			273	6/6	97...10.....0	1.....9.....3
McCHESNEY, Robert			124	6/1	37...14.....4	0...11.....3 3/4

(page 71 contd. Augusta County Land Tax Return of James Ramsay for 1787)

Persons Names Owning Land	No. of Lots	Yearly Rent	Quantity of Land	Rate of Land p Acre	Total Amt. of Value of Land excl. Lots.	Amt. of Tax at 1 1/2 p cent
McCUTCHIN, Samuel (Capt.)			150	6/1	45...12.....6	0...13.....8 1/4
do.			80	2/8	10...13.....4	0.....3.....2 1/4
do.			390	1/9	34.....2.....6	0...10.....2 3/4
McCUTCHIN, John			150	4/4	32...10.....0	0.....9.....9
do.			330	1/8	27...10.....0	0.....8.....4
MURPHEY, William			140	4/4	30.....6.....8	0.....9.....1
MINGA, Henry			127	6/1	38...12.....7	0...11.....7
McKINNEY, John			170	4/9	30.....7.....6	0...12.....1 1/2
do.			200	3/6	35.....0.....0	0...10.....6
do.			187	2/8	24...18.....8	0.....7.....5 3/4
McNUTT, Robert			258	5/8	73.....2.....0	1.....1....11
McNUTT, James			161	6/6	52.....6.....6	0...15.....8 1/2
do.			183	5/3	48.....0.....9	0...14.....5
MARSHAL, George			232	3/11	45.....8.....8	0...13.....7 1/2
McCLURE, John			155	7/	54.....5.....0	0...16.....3
MITCHEL, James Senr.			254	8/8	110.....1.....4	1...13.....3 1/4
do.			259	9/2	118...14.....2	1...15.....7 1/4
do.			370	1/9	32.....7.....6	0.....9.....8 3/4
do.			95	1/9	8.....6.....3	0.....2.....6
MITCHEL, William			176	7/9	68.....4.....0	1.....0.....5
McCUTCHIN, William			100	3/6	17...10.....0	0.....5.....3
do.			100	1/9	8...14.....0	0.....2.....7 1/2
MOORE, William			154	4/4	38.....7.....4	0...10.....0 1/2
do.			10	4/4	2.....3.....4	0.....0.....7 1/2
MATEER, James			200	6/1	60...16.....8	0...18.....3
do.			36	3/6	6.....6.....0	0.....1...10 1/2
MITCHEL, James Junr.			200	7/9	77...10.....0	1.....3.....3
do.			166	7/	58.....2.....0	0...17.....5
MITCHEL, Thomas			234	7/5	86...15.....6	1.....6.....0 1/4
McCUTCHIN, William Senr.			31	2/2	25.....6.....0	0.....7.....6
McCANTREE, Richard			150	2/8	20.....0.....6	0.....6.....0

(page 72. Augusta County Land Tax Return of James Ramsay for 1787)

Persons Names Owning Land	No. of Lots	Yearly Rent	Quantity of Land	Rate of Land p Acre	Total Amt. of Value of Land excl. Lots.	Amt. of Tax at 1 1/2 p cent
MAURY, Samuel			70	2/6	8...15.....0	0.....2.....7 1/2
McFADEN, John			100	3/6	17...10.....0	0.....5.....3
McCUTCHIN, John			330	1/	16...10.....0	0.....7...10 1/2
McCLARY, Hugh			200	6/1	60...16,....8	0...18.....3
NELSON, Alexander	1/3	24				
NELSON, Thomas			103	3/11	20.....3.....5	0.....6.....0 1/2
NORTH, Philip			50	5/3	13.....2.....6	0.....3...11 1/2
PAGE, Thomas	1	1...10				
PHILIPS, John			171	6/1	52.....0.....3	0...15.....7 1/4
do.			86	1/9	7...10.....6	0.....2.....3
do.			50	1/9	4.....7.....6	0.....1.....3 3/4
do.			164	1/6	12.....6.....0	0.....3.....6 1/2
PARIS, John			213	4/4	46.....3.....0	0...13...10
PEARY, James			180	4/4	39.....0.....0	0...11.....8 1/4
PEARY, George			180	4/9	42...15.....0	0...12.....9 3/4

(page 72 contd. Augusta County Land Tax Return of James Ramsay for 1787)

Persons Names Owning Land	No. of Lots	Yearly Rent	Quantity of Land	Rate of Land p Acre	Total Amt. of Value of Land excl. Lots	Amt. of Tax at 1 1/2 p cent
PERREY, Joshua (Capt.)	1	28				
PALMER, William			388	3/6	67...18.....0	1.....0....4 1/2
PATTON, Jacob			127 1/2	6/1	38...15.....7	0...11.....7 1/2
PARRIS, William			184	4/4	46.....0.....0	0...13.....9 1/2
POAGE. William			290	3/11	56...15...10	0...16.....2 3/4
POTTARF, Philip			23	7/	8.....1.....0	0.....2.....4 3/4
RICHIE, Hugh (Doctr.)			60	5/3	15...15.....0	0....4.....8 1/2
do.			100	3/6	17...10.....0	0.....5.....3
READ, Mathew (deced., (Thomas POAGE Admr.)			200	2/8	26...13.....4	0.....8.....0

(page 73. Augusta County Land Tax Return of James Ramsay for 1787)

Persons Names Owning Land	No. of Lots	Yearly Rent	Quantity of Land	Rate of Land p Acre	Total Amt. of Value of Land excl. Lots	Amt. of Tax at 1 1/2 p cent
READ, Robert	1	40	300	8/8	130.....0.....0	1...19.....0
do.			400	2/8	53.....6.....8	0...16.....0
do.			50	4/4	10...16.....8	0.....3.....3
do.			25	4/4	5.....8.....4	0.....1.....7 1/2
RUSK, Margaret			173	7/	60...11.....0	0...18.....1 3/4
RUSK, William			107	4/9	25.....8.....3	0.....7.....7 1/2
do.			190	2/8	25.....6.....8	0.....7.....7
RUSK, David			176	3/6	30...16.....0	0.....9.....2 3/4
RUSK, Robert			160	7/	56.....0.....0	0...16.....9 1/2
do.			120	2/	12.....0.....0	0.....3.....5
RUTLEDGE, Thomas Senr.			220	7/5	81...11.....8	1.....4.....5
RIDDLE, Cornelius (Capt.)			317 3/4	7/5	115.....4.....0	1...14.....6 3/4
RAY, Daniel			100	3/1	15.....8.....4	0.....4.....7 1/2
RICE, William			120	5/3	31...10.....0	0.....9.....5 1/4
ROWEN, James			228	6/1	69.....7.....0	1.....0...10 3/4
RICHARDSON, Philemon			250	7/9	96...17.....6	1.....9.....0 3/4
do.			246	7/9	95.....6.....6	1.....8.....7
do.			80	5/	22.....0.....0	0.....6.....7 1/2
RANDOLPH, William			276	5/8	78.....4.....0	1.....3.....5
do.			55	5/8	15...11.....8	0.....4.....7 1/2
REAUH, William (for Thomas NELSON, deced.)			84	3/11	16.....9.....0	0.....4...11
do.			40	1/9	3...10.....0	0.....1.....0 1/2
SCOTT, Andrew			200	4/9	47...10.....0	0...14.....3
do.			66	2/4	7...14.....0	0.....2.....3 3/4
do.			42	2/2	4...11.....0	0.....1.....7
do.			5 1/3	3/11	1.....0.....0	0.....0.....3
do.			40	2/2	4.....6.....8	0.....1.....3 3/4
SCOTT, Thomas			171	8/8	74.....2.....0	1.....2.....2 3/4
do.			68	2/	6...16.....0	0.....2.....0 1/2
STRICKLING, Joseph (New Grant)			43	1/6	3.....4.....6	0.....1.....0 1/2

(page 74. Augusta County Land Tax Return of James Ramsay for 1787)

Persons Names Owning Land	No. of Lots	Yearly Rent	Quantity of Land	Rate of Land p Acre	Total Amt. of Value of Land excl. Lots	Amt. of Tax at 1 1/2 p cent
SWINK, Henry			109	4/4	23...15.....4	0.....7.....4
SWINK, Laurence			125	4/4	27.....1.....8	0.....8..... 1/2

(page 74 contd. Augusta County Land Tax Return of James Ramsay for 1787)

Persons Names Owning Land	No. of Lots	Yearly Rent	Quantity of Land	Rate of Land p Acre	Total Amt. of Value of Land excl. Lots	Amt. of Tax at 1 1/2 p cent
SWALLOW, Jacob			120	5/3	31...10.....0	0.....9.....5 1/4
SCOTT, Thomas Junr.			302	3/6	52...17.....0	0...15...10 1/4
do.			98	3/6	17.....2.....0	0.....5.....3
SMITH, John			200	7/9	77...10.....0	1.....3.....3 1/4
SAWYER, James			230	7/	80...10.....0	1.....4.....1 3/4
do.			100	2/8	13.....6.....8	0.....4.....0
do.			115	2/8	15.....6.....8	0.....4.....7
SHOUNDS, Leonard			330	3/6	87...15.....0	0...17.....4
SCOTT, Archibald (Revd.)			150	5/3	39.....7.....6	0...11.....9 3/4
SLUSHER, Coonrod			95	3/11	18...12.....1	0.....5.....6 1/2
SLUSHER, Coonrod			320	4/4	69.....6.....8	1.....0.....9 1/2
STEEL, Samuel (B. Smith)			113	6/1	34.....7.....5	0...10.....3 3/4
STEEL, David			186	6/1	56...11.....6	0...16...11 1/2
SHIELDS, William Senr.			100	3/1	15.....8.....4	0.....4.....7 1/2
SHARP, John Senr.			470	4/4	101...16.....8	1...10.....6 1/2
SHARP, John Junr.		2/8	73		9...14.....8	0.....2...11
STEWART, Elizabeth			100	8/8	43.....6.....8	0...13.....0
SCOTT, John			452	2/8	60.....5.....4	0...18.....1
SYLER, Jacob			334	5/3	87...13.....6	1.....6.....3 1/2
STINETT, William			343	3/11	67.....3.....5	1.....1.....1 1/2
SUMMERS, John			200	3/11	39.....3.....4	0...11.....9
SPOTT, George	1	20	30	3/6	5.....5.....0	0.....1.....6 1/2
ST. CLAIR, Alexander	1/2	50	80	13/	52.....0.....0	0...15.....7
do.	1	12...10	50	4/4	10...16.....8	0.....3.....3
do.	1	18	80	2/8	10...13.....4	0.....3.....2 1/2
do.			25	4/4	5.....5.....4	0.....1.....7 1/2
SPROUL, William			490	6/6	159.....5.....0	2.....7.....9 1/4

(page 75. Augusta County Land Tax Return of James Ramsay for 1787)

Persons Names Owning Land	No. of Lots	Yearly Rent	Quantity of Land	Rate of Land p Acre	Total Amt. of Value of Land excl. Lots	Amt. of Tax at 1 1/2 p cent
SPROUL, Alexander			200	6/6	97...10.....0	1.....9.....3
STEWART, Archibald			100	10/6	52...10.....0	0...15.....9
do.			340	1/9	29...15.....0	0.....8...11 1/2
STEWART, Alexander (Major)			180	3/6	31...10.....0	0.....9.....5 1/2
STEWART, Benjamin			497	6/6	161...10.....9	2.....8.....8 1/2
STEEL, James Esqr.			200	8/8	86...13.....4	1.....6.....0
do.			187 1/2	4/4	40...12.....6	0...12.....8 1/2
do.			187 1/2	2/8	25.....0.....0	0.....7.....6
SUMMERS, John			250	4/4	54...13.....4	0...16.....3
SEAWRIGHT, Alexander			252	5/3	66.....3.....0	0...19...10
STEEL, David			244	5/3	64.....1.....0	0...19.....2 1/2
do.			50	7/	17...10.....0	0.....5.....3
STEEL, Samuel			150	4/4	32...10.....0	0.....9.....9
SINK, John			100	1/9	8...15.....0	0.....2.....7 1/2
STEEL, Robert Senr.			160	6/1	48...13.....4	0...14.....7
STEEL, Samuel			260	7/	91.....0.....0	1.....7.....3 1/2
STEEL, James			230	6/1	69...19.....2	1.....0...11 1/2
SHOLTZ, George			154	5/3	40.....8.....9	0...12.....1 1/2
STEEL, Nathaniel			480	8/8	209...14.....8	3...12...11
SHIELDS, William			70	7/	24...10.....0	0.....7.....4
SHIELDS, Thomas			200	7/5	74.....3.....4	1.....1.....8

(page 75 contd. Augusta County Land Tax Return of James Ramsay for 1787)

Persons Names Owning Land	No. of Lots	Yearly Rent	Quantity of Land	Rate of Land p Acre	Total Amt. of Value of Land excl. Lots	Amt. of Tax at 1 1/2 p cent
STIRLING, John			231	6/6	75.....1.....6	1.....2.....6 1/4
SHIELDS, John			129	2/2	13...19.....6	0.....4.....2 1/4
do.			43	2/6	5.....7.....6	0.....1.....7 1/2
SHIELDS, Margaret & Heirs of Thomas			225	5/8	63...15.....0	0...19.....1 1/2
do.			43	1/9	3...15.....3	0.....1.....1 1/2
SHIELDS, William (C. Creek)			200	5/8	59...13.....4	0...17.....0
STIRRETT, Robert			128	2/8	17.....1.....4	0.....5 1 1/2
SCOTT, William (Sadler)			224	4/4	48...10.....8	0...14.....6 1/2
do.			100	1/9	8...15.....0	0.....2.....7 1/2
do.			50	1/5	3...10...10	0.....1.....0 3/4
STEWART. Thomas	1	35	350	7/9	136.....8.....0	2.....0...11
do.			120	3/6	21.....0.....0	0.....6.....3
do.			128	1/9	11.....4.....0	0.....3.....4 1/4

(page 76. Augusta County Land Tax Return of James Ramsay for 1787)

A List of the number of Lots, yearly Rent and amount of Tax on the same omitted to be extended in their proper places

John ABNEY	2	36	1...16.....0
D. for MdDONOUGH Estate	1/2	15	0...15.....0
Robert BEVERLEY	1	5	0.....5.....0
Elizabeth BURNS	2	45	2...5.....0
Elizabeth BLAIR	1/2	16	0...16.....0
William BOWYER (Colo.)	1	35	1...15.....0
Michael BOWYER	1	18	0...18.....0
John BOFONG	1	40	2.....0.....0
William CRAWFORD	1	45	2...5.....0
William DAVIS	1	14	0...14.....0
Robert ESTRAP	1/2	12	0...12.....0
Robert GAMBLE (Colo.)	1/2	55	2...15.....0
David GRINER	1	25	1.....5.....0
do.	1	12	0...12.....0
John GRIFFIN	1/3	15	0...15.....0
Peter HYSKEL	1	38	1...18.....0
Euphemia HUGHS	1	20	1.....0.....0
Daniel KIDD	1	25	1.....5.....0
Francis MARROW	1	24	1.....4.....0
Sampson MATHEWS (Colo)	1	5	0.....5.....0
do.	1	1	0.....1.....0
do.	1	40	2.....0.....0
William McDOWEL	1/2	35	1...15.....0
do.	1	26	1.....6.....0
John McGIBBINS	1	14	0...14.....0
Samuel MERRIT	1	25	1.....5.....0
do.	1	10...10	0...10.....6
Anthony MUSTER	1/2	16	0...16.....0
Alexander NELSON	1/3	24	1.....4.....0
Thomas POAGE	1	1...10	0.....1.....6
Joshua PERRY	1	28	1.....8.....0
Robert READ	1	40	2.....0.....0

(page 76 contd. Augusta County Land Tax Return of James Ramsay for 1787)

Persons Names Owning Land	No. of Lots	Yearly Rent	Quantity of Land	Rate of Land p acre	Total Value of Land excl. of Lots	Amt. of Tax at 1 1/2 p cent
George SPOTTS	1	20				1.....0.....0
Alexander ST. CLAIR	1/2	50				2...10.....0
do.	1	12...10				0...12.....6
do.	1	18				0...18.....0
Thomas STEWART	1	35				1...15.....0

(page 77. Augusta County Land Tax Return of James Ramsay for 1787)

SCOTT, James			216	7/9	83...14.....0	1.....5...11 1/4
do.			176	5/3	46.....4.....0	0...13...10
do.			86	2/8	11.....9.....4	0.....3.....5
TRIMBLE, David			160	7/	56.....0.....0	0...16.....9 1/2
do.			140	2/2	15.....3.....4	0.....4.....6 1/2
do.			110	2/2	11...18.....4	0.....3.....6 3/4
TANDY, Smith			300	5/3	78...15.....0	1.....3.....7 1/2
TRIMBLE, John			48	4/4	10.....8.....0	0.....3.....1 1/4
do.			160	2/8	21.....6...8	0.....6.....4 3/4
TRIMBLE, James (Capt.)			300	7/	105.....0.....0	1...11...6
do.			250	2/8	33.....6...8	0...10.....0
TROTTER, James Senr.			130	7/9	50.....7.....6	0...15.....1 1/4
TRIMBLE, Walter			188	8/8	81.....9.....4	1.....4.....5 1/4
do.			62	3/6	10...17.....0	0.....3.....3
TRIMBLE, Robert			167	10/6	87...13.....6	1.....6.....3
do.			34	1/9	2...19.....6	0.....0...10 1/2
TRIMBLE, John Senr.			343	10/6	180.....1.....6	2...14.....0 1/4
TROTTER, Joseph			150	5/3	39.....7.....6	0...11.....9 3/4
do.			82	1/9	7.....3.....6	0.....2.....2 1/4
do.			22	5/3	5...15.....6	0.....1.....8 3/4
TRIMBLE, James			317	4/4	68...13.....4	1.....0.....7 1/4
TEAFORD, Jacob			200	3/6	35.....0.....0	0...10.....6
THOMPSON, Robert (Capt.)			200	7/9	77...10.....0	1.....3.....3
do.			140	1/9	12.....5.....0	0.....3.....8
THOMPSON, Alexander (Colo.)			302	7/9	117.....0.....6	1...15.....1 1/4
do.			130	1/9	11.....7.....6	0.....3.....5
THOMPSON, William			100	3/6	17...10.....0	0.....5.....3
TEAS, Mary			40	13/	260.....0.....0	3...18.....0

(page 78. Augusta County Land Tax Return of James Ramsay for 1787)

TATE, Robert			186	7/	65.....2.:..0	0...19.....6
do.			146	4/4	31...12.....8	0.....9.....5 3/4
do.			23	7/	8.....1.....0	0.....2.....4 3/4
THOMPSON, Joseph			155	4/4	33...11.....8	0...10.....0 3/4
TATE, Sarah			200	6/1	60...16.....8	0...18.....3 3/4
do.			27	6/1	8.....4.....3	0.....2.....5
TATE, Thomas			200	6/6	65.....0.....0	0...19.....6
TATE, John Senr.			244	7/5	90.....9...8	1.....7.....1 3/4
do.			200	1/5	14.....3.....4	0.....4.....3
do.			400	1/5	28.....6...8	0.....8.....6
TATE, William (Capt.)			160	4/4	34...13.....4	0...10.....4 3/4

(page 78 contd. Augusta County Land Tax Return of James Ramsay for 1787)

Persons Names Owning Land	No. of Lots	Yearly Rent	Quantity of Land	Rate of Land p Acre	Total Amt. of Value of Land excl. of Lots	Amt. of Tax at 1 1/2 p cent
THOMPSON. William			306	6/1	93.....1.....6	1.....7...11
do.			93	1/9	8.....2.....9	0.....2.....4 3/4
TARBUT, Hugh			197	1/9	17...10.....0	0.....5.....3
THOMPSON, Mathew			202	6/1	61.....8...10	0...18.....5
do.			110	3/1	16...19.....2	0.....4...11 1/2
do.			60	1/9	5.....5.....0	0.....1.....6 3/4
do.			50	3/1	7...14.....2	0.....2.....3
THOMPSON, John			255	4/4	55.....5.....0	0...16.....6 3/4
do.			60	3/1	9.....5.....0	0.....2.....8 1/4
THOMPSON, Alexander			150	5/8	42...10.....0	0...12.....9
TELFORD, James			23	1/9	2.....0.....0	· 0.....0.....6 1/2
UTT, John Senr.			180	2/8	24.....0.....0	0.....7.....2 1/4
do.			50	1/9	4.....7.....6	0.....1.....3 1/4
VERNER, Henry			82	3/6	14.....7.....0	0.....4.....3 1/2
VANCE, John (deced), Heirs			305	5/3	80.....1.....3	1.....4.....0 3/4

(page 79. Augusta County Land Tax Return of James Ramsay for 1787)

Persons Names Owning Land	No. of Lots	Yearly Rent	Quantity of Land	Rate of Land p Acre	Total Amt. of Value of Land excl. of Lots	Amt. of Tax at 1 1/2 p cent
VERNER, Henry			107	4/4	23.....3.....8	0.....6...11 1/2
VANLEER, Jacob			490	3/11	95...19.....2	1.....8.....9
do. Exr. of G. ROBINSON			141	5/3	37.....0.....3	0...11.....1 1/4
WHITREL, Martin			20	3/6	3...10.....0	0.....1.....0
WHITE, Isaac Junr.			243	9/7	119.....5...10	1...15...11 1/4
do.			94	1/5	6...13.....2	0.....2.....0
WALACE, John			250	3/6	43...15.....0	0...13.....1 1/2
do.			188	3/6	32...14.....0	0...10.....0
WILSON, William			301	8/8	130.....8.....8	1...19.....1 1/2
WILSON, Robert Junr.			290	8/8	125...13.....4	1...17.....8 1/4
WILLIAM, Moses			300	4/4	65.....0.....0	0...19.....6
WILSON, Mathew			348	7/9	134...17.....0	2.....0.....5 1/2
do.			290	4/4	64...15.....8	0...19.....5
WALACE, Robert			160	8/8	69.....6.....8	1.....0.....9 1/2
WILLIAMS, John			150	2/2	16.....5.....0	0.....4...10 1/2
WISEMAN, Peter			200	3/1	30...16.....8	0.....9.....3
WILLIAMS, Richard			120	3/1	18...10.....0	0.....5.....6 1/2
WILLIAMS, John			327	6/1	99.....9.....3	1.....9...10
WADDLE, John			100	5/3	26.....5.....0	0.....7...10 1/2
WEAVER, George			150	3/6	26.....5.....0	0.....7...10 1/2
do			44	1/9	3...17.....0	0.....1.....1 3/4
WILEY, John			96	3/6	16.....2.....6	0.....4...11 3/4
WASON, Robert			150	3/6	26.....5.....0	0.....7...10 1/2
WILSON, David			461	7/5	170...19.....1	2...11.....3 1/4
WRIGHT, James			260	7/9	100...15.....0	1...10.....2 1/2
WILSON, Robert Senr.			360	4/4	78.....0.....0	1.....3.....4 3/4
WILSON, Andrew			180	2/8	24.....0.....0	0.....7.....2 1/4

(page 80. Augusta County Land Tax Return of James Ramsay for 1787)

Persons Names Owning Land	No. of Lots	Yearly Rent	Quantity of Land	Rate of Land p Acre	Total Amt. of Value of Land excl. Lots	Amt. of Tax at 1 1/2 p cent
WADDLE, James (Revd.)			1400	5/3	367.....0.....0	5...10.....3
do.			17	5/	4.....5.....0	0.....1.....2
do.			400	1/6	30.....0.....0	0.....8.....9
do.			220	1/9	19.....5.....0	0.....6.....0
YOUNG, John (Capt.)			536	6/1	166.....0.....0	2.....8...10 3/4
do.			190	4/6	45.....1.....6	0...13.....6
BOWYER, William (Colo.)			15 1/2	3/6	2...13.....0	0.....0.....9 1/2

Tax on Town Los brot. forward from p.

478...15...10 1/4
 47...15.....6
526...11.....4 1/4

Examed J. LYLE, JUNR., D. C. A. C.

Augusta County 1787. JAMES RAMSAY, Commr. Ent.'d 16 July 1788.

(There is another Land Tax Book for Augusta County for the year 1787, but the first ten pages or so are so faded that is is not feasible to take down the material. However, before the return is finished most of the remaining part can be read with some accuracy. Also, much of this material will probably in the 1788 return of Joseph Bell which, although somewhat faded and torn, will provide more material)

(page 90. Augusta County Land Tax Return of Joseph Bell for 1787)

Persons Names Owning Land	Quantity of Land	Rate of Land p Acre	Total Amount Value of Land	Amount of Tax at 1 1/2 p cent
McCOMB, Andrew	130	7/	45...10.....0	0...13.....7 1/2
do.	40	2/8	5.....6.....8	0.....1.....7
do.	200	7/0	70.....0.....0	1.....1.....0
McMACHEN, John	330	4/4	71...10.....0	1.....1.....5
McKEE, Samuel	230	5/3	60.....7.....6	0...18.....1 1/2
do.	75	3/6	13.....2.....6	0.....3...11 1/2
MIRES, Frederick	399	8/8	172...18.....0	2...11...10 1/2
McCLURE, Josiah	128	5/3	33...12.....0	0...10.....0 1/4
McCOLLOCK, Thomas	16	1/9	1.....8.....0	0.....9.....5
MILLER, Henry	1150	2/8	153.....6.....8	2.....6.....0
do.	518	10/9	45.....6.....6	0...13.....7
do.	593	1/9	51...17.....6	0...15.....6 3/4
do.	490	1/9	42...17.....6	0...12...10 1/4
do.	160	2/8	28.....6.....8	0.....6.....4 3/4
do.	400	1/9	35.....0.....0	0...10.....6
do	212	3/6	37.....2.....0	0...11.....1 1/2
do.	134	3/6	23.....9.....0	0.....7.....0 1/4
do.	170	8/8	73...13.....4	1.....2.....1
do.	238	4/4	51...11.....4	0...15.....5 1/2
do.	200	1/9	17...10.....0	0.....5.....3
do.	208	7/	72...16.....0	1.....1...10
do.	136	4/4	29.....5.....0	0.....8.....9 1/2

(page 90 contd. Augusta County Land Tax Return of Joseph Bell for 1787)

Persons Names Owning Land	Quantity of Land	Rate of Land p Acre	Total Amount of Value of Land	Amount of Tax at 1 1/2 p cent
MILLER, Henry	207	3/6	36.....4.....6	0...10...10 1/2
do.	277	3/6	48.....9.....6	0...14.....6 1/2
do.	52	5/0	13.....0.....0	0.....4.....0
do.	85	1/9	7.....8.....9	0.....1...10 1/4
do (on mortgage)	80	4/4	17.....6.....8	0.....5.....2 1/4
McCLURE, James	370	5/3	97.....2.....6	1.....9.....1 1/2
McDUGHULL, John	400	7/	140.....0.....0	2.....2.....0
do.	200	1/9	17...10.....0	0.....5.....3
McGLAMERY, John	128	4/4	27...14.....8	0.....8.....3 1/2
NICHALL, John	230	7/0	67...10.....0	1.....6.....3
do.	45	2/8	6.....0.....0	0.....1.....9 1/2
NELSON, Alexander	572	8/8	247...17.....4	3...14.....2 3/4
do.	155	5/0	38...15.....0	0...11.....5
do.	278	3/11	54.....8...10	0...16.....4 1/2
OLIVER, James	150	7/9	58.....2.....6	0...17.....5 1/4
do.	150	7/9	58.....2.....6	0...17.....5 1/4
do.	150	1/9	13.....2.....6	0.....3...11 1/4
do.	125	/10	5.....4.....2	0.....1.....6 3/4
do.	186	/10	7...15.....0	0.....2.....3 3/4
POAGE, Thomas	262	10/	143.....0.....2	2.....2...10 1/2
do.	200	10/	109.....3.....4	1...12.....9
do.	200	4/4	43.....6.....8	0...13.....0
do.	98	4/4	21.....4.....8	0.....6.....4 1/2
PATTERSON, John (Deaf)	250	5/3	66...13.....4	1.....0.....0

(page 91. Augusta County Land Tax Return of Joseph Bell for 1787)

Persons Names Owning Land	Quantity of Land	Rate of Land p Acre	Total Amount of Value of Land	Amount of Tax at 1 1/2 p cent
PATTERSON, Thomas	167	15/3	127.....6.....9	1...18.....2 1/2
do.	178	5/3	46...14.....6	0...14.....0
do.	87	5/0	27...15.....0	0.....6.....7
PERRY, John	200	5/3	52...10.....0	0...15.....7
PATTERSON, James Senr.	230	7/	80...10.....0	1...11.....1 1/2
PATTERSON, Joseph Capt.	70	6/3	18.....7.....6	0.....6.....6
PECK, Jacob (Tanner)	320	1/9	28.....0.....0	0.....8.....4 3/4
do.	196	5/1	59...12.....4	0...17...10 1/2
do.	140	1/9	12...15.....0	0.....3.....8 1/2
do.	2	8/8	0...17.....4	0.....0.....3
PILSON, Samuel	148	7/9	52...17.....0	0...15.....8 1/2
do.	170	1/9	4.....7.....6	0.....1.....6
PATTERSON, James (S.R.)	111	10/6	58...13.....4	0...17.....4 1/2
do.	56	1/9	4...18.....0	0.... 1.....5 1/2
PATRICK, John	437	13/	284.....1.....0	4.....6.....2 1/2
do.	280	6/1	85.....3.....4	1.....5.....6 1/2
do.	235	1/9	20...11.....3	0.....6.....2
PORTERFIELD, Robert Majr.	250	6/1	76.....0...10	1.....2.....9 3/4
do.	143	6/1	43.....9...11	0...13.....0 1/2
PATTERSON, William Junr.	200	8/8	86...13.....4	1.....6.....0 1/2

(page 91 contd. Augusta County Land Tax Return of Joseph Bell for 1787)

Persons Names Owning Land	Quantity of Land	Rate of Land p Acre	Total Amt. of Value of Land	Amount of Tax at 1 1/2 p cent
POAGE, John (S.A.C.)	476	3/6	83.....6.....0	1.....4...11 3/4
do.	200	1/9	17...10.....0	0.....5.....3
do. for John ARCHER's Estate	250	6/1	39...,.7.....6	0...11....9 1/2
do. from (?)	13	6/1	3...19...11	0.....1.....2 1/2
ROBERTSON, Mathew	196	17/6	171...10.....0	2...11.....0
do.	170	4/4	36...16.....8	0...11....0 1/2
do.	75	8/8	32...10.....0	0.....9.....9
RUTLEDGE, George	133	10/0	69...16.....0	1.....0...11 1/2
do.	91	4/4	19...15.....2	0.....5...11 3/4
RUSSELL, Andrew	200	7/0	70.....0.....0	1...1.....( )
do.	30	7/0	10...10.....0	0.....3.....1 1/4
RANKIN, James	120	7/0	42.....0.....0	0...12....7 1/2
do.	30	7/0	10...10.....0	0.....3.....1 1/4
do.	380	2/8	50...13.....4	0...15.....2 1/2
RUNKLE, Samuel	160	9/7	76...13.....4	1.....3.....0
do.	200	2/8	26...13.....4	0.....8.....0
do.	127	2/2	13.....5.....8	0.....4.....1 1/2
do.	200	2/8	26...13.....4	0.....8.....0
RALSTON, John	300	2/8	40.....0.....0	0...12.....0
ROBERTSON, Mary (Widow)	200	7/9	77...10.....0	1.....3.....3
RALSTON, William	100	6/1	30.....8.....4	0.....9.....1 1/2
do.	100	2/8	13.....6.....8	0.....4.....0
RALSTON, Samuel	113	6/1	34.....7.....5	0...10.....3 3/4
do.	137	2/2	14...16...10	0.....4.....5 1/2
REED, Robert (S. M.)	81	6/1	24...12.....9	0.....7.....4 1/2
do.	190	1/5	13.....9.....4	0.....4.....0 1/2
REED, Alexander	142	6/1	43.....3.....4	0...12...11 1/2
do.	92	5/3	24.....3.....0	0.....7.....2

(page 92. Augusta County Land Tax Return of Joseph Bell for 1782)

Persons Names Owning Land	Quantity of Land	Rate of Land p Acre	Total Amt. of Value of Land	Amount of Tax at 1 1/2 p cent
RUSSELL, Robert	196	6/1	59...12.....4	0...17...10 1/2
do.	72	2/8	9...12.....0	0.....2...10 1/2
do.	33	2/2	3...11.....6	0.....1.....0 3/4
RUSSELL, Joshua	150	6/6	48...15.....0	0...14.....7 1/2
do.	53	2/2	6.....3.....8	0.....1...10 1/4
RANKIN, Richard Senr.	1300	3/11	254...11.....8	3...16.....4 1/2
REBURN, John	320	5/3	84.....0.....0	1.....5.....2 1/2
RANKIN, Thomas	380	6/1	115...11.....0	1...14.....8
do.	109	13/0	70...17.....0	1.....1.....3
RANKIN, John	110	13/0	71...10.....0	1.....1.....5 1'2
RANKIN, William	109	13/0	70...17.....0	1.....1.....3
RAMSAY, John Senr.	320	8/8	138...13.....0	2.....1.....7
do.	88	10/6	46...10.....0	0...13...10 1/2
do.	97	1/9	8.....9.....9	0.....2.....6 1/2
do.	28	2/8	3...14.....8	0.....1.....1
do.	70	1/9	6.....2.....6	0.....1...10
RAMSAY, Andrew	165	10/11	90.....1.....5	1.....7.....0
do.	146	1/9	12...15.....6	0.....3...10

(page 92 contd. Augusta County Land Tax Return of Joseph Bell for 1787)

Persons Names Owning Land	Quantity of Land	Rate of Land p Acre	Total Amt. of Value of Land	Amount of Tax at 1 1/2 p cent
RAMSAY, John Junr.	408	5/3	107.....2.....0	1...12.....1 1/2
do.	110	1/9	9.....2.....6	0.....2...10 1/2
do.	60	2/8	8.....0.....0	0.....2.....4 3/4
do.	75	1/9	6...11.....3	0.....1...11
ROBERTSON, William Senr.	60	13/0	39.....0.....0	0...11.....9 1/2
do.	280	7/0	98.....0.....0	1.....9.....4 1/2
do.	100	13/0	65.....0.....0	0...19.....6
do.	96	1/9	8.....8.....0	0.....2.....6 1/4
do.	90	1/9	7...17.....6	0.....2.....4 1/2
ROBERTSON, James	350	8/8	151...13.....4	2.....5.....6
RANKIN, Richard Junr.	400	3/0	60.....0.....0	0...18.....0
RUTLEDGE, James	117	10/6	61.....8.....6	0...18.....4 1/2
do.	26	4/4	5...12.....8	0.....1.....8 1/4
STEWART, John	200	7/6	175.....0.....0	2...12.....6
do.	40	7/0	14.....0.....0	0.....4.....2 1/2
do.	196	17/6	171...10.....0	2...11.....5 1/2
do.	30	3/0	4...10.....0	0.....1.....4
STORY, James	175	13/0	113...15.....0	1...14.....1 1/2
STORY, Thomas	100	17/6	87...10.....0	1.....6.....3
STORY, John	100	15/3	76.....5.....0	1.....2...10 1/2
STORY, Ann (Widow)	100	17/6	87...10.....0	1.....6.....3
SURTICE, John	150	4/4	32...10.....0	0.....9.....9
SILLIN, Gasper	100	5/3	26.....5.....0	0.....7...10 1/2
do.	78	2/8	10.....8.....0	0.....3.....1 1/4
SHIERS, John	200	4/4	40.....6.....8	0...13.....0
SMITH, Lewis	923	5/3	242.....5.....9	3...12.....8 1/2
STEVENSON, John	125	7/9	48.....8.....9	0...14.....6 1/2
do.	142	2/8	18...18.....9	0.....5.....8 1/4
STEVENSON, Adam	125	7/9	48.....8.....9	0...14.....6 1/2
do	142	2/8	18...18.....9	0.....5.....8 1/4
do.	100	2/6	12...10.....0	0.....3.....9
SMITH, Zachariah	160	4/4	34...13.....4	0...10.....4 1/2
STUNKARD, William	230	7/0	80...10.....1	1.....4.....1 1/2

(page 93. Augusta County Land Tax Return of Joseph Bell for 1787)

Persons Names Owning Land	Quantity of Land	Rate of Land p Acre	Total Amt. of Value of Land	Amount of Tax at 1 1/2 p cent
SEAWRIGHT, John	400	7/9	155.....0.....0	2.....6.....6
do.	200	1/9	17...10.....0	0.....5.....3
SMITH, Abraham (Rk)	540	6/1	164.....5.....0	2.....9.....3 1/4
SHEETS, Jacob	450	5/3	108...18.....9	1...12.....8
do.	280	3/6	48.....0.....0	0...14.....9
do.	107	2/8	14.....5.....0	0.....4.....4
do.	27	3/0	4.....4.....0	0.....1.....3
SHIRLEY, Valentine	121	15/3	92.....5.....0	1.....7.....8
do.	351 1/4	1/9	30...13.....0	0.....9.....2 1/4
do.	7 1/2	12/2	4...11.....2	0.....1.....4 1/4
STULL, Frederick	419	2/8	55...17.....4	0...16.....9
do.	77	1/9	6...14.....9	0.....2.....0 1/2
STEVEN, Robert	180	1/9	15...15.....0	0.....4.....8 1/2
STEEL, Andrew	300	8/8	130.....0.....0	1...19.....0

(page 93 contd. Augusta County Land Tax Return of Joseph Bell for 1787)

Persons Names Owning Land	Quantity of Land	Rate of Land p Acre	Total Amt. of Value of Land	Amount of Tax at 1 1/2 p cent
STEEL, Samuel Senr.	200	8/8	86...13.....4	1.....6.....0
do.	175	1/9	15.....6.....3	0.....4.....7
do.	232	1/9	20.....7.....9	0.....6.....11/2
STEVENSON, David (Major)	190	17/6	166.....5.....0	2.....9...10 1/2
do.	70	4/4	15.....3...11	0...11.....6 1/4
SPRING, Nicholas	292	5/3	76...13.....6	1.....3.....0
TURK, Thomas Senr.	218 1/2	15/3	166...12.....1	2.....9...11 3/4
do.	150	4/4	32...10.....0	0.....9.....9
do.	400	2/8	53.....6.....8	0...16.....0
do.	190	7/0	61...10.....0	0...18.....5
do.	200	8/8	86...13.....4	1.....6.....0
TURK, Thomas (Capt.).	218 1/2	15/3	166...12.....1	2.....9...11 3/4
do.	150	4/4	32...10.....0	0.....9.....9
THOMPSON, Andrew	270	4/4	58...10.....0	0...17.....6 1/2
do.	122	3/6	21.....7.....0	0.....6.....4 1/2
TEVENBOUGH, Palzer	200	3/11	39.....3.....4	0...11...10 1/2
TROPOAGH, Nicholas	370	4/4	80.....3.....4	1.....4.....0 1/2
TANNER, John	160	5/3	42.....0.....0	0...12.....7
do (not before valued)	11	5/3	2...17.....9	0.....0 10 1/2
USHER, Robert	116	7/9	44...19.....0	0...13.....6
VANCE, David	80	7/9	31.....0.....0	0.....9.....3 1/2
do.	60	1/9	5.....5.....0	0.....7.....6 3/4

(page 94. Augusta County Land Tax Return of Joseph Bell for 1787)

Persons Names Owning Land	Quantity of Land	Rate of Land p Acre	Total Amt. of Value of Land	Amount of Tax at 1 1/2 p cent
WHITE, David	265	13/0	172.....5.....0	2...11.....5 1/4
do.	150	2/8	20.....0.....0	0.....6.....0
do.	92	4/4	19...18.....0	0.....5...11 3/4
WALACE, Jean (Widow)	200	10/6	105.....0.....0	1...11.,...6
do.	200	4/4	43.....6.....8	0...13.....0
WOODS, Mary	110	4/4	29.....6.....8	0.....8.....9 1/2
WILSON, James	115	10/6	60.....7.....6	0...18.....1 1/2
do.	190	1/9	16...12.....6	0.....4...11
WILLIAMS, David	200	5/3	52...10.....0	0...15.....9
WADDLE, Joseph	152	5/3	39...18.....0	0...11...11 1/2
WADDLE, Thomas	263	7/6	101...18.....3	1...10.....6 3/4
do.	66	2/2	7.....3.....0	0.....2.....1 1/2
WADDLE, James	130	7/9	50.....7.....6	0...15.....1 1/2
WALKER, Alexander's Heirs	287	6/1	87.....5...11	1.....6.....2 1/2
do. in Partnership w/ CONNELY	79 1/2	1/9	6...19.....1	0.....2.....1
WILSON, William (Revd.)	430	10/6	225...15.....0	3.....7.....8 1/2
WALKER, Alexander				
(CONNELY's Exr.	429	5/3	111.....0.....6	1...13.....4 1/2
do.	90	2/8	12.....0.....0	0.....3.....7 1/2
YEARACIT, Charles	67	6/1	20.....7.....7	0.....6...1 1/2
do.	124	5/3	32...11.....0	0.....9.....9

(page 94 contd. Augusta County Land Tax Return of Joseph Bell for 1787)

Persons Names Owning Land	Quantity of Land	Rate of Land p Acre	Total Amt. of Value of Land	Amount of Tax at 1 1/2 p cent
YOUNG, William (B. Smith)	228	10/6	119...14.....0	1...15...10 1/2
do.	23	10/6	12.....1....6	0.....3.....7 1/4
do.	53	2/8	7.....1....4	0.....2.....1 1/4
YOUNG, James Junr.	335	7/0	117.....5.....0	1...15.....2
do.	104	2/8	13...17.....4	0.....4...10 1/2
YOUNG, William Senr.	200	7/0	70.....0.....0	1.....1.....0
YOUNG, James Senr.	50	5/3	13.....2....6	0.....3...11 3/4
YOUNG, William	50	5/3	13.....2....6	0.....3...11 3/4
YOUNG, Robert	100	5.3	26.....5.....0	0.....7...10 1/2
do.	100	2/8	13.....6....8	0.....4.....0
do.	199	2/9	19...18.....0	0.....6.....0

Examined J. LYLE, JR. D. C.

Acres of Land	121839	37146...16...11	Tax	557.....5.....1 1/2

JOS: BELL, Commr.

(page 95).

Second Battalion, Augusta County.
Third District Land Book 1788.

A List of the Land within the District of SAMUEL VANCE, Commr., for the Third District of the County of Augusta for the year 1788.

Persons Names Owning Land	Quantity of Land	Rate per Acre	Total Amt. of Value of Land	Amt. of Tax at 1 1/2 p cent
Thomas ADAMS. (all inclusive Survey	995	6/1	302...12...11	4...10.....9 1/2
& out of the New Grant taken is	211	/10	8...15...10	0.....2.....7 3/4
& remainder of 777 New Grant	571	/10	23...15...10	0.....7....2
do. New Grant	800	/10	33.....6.....8	0...10.....0
Richard ADAMS, (Colo.)	525	7/0	183...15.....0	2...15.....1
Archibald ARMSTRONG	213	7/0	74...11.....0	1.....2.....4 1/4
Thomas ANDERSON	520	1/9	45...10.....0	0...13.....7 3/4
Michael ARABAYNS	630	3/6	110.....5.....0	1...13.....0 3/4
do.	118	2/6	10.....2.....6	0.....3.....0 1/4
Henry ANDERSON, (Propr. of James TANNER)	270	1/9	23...12.....6	0.....7.....1
John ARMSTRONG (from John JOURDAN)	45	5/3	11.....6.....3	0.....3.....6 1/2
do. (not valued before)	97	1/6	7.....5.....6	0.....2.....1 1/2
John BROWN (Capt.	215	9/7	103.....0.....5	1...10...11
Robert BRATTON's Estate	425	8/8	184.....3.....4	2...15.....3
William BLACK	125	8/8	54.....3.....4	0...16.....0

(page 95 contd. Augusta County Land Tax Return of Samuel Vance for 1788)

Proprietors Names Owning Land	Quanty of Land	Rate of Land p Acre	Total Amt. of Value of Land	Amount of Tax at 1 1/2 p cent
Alexander BLACK	125	8/8	54.....3.....4	0...16.....0
ditto	34	2/0	3.....8.....0	0.....1.....0
George BENSON	342	6/1	104.....0.....6	1...11.....2 1/2
ditto	263	1/6	19...14.....6	0.....5...11 3/4
Mathias BENSON, SENR.	216	4/4	46...16.....0	0...14.....0 1/2
James BOTKIN	105	5/3	27...11.....3	0.....8.....3
John BOTKIN	114	3/6	19...19.....0	0.....5...11 3/4
Charles BOTKIN	140	1/3	8...15.....0	0.....2.....8 1/2
Joseph (B--------)	114	3/6	19...19.....0	0.....5...11 3/4
John BRADSHAW	100	7/0	35.....0.....0	0...10.....6
ditto	333	1/6	24...19.....6	·0.....7.....8
Theophilus BLAKE	47	2/7	6.....1.....3	0.....1.....9 3/4
John BLAKE	47	2/8	6.....5.....4	0.....1...10 1/2
Leonard BELL	200	4/4	40.....6.....8	0...10.....0
ditto	60	/10	2...10.....0	0.....9.....0
John BELL	271	4/4	58...14.....4	0...17.....7 1/4
Rebecca BLACK (Widow)	230	4/4	49...16.....8	0...14...11 1/4
James BERRY	307	7/0	107.....9.....0	1...12.....2 3/4
Joseph BENETT, Senr.	70	8/8	30.....6.....8	0.....9.....1

(page 96. Augusta County Land Tax Return of Samuel Vance for 1788)

Proprietors Names Owning Land	Quanty of Land	Rate of Land p Acre	Total Amt. of Value of Land	Amount of Tax at 1 1/2 p cent
Jacob BENETT	351	2/8	46...16.....0	0...14.....0 1/2
ditto	48	1/6	3...12.....0	0.....1...10 1/2
Jacob BENETT	62	7/0	21...14.....0	0.....6.....6
David BELL's Estate	150	2/8	20.....0.....0	0.....6.....0
Joseph BELL (Capt.)	97	2/8	12...18.....8	0.....3...10 1/2
ditto	294	1/9	15...16.....6	0.....4.....8
ditto	62	1/8	3...17.....6	0.....1.....2
ditto. (New Grant)	120	1/9	11.....0.....0	0.....3.....8 1/4
George BOFINGBERY	100	5/3	26.....5.....0	0.....7...10 1/2
William BARNETT	400	2/8	53.....6.....8	0...16.....8
John BEVERIDGE	98	2/8	12.....8.....0	0.....3.....8 1/2
Hugh BOTKIN	237	4/4	62.....3.....8	0...18.....7 3/4
George BRATTON	285	8/8	123...10.....0	1...17.....0 1/2
John BYRD	125	10/6	65...12.....6	0...19.....8 1/2
Andrew BOURLAND	327	8/8	141...14.....0	2.....2.....6
John BAXTER	300	2/6	52...10.....0	0...15.....9
ditto	50	1/3	3.....2.....6	0.....1.....0
ditto	142	2/0	12.....8.....0	0.....3.....9
Thomas BLAKE	115	3/6	20.....2.....6	0.....6.....0 1/2
Joseph BROWN	50	1/9	4.....7.....6	0.....1.....3 3/4
Abram BURNER	400	1/6	80.....0.....0	0.....9.....0
John BERY	142	2/0	14.....4.....0	0.....4.....2
James BRATTON, (Capt.)	400	8/8	173.....6.....8	2...10.....0
ditto	325	4/4	70.....8.....4	1.....1.....1 1/2
Henry BUZZARD	82	3/6	12.....6.....0	0.....3.....8
Robert BEVERLEY, Esqr.	200	3/9	37...10.....0	0...11.....0
ditto	120	1/6	9.....0.....0..	0.....2.....9
John BOURLAND's Estate	160	9/7	132.....5.....6	1...19.....8
ditto	16	2/9	2.....4.....0	0.....0.....7 3/4

(page 96 contd. Augusta County Land Tax Return of Samuel Vance for 1788)

Persons Names Owning Land	Quantity of Land	Rate of Land p Acre	Total Amount of Value of Land	Amount of Tax at 1 1/2 p cent
Thomas BULLET's Heirs (Old Grant)	28	3/8	7...18.....4	0.....2.....1 1/2
do (not befoe valued)	50	3/6	8...15.....0	0.....2.....7 1/2
John BELL (Old Grand, not before valued)	128	1/9	11.....4.....0	0.....3.....4 1/2
Coonrod BUCK (from Bernard LANCE's Estate)	80	4/4	17...16.....8	0.....5.....2 3/4
Nathan CRAWFORD	112	4/4	24.....5.....4	0.....7.....4
ditto (from Hugh BROWN)	215	6/1	65.....7...11	0...19.....7 1/2
John CARLILE (Calf Pasture)	250	6/1	76.....0...10	1.....2.....9 3/4
John CHESNUT	232	2/8	30...18.....8	0.....9.....8 3/4
John CARLILE (B: Pasture)	150	9/7	71...17.....6	1.....1.....6 3/4
ditto	50	/10	2.....1.....8	0.....0.....7 1/2

(page 97. Augusta County Land Tax Return of Samuel Vance for 1788)

Persons Names Owning Land	Quantity of Land	Rate of Land p Acre	Total Amount of Value of Land	Amount of Tax at 1 1/2 p cent
Robert CARLILE, SENR.	150	9/7	71...17.....6	1.....1.....6 3/4
Robert CARLILE (Son to John)	300	7/9	116.....5.....0	1...14...10 1/2
James CARLILE	136	9/7	65.....3.....4	0...19.....6 1/2
John CARTMILL	140	5/3	36...15.....0	0...11.....0 1/4
John COWARDIN	206	3/6	36.....1.....0	0...10.....9 3/4
ditto	359	1/9	31.....8.....3	0.....9.....2
ditto	58	1/9	5.....1.....6	0.....1.....6 1/4
Olery COONROD, SENR.	476	6/1	144...15.....8	2.....3.....4
Olery COONROD, JUNR.	206	2/8	27.....9.....4	0.....8.....2 3/4
Christopher CRUMITT	40	2/8	5.....6.....8	0.....1.....7
ditto (New Grant)	87	2/4	10.....3.....0	0.....3.....0 1/2
Robert CUNINGHAM (Hampshire)	300	7/0	105.....0.....0	1...11.....6
James CLARK	240	4/4	52.....0.....0	0...13.....7
Thomas CARTMILL	581	2/8	77.....9.....4	1.....3.....2 3/4
James CARSON	100	1/9	8...15.....0	0.....2.....7 1/2
Alexander CRAWFORD	240	11/5	137.....0.....0	2.....1.....1
Samuel GRAIG	200	5/8	52...10.....0	0...15.....9
John COWGAR	170	4/1	34...14.....2	0...10.....6
John DICKENSON (Colo.)	570	13/0	370...10.....0	5...11.....1 3/4
Thomas DAVIS	135	4/4	29.....5.....0	0.....8.....9 1/4
Thomas DOUGLASS	168	2/8	22.....8.....0	0.....6.....8 1/2
Charles DONELY	484	6/1	147.....4.....4	2.....4.....2
Charles DAVIS	105	/10	4.....7.....6	0.....1.....3 3/4
Hugh DIVER (Rockingham)	150	2/8	20.....0.....0	0.....6.....0
Robert DUFFILL	330	3/6	57...15.....0	0...16...11 1/2
do. (102 acres new Grant formerly valued in the 330 above)				
James DYER (Rockingham)	174	3/6	30.....9.....0	0.....9.....1 1/4
Robert DINWOODY	210	5/3	55.....2.....6	0...16.....6 1/2
James DINWOODY & William	180	1/9	15...15.....0	0.....4.....8 1/2
Michael DOUGHERTY	200	2/8	26...18.....4	0.....8.....0
ditto	150	4/4	32...10.....0	0.....9.....9
John DEAN (Botetourt)	195	1/3	12.....3.....9	0.....3.....7 1/2
Lawrence DRINNEN's Estate	300	2/8	40.....0.....0	0...12.....0

(page 97 contd. Augusta County Land Tax Return of Samuel Vance for 1788)

Persons Names Owning Land	Quanty of Land	Rate of Land p Acre	Total Amount of Value of Land	Amount of Tax at 1 1/2 p cent
Jacob DRINNEN	500	5/3	131.....5.....0	1...19.....4
Thomas DRINNEN	333	1/9	29.....2.....9	0.....8.....9
William DICKEY	100	8/8	43.....6.....8	0...13.....0
John DENISON	400	/10	16...13.....4	0.....4.....9 1/4
ditto	205	1/0	10.....5.....0	0.....3.....3 3/4
Alexander DUNLAP	400	2/4	46...13.....0	0...14.....1 1/2

(page 98. Augusta County Land Tax Return of Samuel Vance for 1788)

Persons Names Owning Land	Quanty of Land	Rate of Land p Acre	Total Amount of Value of Land	Amount of Tax at 1 1/2 p cent
William ERWIN	240	5/3	53...11.....3	0...16.....0 3/4
Charles ERWIN	130	6/1	39...10...10	0...11...11 3/4
Gerard ERWIN	100	8/8	43.....6.....8	0...10.....0
ditto (New Grant)	100	1/3	6.....5.....0	0.....1.....3
John ELLIOTT	340	7/0	119.....0.....0	1...15.....8 1/4
ditto	40	1/6	3.....4.....6	0.....1.....0
Stonhil EYE	100	2/8	13.....6.....8	0.....4.....0
Phillip EACKORD	95	4/4	20...11.....8	0.....6.....2
ditto	50	2/0	5...16.....0	0.....1.....6 1/2
do. (New Grant)	150	2/0	15.....0.....0	0.....4.....6
EBRAM EACKORD	150	2/8	18...15.....0	0.....5.....6 3/4
George EVICK	317	3/0	47...10.....0	0...14.....3
James ERWIN	140	1/3	3...13.....6	0.....1.....1
James ELLIOTT (from James RUCKER, SENR.)	180	2/8	24.....0.....0	0.....7.....2 1/4
John FOWLER from William GERARD)	139	1/9	11...13.....3	0.....3.....8 1/2
James FULTON	241	8/8	104.....8.....8	1...11.....2 1/2
Thomas FEMSTER	290	13/0	188...10.....3	2...16.....6 1/2
ditto	185	2/0	18...10.....0	0.....5.....6 1/2
David FRAME (valued formerly)	270	/10	10...11...10	0.....3.....4 1/2
do. (remainder of New Grant)	880	1/3	50.....0.....0	0...15.....0
Moore FANTELEROY	235	6/6	41.....2.....6	0...12.....4
Petter FLESHER	200	5/0	52...10.....0	0...15.....9
Henry FLESHER (New Grant)	82	2/2	8...16.....8	0.....2.....7 3/4
Robert FLETCHER (Rockbridge)	50	3/6	8...15.....0	0.....2.....7 1/2
ditto	22	2/0	2.....4.....0	0.....0.....8
Coonrod FLESHER	200	3/6	35.....0.....0	0...10.....6
David GIVIN	967	4/4	209...12.....0	3.....2...10 1/2
Joseph GIVIN	216	6/1	65...14.....0	0...19.....8 1/2
ditto	100	1/9	8...15.....0	0.....2.....7 1/2
ditto	18	6/1	5.....9.....6	0.....1.....7 1/2
ditto	260	8/8	112...13.....4	1...13.....9 1/2
ditto	318	6/1	96...14.....6	1.....9.....0 1/4
Christopher GRAHAM	289	10/6	151...14.....6	2.....5.....6 3/4
Thomas GILLASPY	300	4/4	65.....0.....0	0...19.....6
John GILLASPY	190	5/3	49...17.....6	0...14...11 1/2
ditto	108	4/4	23.....8.....0	0.....7.....0 1/2
Hugh GILLASPY's Estate	89	2/8	10...10.....4	0.....3.....2 1/4

(page 98. Augusta County Land Tax Return of Samuel Vance for 1788)

Persons Names Owning Land	Quantity of Land	Rate for Land p Acre	Total Amount of Value of Land	Amount of Tax at 1 1/2 p cent
James GAY	200	7/0	70.....0.....0	1.....1.....0
Elizabeth GRAHAM (Widow)	312	8/8	135.....4.....0	2.....0.....6 1/2
ditto	53	2/0	5....6.....0	0....1.....7 1/2
John GRAHAM	128	8/8	55....9.....4	0...16.....7 1/4
ditto	91	2/0	9.....2.....0	0.....2...10 3/4
John GRAM (B. Pasture)	137	2/8	18.....5.....4	0.....5.....5 3/4
Isabella GAMBEL (Widow)	300	4/4	65.....0.....0	0...19.....6
do. (for Son, William)	150	1/6	11.....5.....0	0.....3.....4 1/2
William GEENS	100	2/8	13.....6.....8	0.....4.....0
ditto	143	7/9	12...10.....3	0.....3....90
John GUM, SENR.	216	3/6	37...16.....0	0...11.....4
ditto	200	1/9	19.....5.....0	0.....5.....9 3/4
Isack GUM (formerly valued)	193	2/8	25...14.....8	0.....7.....8 3/4
do. (remainder of New Grant)	200	/10	8.....6.....6	0.....2.....5 3/4
William GIVENS	354	7/9	137.....3.....6	2.....1.....1 3/4
do. (New Grant)	83	/10	3.....9.....2	0.....0.....8 1/4
do. (New Grant)	48	/10	2.....0.....0	0.....0.....4 3/4
Mary GRIGORY	220	5/3	57...15.....0	0...17.....3 3/4
Samuel GRIGORY	148	5/3	38...17.....0	0...11.....7 3/4
Jacob GILLASPY	400	1/9	30.....0.....0	0.....9.....0
James GRIFFETH	155	5/3	40...13.....9	0...12.....2 1/2
John GRIGORY	100	2/8	13.....6.....8	0.....4.....0
do. (of William GRIGORY not before valued)	50	2/8	6...13.....4	0.....2.....0
Thomas GALFORD	90	/10	3...17.....6	0.....1.....1 3/4
do. (from Lewis TACKETT)	191	1/9	16...14.....3	0.....5.....0
Robert GRAHAM's Estate	128	8/8	55.....9.....4	0...16.....7 1/2
John GEENS	90	1/9	7...17.....6	0.....2.....4 1/2
John GUM, JUNR.	180	2/8	24.....0.....0	0.....7.....2 1/4
Palser HAMMER (from LION and SIMONS)	85	5/8	14.....8.....9	0.....4.....3 1/4
do (remainder of New Grant)	48	1/9	4.....4.....0	0.....1.....3
John HICKLIN	263	7/6	101...18.....3	1...10.....7 1/2
Robert HALL	1250	10/6	656.....5.....0	9...16...10 1/2
Thomas HUGHART (COLO.)	395	10/11	215...12.....1	3.....4.....8
ditto	95	2/8	12...13.....4	0.....3.....9 1/2
Thomas HICKLIN	200	10/6	105.....0.....3	1...11.....6
ditto	150	1/9	12...12.....2	0.....3.....9 1/2
Edward HINDS's Estate	150	4/4	92...10.....0	0.....9.....9

(page 99. Augusta County Land Tax Return of Samuel Vance for 1788)

Persons Names Owning Land	Quantity of Land	Rate for Land p Acre	Total Amount of Value of Land	Amount of Tax at 1 1/2 p cent
Hugh HICKLIN	200	7/0	70.....0.....0	1.....1.....0
James HUGHART	378	4/4	81...18.....0	1.....4.....7 1/2
John HODGE	350	6/1	106.....9.....2	1...11...11 3/4
Andrew HAMILTON	185	7/0	64...15.....0	0...19.....5
ditto	200	/10	8.....6....8	0.....2.....6
Jones HENDERSON	314	6/1	95...10.....2	1.....8.....7 3/4
ditto	100	/10	4.....3.....4	0.....1.....3
Paul HINKLE	97	2/8	12...18.....8	0.....3...10 1/2

(page 99 contd. Augusta County Land Tax Return of Samuel Vance for 1788)

Persons Names Owning Land	Quantity of Land	Rate of Land p Acre	Total Amount of Value of Land	Amount of Tax at 1 1/2 p cent
Henry HEATH (Fort Pitt)	1000	4/4	216...13.....4	3.....5.....0
Nicolas HARPER	200	5/3	32...10.....0	0...15.....9
ditto	227	1/6	17.....0.....6	0.....5.... 1 1/2
Jacob HOOVER	375	6/1	114.....1.....3	1...11.....2 1/2
Bostion HOOVER's Estate	150	2/8	20.....0.....0	0.....6.....0
Adam HARPER (Hampshire)	100	3/6	17...10.....0	0.....3.....3
John HINES	140	2/8	18...10.....4	0.....5.....7
ditto	58	1/8	5.....1.....6	0.....1.....6 1/4
do. (formerly valued, to James WOODS, New Grant)	60	2/8	8.....8.....0	0.....2.....9 3/4
Roger HICKMAN	140	7/0	49.....0.....0	0...14.....8 1/4
Petter HOLL (Capt.)	355	5/3	98...13.....9	1.....8.....1 1/4
ditto	341	1/6	25...11.....6	0.....7.....9
ditto	140	7/0	49.....0.....0	0...14.....8 1/4
do. (from William ROBINSON, 80 acres formerly valued)	150	2/8	20.....0.....0	0.....6.....0
ditto (New Grant)	97	3/9	18.....3.....9	0.....5.....5 1/4
ditto (New Grant)	32	/10	1.....6.....8	0.....0.....3
do. (from John COWGER, New Grant)	395	1/9	34...11.....0	0...10.....4 1/4
do. (the above 395 acres formerly charged to John (?)				
George HOLL (from Petter HOLL)	240	5/3	63.....0.....0	0...15...10 3/4
Jacob HOLL (from do.)	130	5/3	34.....2.....6	0...10.....2 3/4
Adam HOLL (from do.)	143	5/3	37...10.....9	0...11.....3
Michael HOOVER	50	4/4	13...16.....0	0.....3.....8
do (from Petter SMITH)	27	5/0	7.....1.....9	0.....2.....1 1/2
Jonathan HUMPHREYS	300	3/6	52...10.....0	0...15.....9
ditto (the tracts of 76 & 54 acres is valued in the 300 mentioned)				
William HUTCHISON	240	6/1	73.....0.....0	1.....1...10 3/4
Ozborn HAMILTON	94	7/0	32...18.....0	0.....9.....9 1/4
ditto	130	8/8	56.....6.....8	0...16...10 1/2
ditto	21	8/8	9.....2.....0	0.....2.....9
ditto	35	/10	1.....9.....2	0.....0.....5 1/3
Alexander HAMILTON	170	6/1	51...14.....2	0...15.....6
Charles HAMILTON	100	6/1	30.....8.....4	0.....9.....1 1.2
(Credit John HICKLAN, JUNR.)	100	(no such land)		

(page 100. Augusta County Land Tax Return of Samuel Vance for 1788)

Ebram HEMPENSTALL	32	2/0	3.....4.....0	0.....1.....0
William HANDLEY	100	10/6	52...10.....0	0...16.....9
Isack JOHNS	250	2/2	27.....1.....8	0.....8.....1 3/4
Anthony JOHNSON	198	2/8	26.....8.....0	0.....7...11
Andrew JOURDAN (from John JOURDAN)	45	5/0	11.....6.....0	0.....3.....6 1/2
ditto. (from John JOURDAN)	80	1/6	6.....0.....0	0.....1.....9 1/2
Ebram INGRAM, SENR.	150	2/8	20.....0.....0	0.....6.....0
Ebram INGRAM, JUNR.	205	2/8	27.....6.....8	0.....8.....2 1/4

(page 100 contd. Augusta County Land Tax Return of Samuel Vance for 1788)

Persons Names Owning Land	Quantity of Land	Rate for Land p Acre	Total Amount of Value of Land	Amount of Tax at 1 1/2 p cent
Thomas JERVIS	400	1/9	35.....0.....0	0...10.....6
Gabriel JONES (Atorney)	100	5/0	25.....0.....0	0.....7.....6
John KINKADE, Esqr.	286	4/4	61...19.....4	0...18.....6 3/4
William KINKADE, (Capt.)	350	6/1	106.....9.....2	1...11...11 1/2
William KILPATRICK	200	/10	8.....6.....8	0.....2.....6
Thomas KINKADE	300	6/1	91...5.....0	1.....7.....4 1/2
William KINKADE (Stiller)	250	5/3	65...12.....6	0...19.....8 1/2
James KILPATRICK	50	5/3	13.....2...6	0.....3....1 3/4
Andrew KILPATRICK	40	5/3	10...10.....0	0.....3....1 3/4
John KINKADE (Jackson's River)	161	1/3	7...11.....3	0.....2.....3 1/4
Richard KILLINGSWORTH	95	1/3	5...18.....9	0.....1.....6 3/4
John KELLY	295	5/3	67...19.....9	1.....0.....8 1/2
John LAMBERT	30	1/9	2...17.....9	0.....0...10 1/4
Charles LEWIS (Colo.) Estate	1130	12/2	687.....8....4	10...6.....2 1/2
Ralph LAFERTY	40	7/0	14.....0.....0	0.....4.....2
Rebecah LAFERTY	300	7/0	105.....0.....0	1...11.....6
William LOCKRIDGE	250	7/0	87...10.....0	1.....6.....3
Andrew LOCKRIDGE	566	8/8	244...16.....8	3...13.....5 1/2
do. (from John HICKLIN)	196	7/9	75...18...10	1.....2.....8 3/4
John LOCKRIDGE	200	5/3	52...10.....0	0...15.....9
ditto	143	1/6	10...14.....6	0.....3.....2
Joseph LEEZER	44	3/6	7...14.....0	0.....2.....3 3/4
Coonrod LANCE (from Bernard LANCE's Estate)	115	4/4	24...15.....4	0.....7.....5 1/2
George LANCE (from do.)	230	4/4	49...16.....8	0...14...11 3/4
Martin (? LIFE) (from do.)	150	4/4	39.....0.....0	0...11.....8 1/4
Joseph LANCE (from do., the same)	606	4/4	131.....6.....0	1...18.....7 1/2
William LEWIS	250	5/3	65...12.....6	0...19.....8 1/4
ditto	400	6/4	126...13.....4	1...18.....1 1/2

(page 101. Augusta County Land Tax Return of Samuel Vance for 1788)

Thomas LEWIS	1350	5/3	354.....7....6	5.....6.....3 1/2
Allexander LOWRY	50	1/9	4.....7.....6	0.....2.....3 3/4
ditto	161	1/0	8.....0.....0	0.....2.....3 1/2
William LANGSDALE (part New Grant)	66	1/9	7...15.....6	0.....2.....6
do (from Ralph STEWART, the same)	100	2/8	(blurred)	(blurred)
do. (remainder of New Grant)	134	2/8	17...17.....4	0.....5.....4 1/4
John LEWIS (Capt.)	580	17/6	507...10.....0	7...12.....3
ditto	70	1/9	6.....2.....6	0.....1...10
ditto	26	2/0	2...12.....0	0.....0...10
John McDONALD	277	7/0	90...19.....0	1.....7.....6 3/4
Patrick MILLER	193	9/7	92.....9....7	1.....7.....8 3/4
ditto (New Grant)	58	/10	2.....8....4	0.....0.....8 1/2
ditto (New Grant)	58	/10	2.....8....4	0.....0.....8 1/2
Lewis MARTIN	65	1/9	5...13.....9	0.....1.....8 1/4

(page 101 contd. Augusta County Land Tax Return of Samuel Vance for 1788)

Persons Names Owning Land	Quantity of Land	Rate of Land p Acre	Total Amount of Value of Land	Amount of Tax at 1 1/2 p cent
Adam MARTIN	66	1/9	5...15.....9	0.....1....8 3/4
Joseph MALCOM	280	7/9	108...10.....0	1...12.....6 1/2
ditto	130	2/6	16.....5.....0	0.....4...10 1/2
Samuel McDONALD (from William THOMPSON)	195	7/0	68.....5.....0	1.....0....5 1/2
ditto	300	5/3	78...15.....0	1....3....7 1/2
Robert McMULLIN	310	/10	12...18.....4	0.....3...10
William MOORE	94	5/3	24...10.....6	0.....7....4 3/4
John MILLER	290	4/4	62...16.....8	0...18...10
ditto	232	1/6	17.....8.....0	0.....5.....2
ditto	58	1/6	4.....7.....0	0.....1.....3
Robert McCREERY, (Capt.)	260	9/7	124...11.....8	1...17.....4 1/2
ditto	30	2/	3.....0.....0	0.....0...10 1/2
John MONTGOMERY	108	11/2	60.....6.....0	0...18....1
Joseph MAZZE Estate	182	7/9	70...10.....6	1.....1....1 3/4
ditto	80	/10	3.....6.....8	0.....1.....0
John McCLUNG	209	5/3	54...17.....3	0...16.....5 1/2
ditto	81	2/0	8.....2.....0	0.....2.....0
ditto	148	1/9	13.....8.....9	0.....3.....8 1/2
ditto	92	1/9	8.....1.....0	0.....2.....3
Andrew MOODY	80	3/6	14.....0.....0	0.....4.....2 3/4
John McCASHLIN	174	6/1	52...18.....6	0...15...10 1/2
ditto	40	2/0	4.....0.....0	0.....1.....1 3/4
Sampson MATHEWS (Colo.)	2150	6/1	653...19.....2	9...16.....2 1/2
John McCUTCHIN	342	7/9	132...10.....6	1...19....9
ditto	31	2/0	3.....2.....0	0.....1.....0
do. (from William McCUTCHIN)	100	8/8	40.....6....8	0...13....( ) 1/2
Thomas MEEK's Estate	310	7/9	115.....2.....6	1...14.....6 1/2
Samuel McCHESNEY	500	4/4	108.....6.....8	1....12.....6

(page 102. Augusta County Land Tax Return of Samuel Vance for 1788)

Persons Names Owning Land	Quantity of Land	Rate of Land p Acre	Total Amount of Value of Land	Amount of Tax at 1 1/2 p cent
Daniel MEEK	250	6/1	76.....0...10	1.....2.....9 1/2
John MEEK	566	4/4	122...12.....8	1...16.....9 1/2
William MATEER	520	6/1	158.....3.....4	2.....7.....5 1/4
George MATHEWS (Gent.)	200	1/9	17...10.....0	0.....5.....3
John McCOLLOM	150	1/9	13.....2.....6	0.....3...11 1/4
John McCOY (Capt.)	146	10/6	76...10.....0	1.....2...11 1/4
ditto	117	1/9	10.....4.....6	0.....3.....0 3/4
ditto	118	1/9	11...16.....0	0.....3.....5 1/2
Duncan McFARLAND	100	7/9	38...15.....0	0...11.....7 1/2
ditto	119	1/3	7.....8.....0	0.....2.....2
Moses MOORE	1105	3/6	193.....7.....6	2...18.....0
do. (940 acres of New Grant formerly valued in the 1105)				
ditto.	124	2/0	12.....8.....0	0.....3.....9
Levi MOORE	500	2/8	66...10.....4	1.....0.....0
James McCARTY	215	2/8	28...13.....4	0.....8.....7
John MULLENEUX, JUNR.	50	2/8	6...10.....4	0.....2.....0
ditto	60	2/0	6.....0.....0	0.....1...10 1/2
Samuel MOSES	100	/10	4.....3.....4	0.....1.....3

(page 102 contd. Augusta County Land Tax Return for 1788)

Persons Names Owning Land	Quantity of Land	Rate of Land p Acre	Total Amount of Value of Land	Amount of Tax at 1 1/2 p cent
Robert McCRAY	110	1/0	5...10.....0	0.....1.....7 1/2
William McCOY	70	3/6	12.....5.....0	0.....3.....8
James McGLOUHLIN	138	1/9	14.....5....3	0.....4.....3 1/4
Mary MOORE (Widow)	220	4/4	47.....3....4	0...14.....2 1/2
William McCUTCHIN	258	8/8	111...16.....0	1...13.....4 1/2
ditto	50	1/6	3...15.....0	0.....1.....1 1/2
ditto	101	2/0	10.....2.....0	0.....3.....0 3/4
Edward MORTON	125	2/6	15...12.....6	0.....4.....8 1/4
ditto. (New Grant)	200	1/9	17...10.....0	0.....5.....3
HUGH MORISON	95	3/0	14.....5.....0	0.....4.....3 1/4
William NOTINGHAM	328	1/9	28.....5....8	0.....8.....5 3/4
George NICOLAS	267	2/8	35...12.....0	0...10.....8
ditto	123	1/6	9.....4.....6	0....2...10
George NEAGLE	100	1/9	8...15.....0	0.....2.....7 1/2
Henry NULL	100	2/8	13.....6.....8	0.....4.....0
John POAGE	1039	3/6	181...16.....6	2...14.....6
ditto	240	1/6	18.....0.....0	0.....5.....6 1/2
ditto	400	4/4	86...13.....4	1...6.....0
ditto (New Grant)	210	1/9	18.....7.....6	0.....5.....6

(page 103. Augusta County Land Tax Return of Samuel Vance for 1788)

George POAGE (Capt.)	200	4/4	43.....6.....8	0...13.....0
ditto	382	1/0	19.....2.....0	0...5...11
Lofty PULLIN	321	8/8	139.....2.....0	2.....1.....8 3/4
ditto	400	1/3	25.....0.....0	0.....7.....6
John PEEBLES	209	10/6	109...14.....6	1...12...10 3/4
ditto	190	1/3	11...11.....6	0.....3.....6
John PLUNKETT	160	3/6	17...10.....0	0.....5.....3
Christian PICKLE	100	4/4	21...13.....4	0.....6.....6
Henry PENINGER	180	10/6	94...10.....0	1.....8.....4
ditto	98	2/0	9...16.....0	0.....2...11
do. (from George STOUT)	131	5/3	34.....7.....9	0...10.....4
Gerard PECK	53	2/8	7.....1.....4	0.....2.....4 1/2
John PAINTER	45	3/6	7...17.....6	0.....2.....4 1/2
Mathew PATTON	315	3/6	55.....2.....6	0...16.....6 1/4
James RAMSEY	240	7/0	84.....0.....0	1.....5.....2 1/4
ditto	316	7/0	110...12.....0	1...13.....2
William REAH	257	6/1	78.....3....5	1.....3.....5 1/2
ditto	150	/10	6.....6.....0	0.....1...10 1/2
ditto	112	1/6	8.....8.....0	0.....2.....7 1/2
John REDMAN	124	4/4	26...17.....4	0.....8.....0 3/4
Henry ROCKEY	568	3/6	99.....8.....0	1.....9.....9 3/4
JOHN REAH	110	6/1	33.....9....2	0...10.....0 1/2
ditto	50	/10	2.....1.....8	0.....0.....7 1/2
William RAMSEY	72	2/8	9...12.....0	0.....2...10 1/2
ditto (formerly valued by mistake.	60	(part of the 72)		
Joseph RAY	100	2/8	13.....6.....8	0.....4.....0

(page 103 contd. Augusta County Land Tax Return of Samuel Vance for 1788)

Persons Names Owning Land	Quantity of Land	Rate of Land p Acre	Total Amount of Value of Land	Amount of Tax at 1 1/2 p cent
Robert RUSK	500	3/6	87...10.....0	1.....6.....3
ditto	385	1/0	22.....7.....6	0.....6.....7 1/2
Samuel RUCKER (from				
John RUCKER, SENR.)	345	1/6	25...7.....6	0.....7.....9 3/4
James RUCKER, JUNR.	285	2/8	38.....0.....0	0...11.....4 3/4
William RIDER	176	/10	7.....6.....6	0.....2.....2 1/4
John RICE's Estate	50	2/8	6...13.....4	0.....2.....0
Samuel REDMAN	200	3/6	35.....0.....0	0...10.....6
do. (from Petter FLECK)	125	2/6	15...12.....6	0.....4.....8 1/4
Petter ROBISON from				
Ephraim BATES	172	3/6	30.....2.....0	0.....9.....0 1/2
do. (from Mathew PATTON)	197	3/6	34.....9.....6	0...10.....4
Robert RAMSEY (from				
James RUCKER, SENR>)	180	2/8	24.....0.....0	0.....7.....2 1/2

(page 104. Augusta County Land Tax Return of Samuel Vance for 1788)

Persons Names Owning Land	Quantity of Land	Rate of Land p Acre	Total Amount of Value of Land	Amount of Tax at 1 1/2 p cent
Nicolas SYBERT	769	1/6	57...10.....6	0...17.....2 1/2
William SMITH's Estate	180	5/8	47.....5.....0	0...14.....2
Zacharaiah STOUT	92	2/6	6...18.....0	0.....2.....0 3/4
Alexander ST. CLAIR from				
McCLINACHAN)	500	7/0	175.....0.....0	2...12.....6
William STEWART	437	4/4	94...13.....8	1.....8.....4 3/4
ditto	122	1/3	7.....12.....0	0.....1...10 1/2
Petter SIGAFOOSE	200	7/9	77...10.....0	1.....3.....3
ditto	250	3/6	43...15.....0	0...13.....1 1/2
Van SWEARINGIN	116	2/8	15.....9.....4	0.....4.....7 1/2
ditto	100	/10	4.....3.....4	0.....1.....3
Robert STEWART	300	5/3	78...15.....0	1.....3.....7 1/2
Andrew SUTLINTON	310	13/1	202...15...10	3...0...10
do. (credit the Tract of)	337	(no such land)		
ditto	167	1/6	72...10.....6	0.....3.....9 1/2
John SUTLINTON	224	10/6	117...12.....0	1...15.....3 1/4
James STONE	69	2/8	9.....4.....0	0.....2.....9
Robert SHIELDS	150	3/6	26.....5.....0	0.....7...10 1/2
John STEWART	246	5/3	67...11.....7	0...19.....7 1/2
Robert SMITH	300	4/4	65.....0.....0	0...19.....6
Leonard SEIMONS (inslusive Survey)	101	5/3	26...10.....3	0.....7.....7 3/4
do. (remainder of New Grnt)	79	1/9	6...18.....4	0.....1.....4 1/2
ditto	86	1/3	5.....7.....6	0.....1.....7
ditto	27	1/3	1...13.....6	0.....0.....6 1/2
ditto	30	1/3	1...17.....6	0.....0.....5 1/2
Mark SEIMONS (from				
Leonard SEIMONS)	44	5/9	11...11.....0	0.....3.....5
do. (remainder of New Grant)	47	1/9	4.....2.....3	0.....1.....2 3/4
Petter SEIMONS (not valued before)	64	3/6	11.....4.....0	0.....3.....4 1/4
Leonard SEIMONS, JUNR.	26	1/6	1...19.....0	0.....0.....6 3/4
John SOMWALT	150	5/3	39.....7.....6	0...11.....9 3/4
George SOMWALT	150	2/8	20.....0.....0	0.....6.....0
Michael SNARE (Hampshire)	50	3/6	8...15.....0	0.....2.....7 1/2
John SNIDER	50	2/8	6...13.....4	0.....2.....0

(page 104 contd. Augusta County Land Tax Return of Samuel Vance for 1788)

Persons Names Owning Land	Quantity of Land	Rate of Land p Acre	Total Amount of Value of Land	Amount of Tax at 1 1/2 p cent
John SEIMONS	100	4/4	21...13....1	0.....6.....6
Leonard SEIMONS (S. Fork)	50	1/9	4.....7....6	0.....1....3 3/4
George SEIMONS	139	4/4	29...15....4	0.....8...11 1/2
ditto	85	3/0	12...15.....0	0.....3.....9 2/4
John SLAVINS, JUNR. (from Lewis PACKETT)	191	1/9	16...14....3	0.....5.....0
Petter SMITH	73	5/3	19.....3....3	0.....5.....8 3/4

(page 105. Augusta County Land Tax Return of Samuel Vance for 1788)

Persons Names Owning Land	Quantity of Land	Rate of Land p Acre	Total Amount of Value of Land	Amount of Tax at 1 1/2 p cent
Paul SUMMERS	225	4/4	48...15.....0	0...14.....7 1/2
ditto	50	1/3	3.....2....6	0.....0...10 1/2
Patrick SLATERY	300	1/3	18...15.....0	0.....5....6 3/4
ditto	300	/10	12...10.....0	0.....7....2 1/4
Henry STONE	180	2/8	24.....0.....0	0.....7....2 1/4
do. (New Grant)	73	2/8	9...14.....0	0.....2...10 3/4
do. (New Grant)	63	1/9	5...10.....0	0.....1.....7 3/4
Jonis SUCK (Hampshire)	200	3/6	35.....0.....0	0...10.....6
Henry SYBERT	100	2/8	13.....6....8	0.....4.....0
Postian STONE	95	7/0	33.....5.....0	0.....9...11 1/2
John SLAVENS, SENR.	380	1/9	33.....5....5	0.....9...11 1/2
William SHARP	300	4/4	65.....0.....0	0...19.....6
do. (New Grant)	320	2/2	34...10....4	0...19.....4 3/4
do. by do.	270	2/8	31...16....8	0.....9.....6 1/2
do. by do.	200	/10	8.....6....8	0.....2.....6
do. by do.	15	4/4	3.....5.....0	0.....0...11 1/2
Henry SWADLEY	100	3/6	17...10.....0	0.....5....3
Stophill SOMWALT	200	/10	8.....6....8	0.....2.....6
George SHEITZE	50	2/8	6...13....4	0.....2.....0
Daniel SMITH, JUNR.	150	1/9	13.....3....6	0...3...11 1/4
Credit Ralph STEWART 100 acres charged William LANGSDALE New Grant				
Joseph SUTTON	100	1/9	8...15.....0	0.....2.....7 1/2
Daniel STOUT (New Grant, 100 acres formerly valued)	133	1/9	11...12....9	0....3.....5 3/4
James STEPHENSON	286	3/6	50.....1....0	0...15.....0
Thomas SMITH (Major)	303	5/3	79...10.....9	1.....3...10 1/2
Edward STEWART (from John HICKLIN)	130	7/9	50.....7....6	0...15.....4
Edward THOMPSON	50	5/3	13.....2....6	0.....3...11 1/2
Lewis TACKETT	297	1/9	25...19....9	0.....7.....9 1/2
Ezekiel TOWNSEND	40	2/8	5.....6....8	0.....1.....7
Credit James TANER	100	(overcharged)		
James TOWNSEND	80	2/8	10...18....4	0....3.....2 1/4
Credit Christopher TACKETT	375	(no such land)		
Alexander THOMPSON	84	6/1	25...11.....1	0.....7.....8
John VANCE's Estate	187	7/0	65...9.....0	0...19.....7 1/2
Samuel VANCE (Colo.)	577	4/4	125.....0.....4	1...17.....6
Adam VERNOR	117	1/9	10...4....9	0.....3.....2

(page 106. Augusta County Land Tax Return of Samuel Vance for 1788)

Persons Names Owning Land	Quantity of Land	Rate of Land p Acre	Total Amount of Value of Land	Amount of Tax at 1 1/2 p cent
John VACOB	307	7/0	107.....9.....0	1...12.....7 3/4
ditto	16	/10	0...10.....0	0.....0.....2 1/2
Robert VACOB	300	5/3	78...15.....0	1.....3.....7 1/2
ditto	78	8/8	33...16.....0	0...10.....1 1/4
John WILSON, Major	304	8/8	131...14.....8	1...19.....6
William WILSON	304	8/8	121...14.....8	1...19.....6
ditto	262	2/8	34...18.....4	0...10.....5 3/4
ditto	400	1/9	25.....0.....0	0.....7.....6
Stephen WILSON	300	8/8	130.....0.....0	1...19.....0
James WOODS (New Grant for-merly valued)	242	2/8	32.....8.....8	0.....8.....8 /4
do. (the remaining)	63	(charged to John HINER)		
Elizabeth WILSON	175	10/6	91...17.....6	1.....7.....6 3/4
ditto	86	1/9	7.....6.....6	0.....2.....3
William WRIGHT	106	5/3	27...16.....6	0.....8.....4 1/2
Robert WALLACE	240	8/8	104.....0.....0	1...11.....2 1/2
Jacob WARICK	1745	3/6	305.....0.....0	4...11.....7 1/4
John WORMSLEY	150	3/6	26.....5.....0	0.....7...10
ditto	384	1/3	24.....0.....0	0.....7.....2 1/2
William WARD	135	1/9	11...16.....3	0.....3.....6 1/2
Michael WOLFONG	120	3/6	21.....0.....0	0.....6.....3 1/2
Christopher WAGONER	90	2/8	12.....0.....0	0.....3.....7
Alexander WILEY	200	1/9	17...10.....0	0.....5.....3
ditto	91	/10	3...15...10	0.....1.....1 1/2
Joseph WRIGHT	200	2/8	26...13.....4	0.....8.....0
William WARICK	800	2/8	106...13.....4	1...12.....0
William WILSON (B. Pasture)	176	6/1	52.....6.....4	0...15.....8 1/4
Thomas WORMSLEY	45	2/8	6.....0.....0	0.....1.....9 1/2
Philip WIMORE	100	1/9	8...15.....0	0.....2.....7 1/2
ditto	146	1/9	9.....3.....6	0.....2...10 1/2
Abijah WAREING	280	/10	12.....0.....0	0.....3.....7
John WAIDE	100	/10	4.....3.....4	0.....1.....3
John WARICK	200	1/9	17...10.....0	0.....5.....3
Jacob WIMERT	154	1/3	9...12.....6	0.....2...11
Henry WHITEMAN	146	1/6	10...19.....0	0.....3.....2 1/2
Andrew YEAGER	98	2/8	13.....1.....4	0.....3...11
William YOLL	205	6/1	62.....7.....1	0...18.....8

(page 107)

A List of the Land Tax within the District of JAMES RAMSEY, Commissioner in the County of Augusta for 1788

Persons Names Owning Land	No. of Lots	Yearly Rent	Quantity of Land	Rate p Acre	Total Amt. of Value of Land	Amt. of Tax at 1 1/2 p cent
ASKINS, John			127	3/11	24...19.....5	0.....7.....5 3/4
do.			49	3/11	9...11...11	0.....2...10
ARMSTRONG, William			200	6/1	60...16.....8	0...18.....3
do.			328	6/1	99...15.....4	1.....9...11 1/2
ARGABRIGHT, John			150	3/11	29.....7.....6	0.....8.....9 3/4
ARGABRIGHT, Augustine			121	5/3	31...15.....3	0.....9.....7
ALLEN, William or Henry EAGLE			131	6/1	39...10...10	0...11...10 1/2
ABNEY, John	2	L. 30				1...10.....0
do.			230	5/3	60.....7.....6	0...18.....1 1/4
do.			120	2/8	16.....0.....0	0.....4.....9 1/2
do.			6	5/3	1...11.....6	0.....0.....5 1/2
do.			1	8/8	0.....8.....8	0.....0.....1 1/2
do.			275	1/9	24.....1.....0	0.....7.....2
do. (for McDONOUGH's Exrs.)	1/2	15				0...15.....0
ADAIR, Neal			200	3/6	35.....0.....0	0...10.....6
do.			150	1/5	10...12.....6	0.....3.....2 1/2
ALLEN, Monticu			400	8/8	173.....6.....8	2...12.....0
do.			80	8/8	34...13.....4	0...10.....3
ALLEN, Robert Junr.			80	15/3	61.....0.....0	0...18.....3 1/2
do.			100	2/8	13.....6.....8	0.....4.....0
do. (N. G.)			50	1/9	4.....7.....6	0.....1.....1 1/4
do.			50	1/9	4.....7.....6	0.....1.....1 1/4
ALEXANDER, Andrew			204	6/6	66.....6.....0	0...19...10 1/2
ALEXANDER, Hugh			314	8/8	136.....1.....4	2.....0.....9 3/4
do.			50	7/	17...10.....0-	0.....5.....3
ARMSTRONG, William			200	7/	70.....0.....0	1.....1.....0
do.			170	1/9	14...17.....6	0.....4.....5 1/2
ARMSTRONG, Robert			224	7/	78.....8.....0	1.....3.....6 1/2
ALEXANDER, Gabriel			363	7/	127.....1.....0	1...18.....1 1/2
do.			130	1/5	2.....4.....2	0.....2.....9 1/4

(page 108. Augusta County Land Tax Return of James Ramsey for 1788)

Persons Names Owning Land	No. of Lots	Yearly Rent	Quantity of Land	Rate p Acre	Total Amt. of Value of Land	Amt. of Tax at 1 1/2 p cent
ALEXANDER, John			260	3/6	45...10.....0	0...13.....7 3/4
ALEXANDER, Andrew			194	2/8	25...17.....4	0.....7.....9
do.			90	1/4	6.....7.....6	0.....2.....3
ADAIR, John			100	2/	10.....0.....0	0.....3.....0
BURNS, Elizabeth	2	37..10				1...17.....6
BLAIR, Elizabeth	1/2	14....8				0...14.....4 3/4
BRAND, James (Doctr.)			200	6/1	60...16.....8	0...18.....3
BUCHANAN, Patrick (Capt.)			200	3/6	35.....0.....0	0...10.....6
BUCHANAN, John Senr.			125	7/9	48.....8.....9	0...14.....6
BLAIR, William			150	3/11	29.....7.....6	0.....8.....9 1/2
BRAWFORD, Rebecca			200	7/	70.....0.....0	1.....1.....0
BLAIR, Joseph			300	4/4	65.....0.....0	0...19.....6
BERRY, George			249	7/9	96...11.....9	1.....8...11 1/2

(page 108 contd. Augusta County Land Tax Return of James Ramsey for 1788)

Persons Names Owning Land	No. of Lots	Yearly Rent	Quantity of Land	Rate p Acre	Total Amt. of Value of Land	Amt. of Tax at 1 1/2 p cent
BERRY, William Junr.			98	7/	34.....6.....0	0...10.....3 1/2
do.			50	2/2	5.....8.....4	0.....1.....7 1/2
BURGESS, William			240	1/9	21.....0.....0	0.....6.....3 1/2
BROWN, Benjamin			100	8/8	43.....6.....8	0...13.....0
do.			30	7/	10...10.....0	0.....3.....1 3/4
do.			55	2/2	5...19.....2	0.....1.....9 1/2
do.			100	8/8	43.....6.....8	0...13.....0
BROWN, Thomas			300	7/9	116.....5.....0	1...14...10 1/2
do.			70	5/3	18...17.....6	0.....5.....4
BROWN, James			295	6/6	95...17.....6	1.....8.....9
do.			7 1/2	4/9	1...15.....3	0.....0.....6
BURK, Edward			268	3/11	52...12.....7 1/2	0...15..9 1/4
do.			3 1/2	4/4	0...15.....0	0.....0.....2 1/2
BELL, William Senr.			200	2/8	26...13.....4	0.....8.....0
do.			198	1/5	14.....0.....0	0.....4.....2

(page 109. Augusta County Land Tax Return of James Ramsey for 1788)

Persons Names Owning Land	No. of Lots	Yearly Rent	Quantity of Land	Rate p Acre	Total Amt. of Value of Land	Amt. of Tax at 1 1/2 p cent
BELL, James Senr.			300	6/1	91.....5.....0	1.....7...10 1/2
do.			113	2/8	14...11.....4	0.....4.....3
BELL, William Junr.			206	7/5	76.....7...10	1.....2...11
BELL, James (Capt.)			240	5/1	73.....0.....0	1.....1...10 3/4
do.			80	1/9	7.....0.....0	0.....2.....1
do.			100	1/6	7...10.....0	0.....2.....3
do (from MARTIN)			160	1/9	14.....0.....0	0.....4.....2
BROWN, John			155	6/1	47.....2...11	0...14.....1 3/4
BAILER, Jacob			235	4/9	55...16.....3	0...16.....9
BRADY, James			300	1/5	21.....5.....0	0.....6.....4 1/2
BOWYER, William (Colo.)	1	30				1...10.....0
do.			50	8/8	21...13.....4	0.....6.....6
do.			146	4/4	31...12.....8	0.....9.....5 3/4
do.			54	3/6	9.....9.....0	0.....2.....9 1/2
do			15 1/2	3/6	2...13.....0	0.....0.....9 1/2
BOWYER, Michael	1	15..10				0...15.....6
do.			23	3/6	4.....0.....6	0.....1.....2
do.			33	3/6	5...15.....6	0.....1.....8
BUCHANAN, David			415	3/3	67.....8.....9	1.....0.....2 3/4
BUCHANAN, Sarah			150	3/	22...10.....0	0.....6.....9
BELL, Robert (W. C.)			190	2/8	25.....6.....8	0.....7.....7
BUCHANAN, William			370	3/6	64...15.....0	0...19.....4 1/2
BROWN, John Senr.			252	5/3	66.....3.....0	0...19...10
BERRY, Charles			426	7/	149.....2.....0	2.....4.....8 1/2
BEARD, Thomas			318	4/9	75...10.....6	1.....2.....7 1/2
BROOKS, John Senr.			364	8/3	150.....3.....0	2.....5.....0 1/2
BOGESS, Thomas (from G. JAMESON)			178	2/8	23...13.....0	0.....7.....2
BEST, James			275	2/2	29...15...10	0.....8.....1 1/4
BRATTON, Elizabeth			200	3/6	32...10.....0	0.....9.....2
do.			120	1/5	8...10.....0	0.....2.....6 1/2
BRATTON, John			120	4/4	26.....0.....0	0.....7.....9 1/2

(page 110. Augusta County Land Tax Return of James Ramsey for 1788)

Persons Names Owning Land	No. of Lots	Yearly Rent	Quantity of Land	Rate p Acre	Total Amount of Value of land	Amount of Tax at 1 1/2 p cent
BELL, James (S. R.)			247	8/8	107.....0.....8	1...12.....1 1/4
BUMGARNER, Christopher			120	5/3	31...10.....0	0.....9.....3 1/4
BURNS, Richard			280	1/5	19...16.....8	0.....5...11 1/4
BELEW, Abraham			20	3/6	3...10.....0	0.....1.....0 3/4
BOYD, Thomas			240	7/	84.....0.....0	1.....5.....2 1/4
do.			80	1/9	7.....0.....0	0.....2.....1
BOYD, John			115	7/	40.....5.....0	0...12.....0 3/4
do.			20	3/6	3...10.....0	0.....1.....0 1/2
BROWNLEE, John Senr.			222	8/3	91...11.....6	1.....7.....2
do.			62	3/6	10...17.....0	0.....3.....3
BROWNLEE, William			100	8/3	41.....5.....0	0...12.....4 1/2
do.			83	2/8	11.....1.....4	0.....3.....3 3/4
BROWNLEE, John Junr.			132	7/9	51.....3.....0	0...15.....4
do.			18	3/6	3.....3.....0	0.....0...11 1/4
BRIGHT, George			170	7/	59...10.....0	0...17...10
do.			300	1/5	21.....5.....0	0.....6.....4 1/2
do.)			488	1/3	30...10.....0	0.....9.....3
do.) (N. G.)			240	1/3	15.....0.....0	0.....4.....6
do.)			192	1/2	12.....0.....0	0.....3.....2 1/2
BLACK, Cutlive			160	4/	32.....0.....0	0.....9.....7
BRAWFORD, Samuel			200	8/3	82...10.....0	1.....3.....4 1/2
BRAWFORD, John (from Samuel BRAWFORD)			209	8/3	86.....4.....3	1.....6.....6
BURK, John			212	9/5	78...12.....4	0.....3.....7
BLACK, John			121	5/3	31...15.....3	0.....9.....6 1/4
do.			134	8/8	58.....1.....4	0...17.....5
BLACKWOOD, SAMUEL			105	4/4	22...15.....0	0.....6.....9 3/4
BROWN, William			225	5/8	63...15.....0	0...19.....1 1/2
do.			148	5/3	33...17.....0	0...11.....7 3/4
do.			80	1/9	7.....0.....0	0.....2.....1
BELL, James (S.R.)			300	7/9	116.....5.....0	1...14...10 1/2
BELL, John			300	7/9	116.....5.....0	1...14...10 1/2
do.			130	1/5	9.....4.....2	0.....2.....9 1/4

(page 111. Augusta County Land Tax Return of James Ramsey for 1788)

Persons Names Owning Land	No. of Lots	Yearly Rent	Quantity of Land	Rate p Acre	Total Amount of Value of land	Amount of Tax at 1 1/2 p cent
BLACK, William			316	7/5	117.....3.....8	1...15.....1 3/4
BLACK, Samuel			369	7/5	136...16.....9	2.....1.....0 1/2
do.			200	6/1	61.....5.....0	0...18.....4 1/2
do.			200	1/5	14.....3.....4	0.....4.....3
BERRY, John (B. C.)			398	2/2	43.....2.....4	0...12...11
BRENT, James			200	4/4	43.....6.....8	0...13.....0
do.			90	1/9	7...17.....6	0.....2.....4
do.			400	1/5	28.....6.....8	0.....8.....6
BROBACK, Philip			80	2/8	10...13.....4	0.....3.....2 1/4
BOYD, Alexander (from James Carruthers)			113	3/6	19...15.....6	0.....5...11 1/4
BOFANG, JOHN	1	33				1...13.....0
BEARD, Christopher (from J. COLES)			220	5/8	62.....6.....8	0...18.....8 1/2
CALDWELL, John			300	7/9	116.....5.....0	1...14...10 1/2
CHAPMAN, John			110	4/4	26...16.....8	0.....7.....1 3/4

(page 111 contd. Augusta County Land Tax Return of James Ramsey for 1788)

Persons Names Owning Land	No. of Lots	Yearly Rent	Quantity of Land	Rate p Acre	Total Amount of Value of Land	Amount of Tax at 1 1/2 p cent
COOK, John			30	5/3	7...17.....6	0.....2.....4 1/4
COCKS, Jacob			100	2/2	10...16.....8	0.....3.....3
CROW, Benjamin			200	5/3	52...10.....0	0...15.....9
CAMPBELL, James			200	4/4	43.....6.....8	0...13.....0
do.			27	3/11	7.....5.....9	0.....1.....7 1/2
CALLISON, James			276	5/8	78.....4.....0	1.....3.....3
CALE, Peter			214	5/3	55.....3.....6	0...16.....6 1/2
do.			122	2/8	16.....5.....4	0.....4...10 1/2
CUNINGHAM, David			276	7/	79.....2.....0	1.....3.....8 3/4
CUNINGHAM, John (Capt.)			173	6/6	56.....4.....6	0...16...10 1/4
CALE, David Senr.			30	4/4	6...10.....0	·0.....1...11 1/4
COULTER, Michael			436	7/9	168...19.....0	2...10.....8 1/4
do.			100	1/6	7...10.....0	0.....2.....2 3/4
CRAWFORD, William	1	40				2.....0.....0
do.			800	4/4	173.....6.....8	2...12.....0
do.			90	2/8	12.....0.....0	0.....3.....7
do.			130	2/2	14.....1.....8	0.....4.....2 3/4
do.			133	1/9	11...12.....9	0.....3.....5 3/4

(page 112. Augusta County Land Tax Return of james Ramsey for 1788)

Persons Names Owning Land	No. of Lots	Yearly Rent	Quantity of Land	Rate p Acre	Total Amount of Value of Land	Amount of Tax at 1 1/2 p cent
CRAWFORD, John			390	5/3	102.....7.....6	1...10.....8 1/2
do.			201	4/4	43...11.....0	0...13.....0 3/4
do.			95	2/8	12...13.....4	0.....3.....9 1/2
CUNNINGHAM, James Senr,.			90	7/	31...10.....0	0.....9.....5 1/4
do.			49	1/9	4.....5.....6	0.....1.....3
CUMMINS, Robert Senr.			164	6/6	53.....6.....0	0...15.....1 3/4
do.			135	1/6	10.....2.....6	0.....3.....1
CLUNIGER, Valentine			16	4/4	3.....4.....4	0.....1.....0 3/4
CALDWELL, William (T. S.)			130	7/5	48.....4.....2	0...14.....5 1/2
do.			186	6/1	56...11.....6	0...16.....8
CAMPBELL, Sarah			390	7/5	144...12.....6	2.....3.....3 3/4
CUNNINGHAM, John			210	4/4	45...10.....0	0...13.....7 3/4
CLARK, James Junr.			212	5/5	54.....5.....6	0...16.....8 1/4
CALDWELL, John (T. S.)			275	7/5	101...19.....7	1...10.....7
CARRUTHERS, David			200	2/8	26...13.....4	0.....8.....0
COULTER, John Senr.			150	5/3	40.....4.....3	0...12.....0
do.			106	2/6	13.....5.....0	0.....2...11 1/2
COULTER, David			114	3/6	19...19.....0	0.....5...11 3/4
do.			50	5/3	13.....2.....6	0.....4.....0
CHESNUT, William			320	2/8	42...13.....4	0...12.....9 1/2
CAMPBELL, Andrew			30	2/8	4.....0.....0	0.....1.....2 1/4
COULTER, James			300	4/4	32...10.....0	0.....9.....9
CARRUTHERS, Thomas			100	3/6	17...10.....0	0.....5.....3
COOPER, Robert			150	3/6	26.....5.....0	0.....7...10 1/2
CUNNINGHAM, James (Sadler)			220	3/6	38...10.....0	0...11.....6 1/2
CARSON, Samuel			175	8/3	72.....3.....9	1.....1.....7 1/2
CAMPBELL, Mary			100	2/8	13.....6.....8	0.....4.....0
CAMPBELL, Robert			100	2/8	13.....6.....8	0.....4.....0
do.			150	1/9	13.....2.....6	0.....3...11 1/4
CHRISTIAN, John Senr.			208	7/9	80...15...10 1/2	1...4.....2

(page 112 contd. Augusta County Land Tax Return of James Ramsey for 1788)

Persons Names Owning Land	No. of Lots	Yearly Rent	Quantity of Land	Rate p Acre	Total Amount of Value of Land	Amount of Tax at 1 1/2 p cent
CAMPBELL, George			140	1/9	12.....5.....0	0.....3.....8
do.			50	1/9	4.....7.....6	0.....1.....3 3/4

(page 113. Augusta County Land Tax Return of James Ramsey for 1788)

Persons Names Owning Land	No. of Lots	Yearly Rent	Quantity of Land	Rate p Acre	Total Amount of Value of Land	Amount of Tax at 1 1/2 p cent
CHRISTIAN, Robert Junr.			208 1/2	7/9	80...15...10 1/2	1...4...2
CHRISTIAN, Gilbert			269	8/8	116...11.....4	1...14...11 1/2
CHRISTIAN, Patrick			269	8/8	116...11.....4	1...14...11 1/2
CHRISTIAN, Gilbert & Robert			338	8/8	146.....9.....4	2.....3...11 1/4
CHRISTIAN, William			200	8/8	86...13.....4	1...6.....0
CRAWFORD, James (from J. COAL)			400	1/5	28.....6.....8	0.....8.....6
COFFEY, William (B. C. Amhurst)			186	2/8	24...16.....0	0.....7.....5 1/4
COALTER, John Junr.			100	2/8	13.....6.....8	0.....4.....0
COALTER, Joseph			253	3/6	44.....5.....6	0...13.....3 1/4
COMER, Margaret			116	1/9	10.....3.....0	0.....3.....0 1/2
COOK, John			225	2/0	25...10.....0	0.....7.....8
CLARK, James Senr.			200	5/3	52...10.....0	0...15.....9
COBB, William			87	2/6	10...17.....6	0.....3.....3 1/4
CHILMORE, Lewis			101	5/3	26...10.....3	0.....7...11 1/2
DONALDSON, Robert			238	5/3	61...13.....9	0...18.....6
DOWNEY, Martha			700	5/8	198.....6.....8	2...19.....6
DAILEY, John			150	6/6	48...15.....0	0...14.....7 1/2
DAUGHERTY, Hugh			200	3/11	39.....3.....4	0...11.....3
DAVIS, Walter			160	7/9	62.....0.....0	0...18.....7
do.			50	1/9	4.....7.....6	0.....1.....3 3/4
DAVIS, James			322	7/	112...14.....0	1...13.....9 3/4
do.			5	7/	1...15.....0	0.....0.....6 1/2
DOLT, Philip			186	3/11	36.....8.....6	0...10...11
do. (from S. HENRY)			50	2/2	5.....8.....4	0.....1.....7 1/2
DAVIDSON, John			280	2/8	37.....6.....8	0...11.....2 1/4
DOAKE, John			307	7/9	118...19.....3	1...15.....8 1/2
DOAKE, Robert			266	4/4	57...12.....8	0...17.....3 1/2
DOAKE, David			300	7/9	116.....5.....0	1...14...10 1/2
DORSET, Thomas			130	2/8	17.....6.....8	0.....5.....2 1/4
DAVIS, William						
Henry HALL, Tenant	1	12				0...12.....0

(page 114. Augusta County Land Tax Return of James Ramsey for 1788)

Persons Names Owning Land	No. of Lots	Yearly Rent	Quantity of Land	Rate p Acre	Total Amount of Value of Land	Amount of Tax at 1 1/2 p cent
EMMIT, John			60	7/	21.....0.....0	0.....6.....3 3/4
ESTIL, Zechariah			299	8/8	129...11.....4	1...18...10 1/4
ERWIN, James (Capt.)			252	7/9	97...13.....0	1...9.....3 1/2
do.			150	1/9	13.....2.....6	0.....3...11 1/2
do.			190	7/9	78.....2.....6	1...3.....5
do.			2 1/2	7/9	0...19.....3	0.....0.....3 1/4
ERWIN, James Junr.			145	1/9	12...13.....9	0.....3.....9 3/4
do.			150	4/4	32...10.....0	0.....9.....9
ELLIOTT, John			109 1/2	4/4	23...15.....7	0.....7...1 1/2
ELLIOTT, James			300	7/	105.....0.....0	1...11.....6
ESTRAP, Robert	1/2	10				0...10.....0

((page 114 contd.. Augusta County Land Tax Return of James Ramsey for 1788)

Persons Names Owning Land	No. of Lots	Yearly Rent	Quantity of Land	Rate p Acre	Total Amount of Value of Land	Amount of Tax at 1 1/2 p cent
EAGLE, George			100	5/3	26.....5.....0	0.....7...10 3/4
ERWIN, James			156	4/4	33...16.....0	0...10.....1 1/2
EVY, Jacob (from R. ALLEN)			170	6/1	51...14.....2	0...15.....6 1/2
FULTON, David (from S. MATHEWS)			112	6/6	36.....8.....0	0...10...10
FULTON, Andrew			260	5/3	68...15.....6	1.....0.....7 1/2
FISHER, George			200	4/4	43.....6.....8	0...13.....0
FLOYD, Charles,						
William McKENNY, Admr.			90	2/2	9...15.....0	0.....2...11
FISHER, Frederick			60	2/8	8.....0.....0	0.....2.....4 3/4
FULTON, William			200	8/8	86...13.....4	1.....6.....0
FULWIDER, Olbrick			160 1/2	3/6	28.....1.....9	0.....8.....5
do.			40	1/9	3...10.....0	0.....1.....1
do.			30	1/9	2...12.....6	0.....0.....9 1/2
FERGUSON, William			170	4/9	40.....7.....6	0...12.....1 1/2
FULTON, Hugh			250	8/8	108.....6.....8	1...12.....6
FULTON, Mary			287	7/9	149...19.....3	2.....4...11
FULTON, John			309	8/8	133...18.....0	2.....4.....8
FAUL, George			145	7/	50...15.....0	0...15.....2 1/2
do.			154	5/3	40.....8.....6	0...12.....1 1/2
do.			136	3/6	23...16.....0	0.....7.....1 1/2
do.			290	2/2	31.....8.....4	0.....9.....5 1/4

(page 115. Augusta County Land Tax Return of James Ramsey for 1788

Persons Names Owning Land	No. of Lots	Yearly Rent	Quantity of Land	Rate p Acre	Total Amount of Value of Land	Amount of Tax at 1 1/2 p cent
FULWIDER, John			43	3/11	8.....4.....6	0.....2.....5
FRINGER, Peter			266	7/	93.....2.....0	1.....9...7 1/2
do (from Thomas NELSON)			100	3/11	20.....3.....5	0.....6.....0 1/2
FRIDLEY, Jacob			101	3/6	17.....3.....6	0.....5.....1 1/2
GAMBLE, Robert (Colo.)	1	48				2.....8.....0
GRINER, David's Heirs	1	20				1.....0.....0
do.	1	12				0...12.....0
GARBER, Michael	1	30				1...10.....0
GRIFFIN, John	1/3	12				0...12.....0
GILKISON, Hugh			220	7/9	85.....5.....0	1.....5.....6
GIBSON, Samuel			226	8/8	97...18.....8	1.....9.....4 1/2
GILMER, James Senr.			204	7/9	79.....1.....0	1.....3.....8 1/2
GILKISON, William			265	5/3	69...11.....6	1.....0...10 1/4
GIBSON, Robert			142	5/3	37.....5.....6	0...11.....2
GREAVES, William			100	3/11	19...11.....8	0.....5...10 1/2
GLEAB LAND			200	7/	70.....0.....0	1.....1.....0
GIBSON, Alexander Senr.			200	7/9	85.....5.....0	1.....5.....6 3/4
do.			159	7/	55...13.....0	0...16.....8 1/2
do.			50	2/2	5.....8.....4	0.....1.....7 1/2
do.			205	4/4	44.....8.....4	0...13.....4
do.			50	3/1	7...10.....2	0.....2.....3 3/4
do.			20	1/9	1...15.....0	0.....0.....6 1/4
do.			20	1/9	1...15.....0	0.....0.....6 1/4
GARDNER, Francis			199	5/3	52.....4.....9	0...15.....8
do.			136	1/9	11...18.....0	0.....3.....6 3/4

(page 115 contd. Augusta County Land Tax Return of James Ramsey for 1788)

Persons Names Owning Land	No. of Lots	Yearly Rent	Quantity of Land	Rate p Acre	Total Amount of Value of Land	Amount of Tax at 1 1/2 p cent
GARDNER, Samuel			250	3/6	43...15.....0	0...13.....1 1/2
GREENWOOD, Margaret &						
Heirs of Josiah GREENWOOD			105	6/6	33.....1....6	0.....9...11
GUTHERY, William			490	5/8	138..16....8	2.....1.....7 3/4
GROVE, Windle			114	7/	39...18.....0	0...11...11 1/2
GRAHAM, William			350	2/8	46...13.....4	0...14.....0

(page 116. Augusta County Land Tax Return of James Ramsey for 1788)

Persons Names Owning Land	No. of Lots	Yearly Rent	Quantity of Land	Rate p Acre	Total Amount of Value of Land	Amount of Tax at 1 1/2 p cent
GRASS, Jacob Senr.			10	4/4	2.....3.....4	0.....0.....7 3/4
GABBERT, Jacob			210	5/3	55.....2....6	0...16.....6 1/2
HYSKEL, Peter	1	60				3.....0.....0
do.			13	4/4	2...16....4	0.....0...10
HUGHS, Euphemia	1	16				0...16.....0
do.			30	4/4	6...10.....0	0.....1...11 1/2
HANDREL, Lawrence & George			185	5/3	48...11....3	0...14.....7
do.			95	4/4	20...11....8	0.....6.....2
HAWK, Henry			213	4/4	46.....3....0	0...13...10
HIZER, Samuel			110	4/4	23...16....8	0.....7.....1 3/4
HUDSON, George			183	6/6	59.....9....6	0...17...10 3/4
HANKEY, Simon			50	2/2	5.....8....4	0.....1.....7 1/2
HENDERSON, Joseph			520	3/6	91.....7....3	1.....7.....3 1/2
HANGER, Frederick Senr.			225	4/4	48...15.....0	0...14.....7 1/2
HAMILTON, Arthur			232	5/3	60...18.....0	0...18.....8 3/4
HAMILTON, James			153	5/3	40.....3....1	0...10.....8
HAMILTON, John			200	5/3	60.....0.....0	0...16.....8
HAWTHORN, James			530	6/1	161.....4....2	2.....8.....4 1/4
do.			220	10/6	115...10.....0	1...14.....7 3/4
do.			50	1/9	4.....7....6	0.....1.....3 1/4
HANNA, Robert			100	3/1	15.....8....4	0.....4.....7 1/2
do.			60	2/2	6...10.....0	0.....1...11 1/4
HAYS, James			170	2/8	22...13....4	0.....6.....9 1/2
do.			50	8/8	17...10.....0	0.....5.....3
HILL, James			84	2/2	9.....2....0	0.....2.....8 3/4
do.			33	2/2	3...11....6	0.....1.....0 3/4
do.			17	2/2	1.....6...10	0.....0.....6 1/2

(page 117. Augusta County Land Tax Return of James Ramsey for 1788)

Persons Names Owning Land	No. of Lots	Yearly Rent	Quantity of Land	Rate p Acre	Total Amount of Value of Land	Amount of Tax at 1 1/2 p cent
HANGER, Peter Senr.			280	5/3	73...10.....0	1.....2.....0 1/2
do.			213	5/3	95...16....6	1.....8.....8
do.			85	2/8	11.....6....8	0.....3.....4 3/4
do.			187	6/1	56...17....6	0...17.....0 3/4
do.			280	3/6	49.....0.....0	0...14.....8 3/4
do.			124	2/8	16...10....8	0.....4...11 1/2
do.			438	2/6	54...12....6	0...16.....4 3/4
do.			10	4/4	2.....3....4	0.....0.....7 1/2
HANLEY, John Senr.			150	7/	52...10.....0	0...15.....9
HUNTER, William			240	2/2	26.....0.....0	0.....7.....9 1/2
HINDS, Thomas			120	2/8	16.....0.....0	0.....4.....9 1/2

(page 117 contd. Augusta County Land Tax Return of James Ramsey for 1788)

Persons Names Owning Land	No. of Lots	Yearly Rent	Quantity of Land	Rate p Acre	Total Amount of Value of Land	Amount of Tax at 1 1/2 p cent
HULL, Francis			150	6/1	45...12.....6	0...13.....8 1/2
do.			47	2/8	6.....5.....4	0.....1...10 1/2
HARRIS, Robert			200	4/9	47...10.....0	0...14.....3
do.			200	4/9	47...10.....0	0...14.....3
HUNT, Charles			100	2/8	13.....6.....8	0.....4.....0
do.			20	8/8	8...13.....4	0.....2.....7
HARRISON, David			47	5/3	12.....6.....9	0.....3.....8 1/2
do.			153	2/8	20.....8.....0	0.....6.....1 1/4
HENDERSON, William			390	7/	136...10.....0	2.....0...11 1/2
HENDERSON, David			278 1/2	7/9	107...18.....4	1...12.....4 1/2
HALL, Edward			220	8/8	95...6.....8	1...1.....8.....7
do.			125	2/8	16...13.....4	0.....5.....0
do.			100	2/8	13...6.....8	0.....4.....0
do.			20	1/9	1...15.....0	0.....0.....6
do.			38	1/9	3...6.....6	0.....1.....0
do.			32	5/	8.....0.....0	0.....2.....5
HUTCHISON, George			150	3/7	29...7.....6	0.....9.....4 1/2
HENDERSON, David Senr.			100	1/	5.....0.....0	0.....1.....6
HENRY, Samuel			270	3/11	52...17.....6	0...15...11
do.			300	4/9	71.....5.....0	1.....1.....4 1/2

(page 118. Augusta County Land Tax Return of James Ramsey for 1788)

Persons Names Owning Land	No. of Lots	Yearly Rent	Quantity of Land	Rate p Acre	Total Amount of Value of Land	Amount of Tax at 1 1/2 p cent
HENRY, James (Weaver)			100	7/	35.....0.....0	0...10.....6
HAYS, Samuel			209	8/8	90...11.....4	1.....7.....2
HUMPHREY, David			300	7/	105.....0.....0	1...11.....6
HALL, Patrick			166	7/	58.....2.....0	0...17.....5
do.			2	7/	0...14.....0	0.....0.....2 1/2
HENRY, James (B. Smith)			334	7/	119.....0.....0	1...15.....8 1/2
do.			250	4/4	50.....3.....4	0...15.....1 3/4
do.			250	7/	87...10.....0	1.....6.....3
do.			250	8/8	108.....6.....8	1...12.....6
do.			100	3/6	17...10.....0	0.....5.....3
HAYS, Patrick			212	7/9	62.....3.....0	0...18.....4
HOFFMAN, Gasper			100	5/3	26.....5.....0	0.....7...10 1/2
HUNTER, Samuel			196	7/	68...12.....0	1.....0.....6 3/4
do.			255	8/3	105.....3.....9	1...11.....6 1/2
do. (from CAMPBELL)			200	6/1	60...18.....8	0...18.....3
do. (from CAMPBELL)			200	6/1	60...18.....8	0...18.....3
HUNTER, John			240	5/8	68.....0.....0	1.....0.....4 1/2
HAMILTON, Robert			160	3/11	31.....6.....8	0.....9.....4 3/4
HUGHS, Thomas			150	4/4	33...16.....0	0...10.....1 1/2
HOOFMAN, John			188	2/8	25.....0.....8	0.....7.....6
HANLEY, William			100	10/6	52...10.....0	0...15.....9
HAUPH, Randle			200	6/1	60...16.....8	0...18.....3
do.			100	3/11	19...11.....8	0.....5...10 1/2
do.			200	6/1	60...16.....8	0...18.....3
HANGER, Frederick			150	4/4	32...10.....0	0.....9.....9
HEIZER, John			120	5/3	31...10.....0	0.....9.....5 1/2
HATTON, Mark (for Samuel BLACKWOOD's Heirs			100	6/6	32...10.....0	0.....9.....9

(page 118 contd. Augusta County Land Tax Return of James Ramsey for 1788)

Persons Names Owning Land	No. of Lots	Yearly Rent	Quantity of Land	Rate p Acre	Total Amount of Value of Land	Amount of Tax at 1 1/2 p cent
INGLEMAN, William			180	4/4	39.....0.....0	0...11.....8 1/4
INGLEMAN, Peter			230	4/4	49...16.....8	0...14.....9
INNMAN, William			200	1/9	17...10.....0	0.....5.....3

(page 119. Augusta County Land Tax Return of James Ramsey for 1788)

Persons Names Owning Land	No. of Lots	Yearly Rent	Quantity of Land	Rate p Acre	Total Amount of Value of Land	Amount of Tax at 1 1/2 p cent
JACKSON, John (Doctr.)			278	6/1	84...12.....2	1.....5.....4 1/2
JONES, Gabriel (Attorney)			200	7/	70.....0.....0	1.....1.....0
do.			902	/10	37...11.....8	0...11.....3 1/4
JAMESON, John			200	8/8	86...13.....4	1.....4.....7
do.			40	2/8	5.....6.....8	0.....1.....7
KIRK, James			215	7/	75.....5.....0	1.....2.....6 3/4
KIRK, John			150	3/6	26...12.....0	0.....7...11
do.			76	7/	26.....6.....0	0.....7...10 1/2
KIRKPATRICK, John			110	5/3	55.....2.....6	0...16.....7 1/2
do.			100	2/8	13.....6.....8	0.....4.....6 1/4
KILLER, George			100	4/9	23...15.....0	0.....7.....1 1/4
do.			90	1/9	7...17.....6	0.....2.....4 1/4
do.			32	2/8	4.....5.....4	0.....1.....3 1/4
KIDD, Daniel	1	22				1.....2.....0
do.			173	6/1	52...12.....5	0...15.....9 1/2
do.			87	4/4	18...17.....0	0.....5.....7 3/4
KERR, James (for Joseph MARTIN)			750	7/9	290...12.....6	4.....7.....2 1/4
KENNEDY, James (Rockbridge)			26	3/6	4...11.....0	0.....1.....4 1/4
KERR, William			188	6/1	57.....3.....8	0...17.....1 3/4
KING, John			169	3/6	27.....9.....3	0.....8.....2 3/4
do.			190	2/2	20.....4.....8	0.....6.....2
KILLER, Michael			150	1/8	12.....9.....0	0.....3...10
KENNEDY, William			370	1/8	25...16.....8	0.....7.....8 1/2
LIVINGSTON, William			130	4/4	28.....3.....4	0.....8.....5 1/4
do.			20	8/8	8...13.....4	0.....2.....7
do.			15	3/6	2...12.....6	0.....0.....9 1/2
LEDGERWOOD, William			187	7/	65.....9.....0	0...19.....7

(page 120. Augusta County Land Tax Return of James Ramsey for 1788)

Persons Names Owning Land	No. of Lots	Yearly Rent	Quantity of Land	Rate p Acre	Total Amount of Value of Land	Amount of Tax at 1 1/2 p cent
LOCKHART, James			130	2/8	17.....6.....8	0.....5.....2 1/4
LOVINGOOD, Herman			210	6/1	63...17.....6	0...19.....2
do.			210	2/8	28.....0.....0	0.....8.....4 3/4
do.			50	1/9	4.....7.....6	0.....1.....3 3/4
do.			50	2/8	6...13.....4	0.....2.....0
do.	-		70	2/6	8...15.....0	0.....2.....7 1/2
LOGAN, William			140	5/3	36...15.....0	0...11.....0 1/4
do.			25	3/6	4.....7.....6	0.....1.....3 3/4
LOGAN, John			140	5/3	36...15.....0	0...11.....0 1/4
do.			25	3/6	4.....7.....6	0.....1.....3 3/4
LESLEY, Thomas			144	2/2	15...12.....0	0.....4.....8
LODOWICK, George			108	6/6	35.....2.....0	0...10.....6 1/2

(page 120 contd. Augusta County Land Tax Return by James Ramsey for 1788)

Persons Names Owning Land	No. of Lots	Yearly Rent	Quantity of Land	Rate p Acre	Total Amount of Value of Land	Amount of Tax at 1 1/2 p cent
LEREW, Abraham			171	7/2	61.....5.....6	0...18.....4 1/2
do.			150	7/9	58.....2.....6	0...17.....5 1/4
LONG, Alexander			10	2/8	1.....6.....8	0.....0.....4 3/4
do.			400	1/5	28.....6.....8	0.....8.....6
LONG, Francis			100	8/8	43.....6.....9	0...13.....0
LONG, James			145	8/8	62...16.....8	0...18...10
LONG, Samuel			145	8/8	62...16.....8	0...18...10
LONG, David			200	7/	70.....0.....0	1.....1.....0
LONG, Joseph			200	7/	70.....0.....0	1.....1.....0
LOCKHART, William			300	1/5	21.....5.....0	0.....6.....4 1/2
LEDICK, George			100	4/	20.....0.....0	0.....6.....0
do.			8	10/	4.....0.....0	0.....1.....2 1/2
LYONS, Henry			300	2/6	43...15.....0	0...13.....1 1/2
MATHEWS, George (Genl)			150	2/8	20.....0.....0	0.....6.....0
do.			560	3/6	98.....0.....0	1.....9.....4 1/2
do.			16	4/4	3.....9.....6	0.....1.....0 1/2
do.			86 1/2	6/1	26.....6.....2	0.....7...10 3/4
MILLER, George			192	6/1	58.....8.....0	0...17.....6 1/4
do.			45	2/2	5.....5.....0	0.....1.....6 3/4

(page 121. Augusta County Land Tax Return by James Ramsey for 1788

Persons Names Owning Land	No. of Lots	Yearly Rent	Quantity of Land	Rate p Acre	Total Amount of Value of Land	Amount of Tax at 1 1/2 p cent
MARSHAL, John			269 1/2	5/3	70...14...10	1.....1.....2 1/2
McCLANAHAN's Heirs			310	7/	103...10.....0	1...11.....0 1/2
do.			109	1/9	16...12.....6	0.....4...11 3/4
McCORCLE, Samuel			321	3/1	49.....9.....9	0...14...10 3/4
McPHEETERS, Alexander Senr.			303	7/	106.....1.....0	1...11...9
McPHEETERS, Alexander Junr.			28	3/11	5.....9.....0	0.....1.....9 3/4
McPHEETERS, John			388	7/9	150.....7.....0	2.....5.....1 1/4
do.			321	6/6	102.....7.....0	1...10.....8 1/2
McKITRICK, Robert			200	6/1	60...16.....8	0...18.....3
do.			170	2/8	22...13.....4	0.....6.....9 1/2
do.			90	1/9	7...17.....6	0.....2.....4 1/2
do.			100	6/1	30.....8.....4	0.....9.....1 1/2
MOFFETT, James			200	6/1	60...16.....8	0...18.....3
McCUTCHIN, Samuel Senr.			237	7/9	91...16.....9	1.....7.....5 1/2
MINER, Thomas			122	2/8	16.....5.....4	0.....4...10 1/2
do.			50	1/9	4.....7.....6	0.....1.....4 3/4
do.			149	1/9	11.....3.....6	0.....3...10 3/4
do. (New Grant)			80	1/9	7.....0.....0	0.....2.....1 1/4
McCROSKEY, David			181	3/6	31...13...10	0.....9.....4 1/2
MOFFETT, John Senr.			234	8/8	101.....8.....0	1...10.....5 1/2
McCLANAHAN, Alexander (Colo)			560	6/6	182.....0.....0	2...14.....7
do.			200	1/9	17...10.....0	0.....5.....3
do.			222	7/9	86.....0.....6	1.....5.....9 1/4
do. (New Grant)			57	2/9	7...16.....7	0.....2.....4 1/4
do.			387	3/6	67...17...11	1.....0.....2 1/2
McCLANAHAN, Robert			340	3/1	55.....5.....0	0...16.....6 3/4
McKINNEY, Alexander			310	3/1	47...15...10	0...14.....2
McKEE, Alexander			355	5/3	93.....3.....9	1.....7...11 1/2

(page 121 contd. Augusta County Land Tax Return by James Ramsey for 1788)

Persons Names Owning Land	No. of Lots	Yearly Rent	Quantity of Land	Rate p Acre	Total Amount of Value of Land	Amount of Tax at 1 1/2 p cent
McPHEETERS, William			367	9/7	175...17.....1	2...12.....9
McCLINTOCK, William Senr.			172	4/4	38.....7.....0	0...11.....6
McCLINTOCK, William Junr.			100	3/1	19...11.....8	0.....5...10 1/2

(page 122. Augusta County Land Tax Return by James Ramsey for 1788)

Persons Names Owning Land	No. of Lots	Yearly Rent	Quantity of Land	Rate p Acre	Total Amount of Value of Land	Amount of Tax at 1 1/2 p cent
McPHEETERS, William & Robert TRIMBLE			121	3/	18.....3.....0	0.....5.....4 1/2
McCUTCHIN, John			215	7/9	83.....6.....3	1.....5.....0
McCUTCHIN, William			290	7/9	112.....7.....6	1...13.....9 1/2
MARROW, Francis	1	24				·1.....4.....0
do.			15	3/6	2...12.....6	0.....0.....9 1/2
McDAVID, Patrick			50	8/8	21...13.....4	0.....6.....6
do.			25	4/4	5.....8.....4	0.....1.....7 1/2
MOFFETT, William			244	7/9	94...11.....0	1.....8.....3 3/4
MATHEWS, Sampson (Colo.)	4	5				0.....5.....0
do.	1	1				0.....1.....0
do.	1	40				2.....0.....0
do.			196 1/2	2/8	26.....4.....5	0.....7...10 1/2
do.			196 1/2	2/8	26.....4.....5	0.....7...10 1/2
do.			196 1/2	2/8	26.....4.....5	0.....7...10 1/2
McDOWEL, William	1/2	30				1...10.....0
do.	1/2	50				2...10.....0
do.	1	5				0.....5.....0
do. (from T. POAGE)	1	1				0.....1.....0
do.			27	4/4	5...17.....0	0.....1.....9
do.			257	3/6	43...19.....0	0...13.....9
McDOWEL, Hugh	1/2	30				1...10.....0
do.	1	26				1.....6.....0
do.			204	5/	51.....0.....0	0...15.....3 3/4
McGIBBINS, John			109 1/4	4/4	23...11.....7	0.....7.....1 1/4
McGONIGLE, James	1	16				0...16.....0
MERRIT, Samuel	1	30				1...10.....0
do.			254	3/6	43...19.....0	0...13.....9
MUSTER, Anthony	1/2	14				0...14.....0
do. & William CHAMBERS	1	15				0...15.....0
do.			275	3/6	48.....2.....6	0...14.....6 1/2

(page 123. Augusta County Land Tax Return by James Ramsey for 1788)

Persons Names Owning Land	No. of Lots	Yearly Rent	Quantity of Land	Rate p Acre	Total Amount of Value of Land	Amount of Tax at 1 1/2 p cent
McCHESNEY, JAMES			223	6/1	67...16.....7	1.....0.....4 1/2
do.			273	6/6	97...10.....0	1.....9.....3
McCHESNEY, Robert			124	6/1	37...14.....4	0...11.....3 3/4
McCUTCHIN, Samuel (Capt.)			150	6/1	45...12.....6	0...13.....8 1/4
do.			80	2/8	10...13.....4	0.....3.....2 1/4
do.			390	1/9	34.....2.....6	0...10.....2 3/4
McCUTCHIN, John			150	4/4	32...10.....0	0.....9.....9
do.			330	1/8	27...10.....0	0.....8.....4
MURPHEY, William			140	4/4	30.....6.....8	0.....9.....1
MINGA, Henry			127	6/1	38...12.....7	0...11.....7

(page 123 contd. Augusta County Land Tax Return by James Ramsey for 1788)

Persons Names Owning Land	No. of Lots	Yearly Rent	Quantity of Land	Rate p Acre	Total Amount of Value of Land	Amount of Tax at 1 1/2 p cent
McKINNEY, John (Capt.)			170	4/9	40.....7.....6	0...12.....0
do.			200	3/6	35.....0.....0	0...10.....6
do.			187	2/8	24...18.....8	0.....7.....5
McNUTT, Robert			258	5/8	73.....2.....0	1...11.....1
McNUTT, James			161	6/6	52.....6.....6	0...15.....8 1/2
do.			183	5/3	48.....0.....9	0...14.....5
MARSHAL, George			232	3/11	45.....8.....8	0...13.....7 1/2
McCLURE, John			155	7/	54.....5.....0	0...16.....3
MITCHEL, James Senr.			254	8/8	110.....1.....4	1...13.....3 1/4
do.			259	9/2	118...14.....2	1...15.....7 1/4
do.			370	1/9	32.....7.....6	0.....9.....8 3/4
do.			95	1/9	8.....6.....3	0.....2.....6
MITCHEL, William			176	7/9	68.....4.....0	1.....0.....5
McCUTCHIN, William			100	3/6	17...10.....0	0.....5.....3
do.			100	1/9	8...15.....0	0.....2.....7 1/2
MOORE, William			154	4/4	38.....7.....4	0...10.....0 1/2
do.			10	4/4	2.....3.....4	0.....0.....7 1/2
MITCHEL, James Junr.			200	7/9	77...10.....0	1.....3.....3
do.			166	7/	58.....2.....0	0...17.....5
MATEER, James			200	6/1	60...16.....8	0...18.....3
do.			36	3/6	6.....6.....0	0.....1...10 1/2

(page 124. Augusta County Land Tax Return by James Ramsey for 1788)

Persons Names Owning Land	No. of Lots	Yearly Rent	Quantity of Land	Rate p Acre	Total Amount of Value of Land	Amount of Tax at 1 1/2 p cent
MITCHEL, Thomas			234	7/5	86...15.....6	1.....6.....0 1/4
McCUTCHIN, William Senr.			231	2/2	25.....6.....0	0.....7.....6
McCANTREE, Richard			150	2/8	20.....0.....0	0.....6.....0
MAURY, Samuel			70	2/6	8...15.....0	0.....2.....7 1/2
McFADDEN, John			100	3/6	17...10.....0	0.....5.....3
McCLARY, Hugh			200	6/1	60...16.....8	0...18.....3
McCLANAHAN, Elijsh			387 1.2	4/4	83.....9.....6	1.....5.....0
NELSON, Alexander	1/3	20				1.....0.....0
NORTH, Philip			50	5/3	13.....2.....6	0.....3...11 1/2
OTT, JOHN			150	2/8	20.....0.....0	0.....6.....0
OLINGER, Philip Senr.			180	7/	63.....0.....0	0...18...10 3/4
OLINGER, Philip Junr.			144	6/6	46...16.....0	0...14.....0 1/2
PATTERSON, William (Rockbridge)			100	5/3	26.....5.....0	0.....7.....9 1/2
PATTERSON, Robert			202	7/9	78.....5.....6	1.....3.....4
PHILIPS, John			171	6/1	52.....1.....3	0...15.....7 1/4
do.			86	1/9	7...10.....6	0.....2.....3
do.			50	1/9	4.....7.....6	0.....1.....3 3/4
do.			164	1/6	12.....6.....0	0.....3.....6 1/2
PARIS, John			213	4/4	46.....3.....0	0...13...10
PEARY, George			180	4/9	42...15.....0	0...12.....9 3/4
PEARY, Joshuah (Capt.)	1	25				1.....5.....0
PALMER, William			388	3/6	67...18.....0	1.....0.....4 1/2
PATTON, Jacob			127 1/2	6/1	38...15.....7	0...11.....7 1/2
PARRIS, William			184	4/4	46.....0.....0	0...13.....9 1/2

(page 124 contd. Augusta County Land Tax Return by James Ramsey for 1788)

Persons Names Owning Land	No. of Lots	Yearly Rent	Quantity of Land	Rate p Acre	Total Amount of Value of Land	Amount of Tax at 1 1/2 p cent
POAGE, William			290	3/11	56...15...10	0...16.....2 3/4
POTTER, Philip (from R. TATE)			23	7/	8.....1.....0	0.....2.....4 3/4
RICHIE, Hugh (Doctr.)			60	5/3	15...15.....0	0.....4.....8 1/2
do.			100	3/6	17...10.....0	0.....5.....3
READ, Mathew (deced)						
Thomas POAGE Admintr.)			200	2/8	26...13.....4	0.....8.....0

(page 125. Augusta County Land Tax Return by James Ramsey for 1788)

Persons Names Owning Land	No. of Lots	Yearly Rent	Quantity of Land	Rate p Acre	Total Amount of Value of Land	Amount of Tax at 1 1/2 p cent
READ, Robert (deced)	1	36				1...16.....0
do.			300	8/8	130.....0.....0	1...19.....0
do.			400	2/8	53...6.....8	0...16.....0
do.			50	4/4	10...16.....8	0.....3.....5
do.			25	4/4	5.....8.....4	0.....1.....7 1/2
RUSK, Margaret			173	7/	60...11.....0	0...18.....1 3/4
RUSK, William			107	4/9	25.....8.....3	0.....7.....7 1/2
do.			190	2/8	25.....6.....8	0.....7.....7
RUSK, David			176	3/6	30...16.....0	0.....9.....2 3/4
RUSK, Robert			160	7/	56.....0.....0	0...16.....9 1/2
do.			120	2/	12.....0.....0	0.....3.....5
RUTLEDGE, Thomas Senr.			220	7/5	81...11.....8	1.....4.....5
RIDDLE, Cornelius (Capt.)			317 3/4	7/9	115.....4.....0	1...14.....6 3/4
RAY, Daniel			100	3/1	15.....8.....4	0.....4.....7 1/2
RICE, William			120	5/3	31...10.....0	0.....9.....5 1/4
ROWEN, James			228	6/1	69.....7.....0	1.....0...10 3/4
RICHARDSON, Philemon			250	7/9	96...17.....6	1.....9.....0 3/4
do.			246	7/9	95.....6.....6	1.....8.....7
do.			80	5/	22.....0.....0	0.....6.....7 1/2
RANDOLPH, William			276	5/8	78.....4.....0	1.....3.....5
do.			55	5/8	15...11.....8	0.....4.....7 1/2
REAUGH, William (for NELSON's Heirs)			84	3/11	16.....9.....0	0.....4...11
do.			40	1/9	3...10.....0	0.....1...0 1/2
SCOTT, Andrew			200	4/9	47...10.....0	0...14.....3
do.			66	2/4	7...14.....0	0.....2.....3 3/4
do.			42	2/2	4...11.....0	0.....1.....7
do.			5 1/3	3/11	1.....0.....0	0.....0.....3 1/2
do.			40	2/2	4.....6.....8	0.....1.....3 3/4

(page 126. Augusta County Land Tax Return by James Ramsey for 1788)

Persons Names Owning Land	No. of Lots	Yearly Rent	Quantity of Land	Rate p Acre	Total Amount of Value of Land	Amount of Tax at 1 1/2 p cent
SCOTT, Thomas			171	8/8	74.....2.....0	1.....2.....2 3/4
do.			68	2/	6...16.....0	0.....2.....0 1/2
STRICKLING. Joseph			43	1/6	3.....4.....6	0.....1...0 1/2
SWINK, Henry			109	4/4	27.....5.....0	0.....8.....2
SWINK, Lawrence			145	4/4	31.....8.....8	0.....9.....4
SWALLOW, Jacob			120	5/3	31...10.....0	0.....9.....5 1/4
SCOTT, Thomas Junr.			302	3/6	52...17.....0	0...15...10 1/4
do.			98	3/6	17.....2.....0	0.....5.....2
SMITH, John			200	7/9	77...10.....0	1.....3.....3 1/4

(page 126 contd. Augusta County Land Tax Return by James Ramsey for 1788)

Persons Names Owning Land	No. of Lots	Yearly Rent	Quantity of Land	Rate p Acre	Total Amount of Value of Land	Amount of Tax at 1 1/2 p cent
SAWYER, James			230	7/	80...10.....0	1.....4.....1 3/4
do.			100	2/8	13.....6.....8	0.....4.....0
do.			115	2/8	15.....6.....8	0.....4.....7
SCOTT, Archibald (Revd.)			150	5/3	39.....7.....6	0...11.....9 3/4
do.			95	3/11	18...12.....1	0.....5.....6 1/2
SLUSHER, Coonrod			320	4/4	66.....6.....8	1.....0.....9 1/2
STEEL, Samuel (B. Smith)			113	6/1	34.....7.....5	0...10.....3 3/4
SANCEBAK, John			186	6/1	56...11.....6	0...16...11 1/2
SHIELDS, William Senr.			100	3/1	15.....8.....4	0.....4.....7 1/2
SHIELDS, William Junr.			84	2/8	7...14.....0	0.....2.....3 3/4
SHARP, John Senr.			470	4/4	101...16.....8	1...10.....6 1/2
SHARP, John Junr.			73	2/8	9...14.....8	0.....2...11
do. (from A. HAYS)			35	2/8	2...11.....3	0.....0.....9
STEWART, Elizabeth			100	8/8	43.....6.....8	0...13.....0
SCOTT, John			452	2/8	60.....5.....4	0...18.....1
SYLER, Jacob			334	5/3	87...13.....6	1.....6.....3 1/2
STINETT, William			343	3/11	67.....3.....5	1.....1.....1 1/2
SUMMERS, John			200	3/11	39.....3.....4	0...11.....9
SPOTTS, George	1	16				0...16.....0
do.			30	3/6	5.....5.....0	0.....1.....6 1/2
SPROUl, William			490	6/6	159.....5.....0	2.....7.....9 1/2
SPROUL, Alexander			300	6/6	97...10.....0	1.....9.....3

(page 127. Augusta County Land Tax Return of James Ramsey for 1788)

Persons Names Owning Land	No. of Lots	Yearly Rent	Quantity of Land	Rate p Acre	Total Amount of Value of Land	Amount of Tax at 1 1/2 p cent
ST. CLAIR, Alexander	1/2	45				2.....5.....0
do.	1/2	36				1...16.....0
do.	1	10				0...10.....0
do.	1	24				1.....4.....0
do.	1	18				0...18.....0
do.			80	13/	52.....0.....0	0...15.....7
do.			50	4/4	10...16.....8	0.....3.....3
do.			80	2/8	10...13.....4	0.....3.....2 1/2
do.			25	4/4	5.....8.....4	0.....1.....7 1/2
STEWART, Archibald			100	10/6	52...10.....0	0...15.....9
do.			340	1/9	29...15.....0	0.....8...11 1/2
STEWART, Alexander (Major)			180	3/6	31...10.....0	0.....9.....5 1/2
STEWART, Benjamin			497	6/6	161...10.....9	2.....8.....8 1/2
STEEL, James Esqr.			200	8/8	86...13.....4	1.....6.....0
do.			187 1/2	4/4	40...12.....6	0...12.....8 1/2
SUMMERS, John			250	4/4	54...13.....4	0...16.....3
SEARIGHT, Alexander			252	5/3	66.....3.....0	0...19...10
STEEL, David (Miller)			144	5/3	37...16.....0	0...11.....5 3/4
do.			50	7/	17...10.....0	0.....5.....3
do.			120	4/4	25...10.....0	0.....7.....6
SINK, John			100	1/9	8...15.....0	0.....2.....7 1/2
STEEL, Robert Senr.			160	6/1	48...13.....4	0...14.....7
STEEL, Samuel			260	7/	91.....0.....0	1.....7.... 3 1/2
STEEL, James			230	6/1	69...19.....2	1.....0...11 1/2
SHOLTZ, George			154	5/3	40.....8.....9	0...13.....1 1/2
STEEL, Nathaniel			484	8/8	209...14.....8	3.....2...11

(page 127 contd. Augusta County Land Tax Return of James Ramsey for 1788)

Persons Names Owning Land	No. of Lots	Yearly Rent	Quantity of Land	Rate p Acre	Total Amount of Value of Land	Amount of Tax at 1 1/2 p cent
SHIELDS, William			70	7/	24...10.....0	0.....7....4
SHIELDS, Thomas			200	7/5	74.....3.....4	1.....1.....8
STIRLING, John			231	6/6	75.....1.....6	1.....2 6 1/4
SHIELDS, John			129	2/2	13...19.....6	0.....4.....2 1/4
do.			43	2/6	5.....7.....6	0.....1.....7 1/2

(page 128. Augusta County Land Tax Return of James Ramsey for 1788)

Persons Names Owning Land	No. of Lots	Yearly Rent	Quantity of Land	Rate p Acre	Total Amount of Value of Land	Amount of Tax at 1 1/2 p cent
SHIELDS, Margaret & Heirs of Thomas SHIELDS)			225	5/8	59...13.....4	0...17.....0
STIRRETT, Robert			128	2/8	17.....1.....4	0.....5.....1 1/2
SCOTT, William (Sadler)			224	4/4	48...10.....8	0...14.....6 1/2
do.			100	1/9	8...15.....0	0.....2.....7 1/2
do.			50	1/5	3...10...10	0.....1.....0 3/4
STEWART, Thomas			352	7/9	136.....8.....0	2.....0...11
do.	1	30				1...10.....0
do.			120	3/6	21.....0.....0	0.....6.....3
do.			128	1/9	11.....4.....0	0.....3.....4 1/4
SCOTT, James			216	7/9	83...14.....0	1.....5.....11
do.			176	5/3	46.....4.....0	0...13...10
do.			86	2/8	11.....9.....4	0.....3.....5
TRIMBLE, David			160	7/	56.....0.....0	0...16.....9
do.			140	2/2	15.....3.....4	0.....4.....6 1/2
do.			110	2/2	11...18.....4	0.....3.....6 3/4
TANDY, Smith			300	5/3	78...15.....0	1.....3.....7 1/2
TRIMBLE, John			48	4/4	10.....8.....0	0.....3.....1 1/4
do.			160	2/8	21.....6.....8	0.....6.....4 3/4
TRIMBLE, James (Capt.)			300	7/	105.....0.....0	1...11.....6
do.			250	2/8	33.....6.....8	0...10.....0
TROTTER, James Senr.			130	7/9	50.....7.....6	0...15.....1 1/4
TRIMBLE, Walter			188	8/8	81.....9.....4	1.....4.....5 1/4
do.			62	3/6	10...17.....0	0.....3.....3
TRIMBLE, Robert			167	10/6	87...13.....6	1.....6.....3
do.			34	1/9	2...19.....6	0.....0...10 1/2
TRIMBLE, John Senr.			343	10/6	180.....1.....6	2...14.....0 1/4
TROTTER, Joseph			150	5/3	39.....7.....6	0...11.....9 /4
do.			82	1/9	7.....3.....6	0.....2.....2 1/4
do.			22	5/3	5...15.....6	0.....1.....8 3/4
TRIMBLE, James			317	4/4	68...13.....4	1.....0.....7 1/4
TEAFORD, Jacob			200	3/6	35.....0.....0	0...10.....6
do. (from CARTMILL)			205	3/6	35...17.....6	0...10.....9

(page 129. Augusta County Land Tax Return of James Ramsey for 1788)

Persons Names Owning Land	No. of Lots	Yearly Rent	Quantity of Land	Rate p Acre	Total Amount of Value of Land	Amount of Tax at 1 1/2 p cent
THOMPSON, Robert			200	7/9	77...10.....0	1.....3.....3
do.			140	1/9	12.....5.....0	0.....3.....8
do. (from S. HENRY)			90	3/11	17...12.....6	0.....5.....2 3/4
THOMPSON, Alexander (Colo.)			302	7/9	117.....0.....6	1...15.....1 1/4
do.			130	1/9	11.....7.....6	0.....3.....5
THOMPSON, William			100	3/6	17...10.....0	0.....5.....3

(page 129 contd. Augusta County Land Tax Return of James Ramsey for 1788)

Persons Names Owning Land	No. of Lots	Yearly Rent	Quantity of Land	Rate p Acre	Total Amount of Value of Land	Amount of Tax at 1 1/2 p cent
TEASE, Mary			400	13/	260.....0.....0	3...18.....0
TATE, Robert			186	7/	65.....2.....0	0...19.....6
do.			146	4/4	31...12.....8	0.....9.....5 3/4
THOMPSON, Joseph			155	4/4	33...11.....8	0...10.....0 3/4
TATE, Sarah (Widow)			200	6/1	60...16.....8	0...18.....3
do.			27	6/1	8.....4.....3	0.....2.....5
TATE, Thomas			200	6/6	65.....0.....0	0...19.....6
TATE, John Senr.			244	7/5	90.....9.....8	1.....7.....1 3/4
do.			200	1/5	14.....3.....4	0.....4.....3
do.			400	1/5	28.....6.....8	0.....8.....6
TATE, William (Capt.)			160	4/4	34...13.....4	0...10.....4 3/4
THOMPSON, William			306	6/1	93.....1.....6	1.....7...11
do.			93	1/9	8.....2.....9	0.....2.....4 3/4
TARBUT, Hugh			314	7/5	116.....8...10	1...14...11
do.			317	1/6	23...15.....6	0.....7.....1 1/2
TARBUT, Robert			197	1/9	17...10.....0	0.....5.....3
THOMPSON, Mathew			202	6/1	61...8...10	0...18.....5
do.			110	3/1	16...19.....2	0.....4...11 1/2
do.			60	1/9	5.....5.....0	0.....1.....6
do.			50	3/1	7...14.....2	0.....2.....3
THOMPSON, John			255	4/4	55.....5.....0	0...16.....6 3/4
do.			60	3/1	9.....5.....0	0.....2.....8 1/4
THOMPSON, Alexander			150	5/8	42...10.....0	0...12.....9
TELFORD, James			23	1/9	2.....0.....0	0.....0.....6 1/2
VANCE, Henry			82	3/6	14.....7.....0	0.....4.....3 1/2

(page 130. Augusta County Land Tax Return of James Ramsey for 1788)

Persons Names Owning Land	No. of Lots	Yearly Rent	Quantity of Land	Rate p Acre	Total Amount of Value of Land	Amount of Tax at 1 1/2 p cent
VANCE, John's Heirs			305	5/3	80.....1.....3	1.....4.....0 3/4
VERNER, Henry			107	4/4	23.....3.....8	0.....6...11 1/2
VANLEER, Jacob			490	3/11	95...19.....2	1.....8.....9
do. Exr. of G. ROBINSON)			141	5/3	37.....0.....3	0...11.....1 1/4
WHITREL. Martin			20	3/6	3...10.....0	0.....1.....0
WHITE, Isaac			243	9/7	119.....5...10	1...15...11 1/4
do.			94	1/5	6...13.....2	0.....2.....0
WALACE, John (B. C.)			250	3/6	43...15.....0	0...13.....1 1/2
WALACE, John Senr.			188	3/6	32...14.....0	0...10.....0
WILSON, William			301	8/8	130.....8.....8	1...19.....1 1/2
WILSON, Robert Junr.			290	8/8	125...13.....4	1...17.....8 1/4
WILLIAMS, Moses			300	4/4	65.....0.....0	0...19.....6
WILSON, Mathew			348	7/9	134...17.....0	2.....0.....5 1/2
do.			290	4/4	64...15.....8	0...19.....5
WALACE, Robert			160	8/8	69.....6.....8	1.....0.....9 1/2
WILLIAMS, John			150	2/2	16.....5.....0	0.....4...10 1/2
WISEMAN, Peter			200	3/1	30...16.....8	0.....9.....3
WILLIAMS, Richard			120	3/1	18...10.....0	0.....5.....6 1/2
WADDLE, John			100	5/3	36.....5.....0	0.....5...10 1/2
WILLIAMS, John			327	6/1	99.....9.....3	1.....9...10

(page 130 contd. Augusta County Land Tax Return by James Ramsey for 1788)

Persons Names Owning Land	No. of Lots	Yearly Rent	Quantity of Land	Rate p Acre	Total Amount of Value of Land	Amount of Tax at 1 1/2 p cent
WEAVER, George			150	3/6	26.....5.....0	0.....7...10 1/2
do.			44	1/9	3...17.....0	0.....1.....1 3/4
WILEY, John			99	3/6	16.....2.....6	0.....4...11 3/4
WASON, Robert			150	3/6	26.....5.....0	0.....7...10 1/2
WILSON, David			461	7/5	170...19.....1	2...11.....3 1/4
WRIGHT, James			260	7/9	100...15.....0	1...10.....2 1/2
WILSON, Robert Senr.			360	4/4	78.....0.....0	1.....3.....4 3/4
WILSON, Andrew			180	2/8	24.....0.....0	0.....7.....2
WADDLE, James (Revd.)			1400	5/3	367.....0.....0	5...10.....3
do.			17	5/	4.....5.....0	0.....1.....2
do.			400	1/6	30.....0.....0	0.....8.....0
do.			220	1/9	19.....5.....0	0.....6.....0
YOUNG, John (Capt.)			336	6/1	163.....0.....0	2...8...10 3/4
do.			190	4/6	45.....1.....6	0...13.....6 1/4

JAMES RAMSAY, Commr.

Amount of Land Tax	L 474.....3.....6
Amount of Lots	L 50...18.....4
Total:	L 525.....1...10

(Augusta County Land Tax Books for 1782-1802 will continue in another book beginning with the Land Tax returned by JOSEPH BELL, Commissioner, for the year 1788.)

ABNEY.
  John 1, 49, 50, 63, 83,
  John (Exr. for McDONOUGH) 49,
  John (Hatter) 1,
ADAIR
  John 50, 83,
  Neal 2, 50, 83,
ADAMS.
  Richard 40,
  Richard (Colo.) 71,
  Thomas 71,
  Thomas (Colo.) 40,
ADARE.
  John (N. Mtn.) 29,
AFFREEL.
  Daniel 1, 49,
  Jeremiah 1, 49,
AGNEW.
  James 1,
AILOR.
  Anthony 2,
ALEXANDER.
  Andrew 2, 50, 83,
  Andrew Junr. 2,
  Elizabeth (Widow) 2,
  (Fr-------) 2,
  Gabriel 2, 50, 83,
  Hugh 50, 83,
  James (Long Meadow) 2,
  James Junr. 2,
  James Senr. 2,
  James C. 2,
  John 37, 50, 83,
  John (South River) 2,
  Robert Junr. (S. River) 2,
  Robert Senr. 2,
ALLEN.
  Elizabeth 50,
  Heirs of 2,
  James Junr. 2,
  James Senr. 2,
  Mounticue 37, 50,
  Robert 2, 37,
  Robert Junr. 50, 83,
  William 36, 37, 49, 83,
  William (Smokey Row) 1,
ALLISON.
  John Junr. 38,
  John Senr. 1,
  William 1,
ANDERSON.
  (A--------) Capt. 1,
  George Junr. 1,
  George Senr. 1,
  Henry 71,
  James (Son of James) 1,
  Joseph Senr. 1,
  Margaret (Widow) 1,
  Samuel 1, 37,
  Samuel Junr. 1,
  Thomas 40, 71,
  William 36, 38,   (Anderson, contd.)

ANDERSON (contd.)
  William Senr. 1,
ANGLEMAN.
  James 36,
ARABAYNS.
  Michael 71,
ARCHER.
  John's Estate 68,
ARGENBRIGHT.
  Augustine 37, 49, 83,
  John 1, 49, 83,
ARMAGAST.
  Michael 29, 40,
ARMSTRONG,
  Able 1,
  Archibald 40, 71,
  John 71,
  Robert 2, 50, 83,
  William 2, 49, 50, 83,
  William (N. Mtn.) 1,
ASH.
  Charles 39, 40,
ASKINS,
  John 1, 33, 49, 83,
  John (Shoemaker) 1, 49,

BAILOR
  Jacob 3, 51, 84,
BAITES.
  Ephraim 41,
BAKER.
  Humphrey 38,
BANCE.
  John 37,
BARNETT.
  William 40, 72,
BARRET.
  Alexander 34,
  Alexander (Doctr.) 5,
BARRIGER.
  Jacob (B. Smith) 4,
BASKINS.
  Charles (Capt.) 3,
BAXTER.
  John 30, 33, 40, 41, 72,
BEARD.
  Edward 4,
  Christopher 85,
  Thomas 4, 51, 84,
  William 4, 33, 35,
  William Senr. 51,
BELL.
  David 36,
  David's Estate 40, 72,
  Flowrance 2, 36,
  James 29, 51,
  James (Capt.) 3, 51, 84,
  James (S. River) 5, 52, 85,
  James (an Exr. of Francis Gardner) 11,
  James Junr. (S. River) 4,
  James Senr. 3, 50, 84,
  John 29, 40, 72, 73, 85,   (Bell, contd.)

BELL (contd.)
 John (Long Glade) 3,
 John (S. River) 5, 52,
 Joseph 29, 35, 36,
 Joseph (Capt.) 40, 72,
 Joseph (Commissioner) 2, 66,
 Leonard 40, 72,
 Robert 22, 51,
 Robert (W. Creek) 4, 84,
 Samuel (M. River) 4,
 William 36,
 William (Son of Samuel) 4,
 William (an Exr. of Francis Gardner) 11,
 William Junr. 3, 51, 84,
 William Senr. 3, 50, 84,
BELOW / BELEW
 A. 4,
 Abraham 51, 84,
BENNETT.
 Jacob 40, 72,
 John 33, 40,
 Joseph Senr. 40, 72,
BENSON / BENSTON.
 George 30, 40, 72,
 Mathias Senr. 40, 72,
BERRICK.
 Phillip 2,
BERRY. / BERY
 Charles 4, 51, 84,
 George 3, 50, 83,
 James 40, 52, 72,
 John 30, 41, 72,
 John (B. Creek) 5, 52, 85,
 William Junr. 3, 50, 84,
BEST.
 James 4, 51, 84,
BEVERIDGE.
 John 72,
BEVERLEY.
 Robert Esqr. 39, 41, 50, 63, 72,
BING.
 John 2,
BIRKETT
 Frederick 36,
BLACK.
 Alexander 30, 40, 72,
 Cutlive 5, 51, 85,
 Elizabeth (Widow) 3, 36,
 John 5, 52, 85,
 John (S. River) 4,
 Peter 4,
 Rebecca (Widow) 72,
 Samuel 5, 52, 85,
 William 5, 40, 52, 71, 85,
 William (deced) 14,
BLACKWOOD.
 Samuel 5, 52, 85,
 Samuel's Heirs 90,
BLAIR.
 Elizabeth 50, 63, 83,
 James 36, 37,
 John 36,   (Blair, contd.)

BLAIR (contd.)
 John (Taylor) 3,
 Joseph 50, 83,
 Joseph (Lieut.) 3,
 William 3, 37, 50, 83,
 William (Tanner) 3,
 William Senr. 4,
BLAKE.
 John 40, 72,
 Theophilus 40, 72,
 Thomas 41, 72,
BLEAKLY.
 Thomas 28,
BODKIN.
 John 30,
BOFANG.
 John 52, 63, 85,
BOGESS.
 Thomas 84,
BOLLING.
 Archibald 38,
BOMAN.
 Jacob 39,
BOTKIN.
 Charles 40, 72,
 Hugh 40, 72,
 James 40, 72,
 John 40, 72,
BOURLAND.
 Andrew 40, 72,
 John's Estate 72,
BOWYER.
 Michael 3, 51, 63, 84,
 William (Colo.) 3, 51, 63, 66, 84,
BOYD.
 Alexander 85,
 John 4, 51, 85,
 Thomas 4, 51, 85,
BRADSHA(W)
 John 39, 40, 72,
BRADY.
 James 3, 51, 84,
BRAND.
 James (Doctr.) 50, 83,
BRATCHEY.
 Thomas 2,
BRATTON.
 Elizabeth (Widow) 4, 51, 84,
 George 40, 72,
 James (Capt.) 41, 72,
 John 51, 84,
 Robert (deced) Estate 40, 71,
BRAWFORD,
 John 85,
 Rebecca (Widow) 3, 50, 83,
 Samuel 5, 51, 85,
BREDON
 Edd. 2,
 George (Harrison Co.) 34,
BRENT.
 James 5, 85,

BRIGHT.
George 5, 51, 85,
BROBACK.
Philip 52, 85,
BROCK.
John 3, 37,
BROOKS.
John Junr. 4,
John Senr. 4, 51, 84,
BROWN,
Benjamin 3, 35, 50, 84,
Charles 3,
Francis 4,
Hugh 3, 4, 35, 41, 73,
James 50, 84,
John 3, 4, 37, 51, 71, 84,
John (Capt.) 40,
John Senr. 84,
Joseph 41, 72,
Thomas 3, 50, 84,
William 5, 52, 85,
BROWNLEE.
Alexander 35,
Alexander Senr. 4,
John 51,
John Junr. 4, 85,
John Senr. 4, 51, 85,
William 4, 51, 85,
BRUBANK.
William 38,
BUCHANAN
David 3, 51, 84,
James (deced) 3,
John Senr. 2, 50, 83,
Patrick 27, 83,
Patrick (Capt) 2, 50,
Sarah (Widow of James) 3, 51, 84,
William 4, 51, 84,
BUCK.
Coonrod 73,
BUFFINBERGER
George 40,
BUFFINBURY.
Jonathan (Harrison Co.) 38,
BULLETT.
Thomas's Heirs 73,
BUMGARDNER.
Christopher 4, 33, 51, 85,
BURGIS. / BURGESS
William 3, 50, 84,
BURK(E)
Edward 84,
John 5, 51, 85,
William 3, 35, 50,
BURKET.
Frederick 4,
BURNER.
Abraham 33, 41, 72,
BURNS.
Elizabeth 50, 63, 83,
Richard 4, 51, 85,

BURNSIDE.
John 4,
BURTON.
Edmund 4, 36,
Edward 4,
BUZZARD.
Henry 38, 41, 72,
BYERS.
David 2,
BYRD / BIRD.
John 40, 72,

CAAL.
James 8,
CALDBREATH.
Thomas 6,
CALDWELL.
John 5, 52, 85,
John (T. Spring) 7, 53, 86,
Robert 6, 8,
William (T. Spring) 6, 53, 86,
CALE / CAIL
David Senr. 52, 86,
Jacob 52,
Peter 6, 52, 86,
CALL.
Timothy 5,
CALLISON.
James 6, 52, 86,
CAMBLE.
John (Buchanan's Co.) 6,
CAMERON.
Charles (Commission) 40,
CAMP.
John (Capt., an Exr. of Alexander Walker,
Senr.) 28,
CAMPBELL.
Andrew 7, 53, 86,
George 53, 87,
George (Legatee of Robert) 7,
Hugh 6,
James 36, 52, 53,
James (S. River)
James (Trimbles Co,) 5,
John 14, 53,
John (B. Pasture) 73,
John (Calf Pasture) 73,
John (Capt.) 7,
John (S. River) 7,
Mary (Widow) 7, 53, 86,
Robert 7, 53, 86,
Robert (Heir to Robert, deced) 7,
Robert (Lieut.) 7,
Robert (deced) 7,
Sarah (Widow) 6, 53, 86,
William (Dickey's Co.) 6,
CARLILE
James 41, 73,
John (B. Pasture) 41,
John (C. Pasture) 41,
Robert (Son to John) 41, 73,
Robert Senr. 32, 41, 73,

CAROL.
 Jacob 30,
 Samuel 30,
CARRUTHERS.
 David 7, 53, 86,
 James 7, 53, 85,
 Thomas 7, 53, 86,
CARSON.
 Isaac 5,
 James 41, 73,
 Samuel 53, 86,
 Samuel (B. Smith) 7,
CARTMELL / CARTMILL
 97,
 John 41, 73,
 Samuel 35, 53,
 Thomas 41, 73,
CHAMBERS.
 William 59, 93,
CHAPMAN.
 John 5, 52, 85,
CHESNUT.
 John 41, 73,
 William 7, 53, 86,
CHILMORE.
 Lewis 33, 53. 87,
CHRISTIAN.
 Gilbert 8, 53, 87,
 Gilbert (Legatee of John) 8,
 John (deced) 8, 53,
 John (Legatee of John) 8, 53,
 John Senr. 7, 53, 86,
 Patrick 8, 53, 87,
 Robert 87,
 Robert (Legatee of John) 8, 53,
 Robert Junr. 7, 53, 87,
 William 8, 53, 87,
CIREL.
 Samuel 38,
CLARK.
 James 41, 73,
 James Junr. 6, 53, 86,
 James Senr. 53, 87,
 John 6, 37,
 Robert 6, 37,
CLEMONS.
 Gasper 5,
 John 5,
CLONINGER / CLUNIGER
 Valentine 6, 35, 53, 86,
COAL.
 J. 87,
 James 53,
COBB.
 William 39, 53, 87,
COCKRAN.
 Robert (Sadler) 29, 32,
COCKS.
 Jacob 52, 86,
COFFEY.
 William 53,
 William (B. Creek) 8, 87,

COLES.
 J. 85,
COLLINS.
 John (Weaver) 7,
COMER.
 Margaret 53, 87,
CONELLY.
 Arthur 7,
 Thomas 7,
CONNER.
 Margarett (Widow) 8,
CONOLY
 Arthur (an Exr. of Alexander Walker, Senr.) 28,
 Thomas 28,
CONROD.
 Frederick 6,
 Olery Junr. 41, 73,
 Olery Senr. 41, 73,
COOK.
 Jacob 5,
 James (Capt.) 6,
 James (deced) 7,
 John 5, 29, 52, 53, 86, 87,
COOPER.
 James 7, 53,
 Robert 86,
COUL.
 David Senr. 6,
 Jacob 6,
COULTER / COALTER
 David 7, 37, 53, 86,
 James 7, 53, 86,
 John 37, 87,
 John Junr. 8, 53,
 John Senr. 7, 53, 86,
 Joseph 8, 53, 87,
 Michael 6, 52, 86,
COURSEY.
 James 6,
COWARDINE.
 John 41, 73,
COWGAR.
 John 41, 73, 76,
COWMAN.
 John 6, 37,
COWSEY.
 James 35,
CRAIG(E)
 George 5,
 George (S. River) 7, 39,
 James 38, 39,
 James Senr. 7,
 Robert 7, 29, 35,
 Samuel 41, 73,
CRAWFORD.
 Alexander's Estate 41, 73,
 George (deced)
 George (an Exr. of George) 7,
 James 5, 35, 87,
 James (an Exr. of George) 7,
 James Junr. 33,
 John 36, 52, 86,   (Crawford, contd.)

CRAWFORD (contd.)
John (B. Smith) 6,
Nathan 41, 73,
Nathaniel 35, 36,
Patrick 5,
William 6, 52, 63, 86,
CROW.
Benjamin 5, 52, 86,
CRUMMET / CRUMITT
Christopher 41, 73,
CUBB.
Marquis 5,
CUMMINS.
Robert Senr. 6, 52, 86,
CUNNINGHAM.
Alexander (deced) 6, 34,
David 6, 52, 86,
James 53,
James (Sadler) 7, 34, 86,
James Senr. 6, 52, 86,
John 6, 53, 86,
John (Capt.) 6, 37, 52, 86,
John (Admr. of Alexander) 34,
Robert (Hampshire) 41, 73,
William (Harrison Co.) 34,
CURRY.
Alexander 8,
James Senr. 6,
Robert 6,
Robert Junr. 6,
Samuel 5,
William Senr. 6,

DALHOUSE.
John 8,
DANIEL.
Hugh 28,
DAUGHERTY.
Hugh 54, 87,
DAVIDSON.
John 8, 87,
DAVIS.
Charles 41, 73,
James 37, 54, 87,
John 35,
Thomas 41, 73,
Walter 8, 37, 54, 87,
William 54, 63, 87,
DAVISON.
John 54,
DAYLEY / DAILEY
John 8, 53, 87,
DEAN.
Adam 38,
John 42,
John (Botetourt) 73,
DENISON.
John 30, 42, 74,
DEVITT.
Tully 37,
DICKENSON.
John (Colo.) 41, 73,

DICKEY.
James 8,
John (Capt.) 8,
John (Capt., Exr. of Archibald Henderson) 8,
Michael 8,
William 42, 74,
DICKSON.
John 8, 38,
Thomas 8,
DINWIDDIE / DINWOODY.
James 41, 73,
Robert 41, 73,
William 41, 73,
DIVER.
Hugh (Rockingham) 41, 73,
DIXON.
Archibald 8, 29,
DOAK (E).
David 8, 54, 87,
John 8, 54, 87,
Robert 8, 54, 87,
DOLT.
Philip 87,
DONAGHU
Hugh 8, 37,
James 8,
DONAHO.
13,
Hugh 29,
DONALDSON.
Robert 8, 53, 87,
DONNALLY / DONELY
Charles 41, 73,
DORAN.
Jacob 8, 29, 37,
DORSETT.
Thomas 36, 54, 87,
DOUGHERTY.
Hugh 8,
Michael 39, 41, 42, 73,
DOUGLASS
Thomas 41, 73,
DOWEL
Philip 8, 54,
DOWNEY.
Martha (Widow) 8, 53, 87,
DRINNEN.
Jacob 42, 74,
Laurance 42, 73,
Thomas 42, 74,
DUFFILL.
Robert 41, 73,
DUNLAP.
Adam 8, 36,
Alexander 42, 74,
William 8, 37,
DYER.
James (Rockingham) 41, 73,

EAGER.
Robert (deced) 36,

EAGLE.
  George 37, 54, 88,
ECCORD / EACKORD
  Abraham / Ebram 30, 42, 74,
  Philip 30, 42,
EDMISTON.
  Matthew 9,
EDWARDS.
  Arthur 9, 35,
  Thomas 36, 37,
EHART.
  Francis 9,
ELLIOTT.
  James 9, 54, 74, 87,
  John 9, 42, 54, 74, 87,
  John (L. River) 30,
ELLIS.
  James 38,
EMMITT.
  John 54, 87,
EOVICK / EVICK
  George 35, 74,
ERWIN.
  Andrew 9,
  Charles 42, 74,
  Edward 9, 37, 38,
  Edward (N. River) 9,
  Edward Junr. 9,
  Francis 9,
  Gerard 74,
  James 42, 54, 74, 88,
  James (Capt.) 54, 87,
  James Junr. 54, 87,
  Jane (Widow) 9,
  Janett 42,
  John 9, 33,
  Samuel (M. River) 9,
  William 42, 74,
ESDALE / ESTILL
  Rebecca 9, 54,
  Zachariah 87,
ESTROP.
  Robert 9, 54, 63, 87,
EVE
  Stuffell 42,
EVINS.
  Griffeth (Trimble's Co.) 9,
EVY,
  Jacob 88,
EWING.
  James 37,
  James (Capt.) 9,
  James Junr. 9,

                          -

FAULL.
  George 36, 54, 88,
FEMSTER
  Thomas 31, 42, 74,
FENTLEYROY
  Moore 31, 42, 74,
FERGUSON.
  William (Shoemaker) 10, 88,

FERIS.
  John 9,
FINDLEY.
  John (S. River) 10,
  John (Wheelright) 10,
  John Senr. 9,
  Robert Junr. 10, 37,
  Robert Senr. 10, 37,
  William Junr. (Capt.) 10,
FISHBURN.
  Teeter 37,
FISHER.
  Frederick 9, 54, 88,
  George 9, 54, 88,
FLECK.
  Petter 80,
FLEMING.
  William (Copper Smith) 9,
FLESHER.
  Conrod 42, 74,
  Henry 74,
  Peter 42, 74,
  Rober (R. Bridge) 42,
FLETCHER.
  Robert 30,
  Robert (Rockbridge) 74,
FLOYD.
  Charles 9,
  Charles (deced) 54, 88,
FOSTER.
  James 10,
  Thomas 9,
  William 36,
  William Junr. 10,
FOWLER.
  John 74,
FRAIM / FRAME
  David 37, 42, 74,
  Thomas 9,
FRAIZER.
  James (Long Meadow) 9,
  Samuel Junr. 9, 33,
  Samuel Senr. 9,
FRANCIS.
  John Senr. 9,
FRIDLEY,
  Jacob 88,
FRINGER.
  Peter 54, 88,
FUDGE.
  John 9, 36,
FULTON.
  Andrew 54, 88,
  David 88,
  Hugh 10, 54, 88,
  James 37, 42, 74,
  John 10, 38, 54, 88,
  Mary (Widow) 10, 54, 88,
  William 9, 54, 88,
FULWATER.
  John 36,

FULWIDER.
    John 54, 88,
    Ulrich 10, 54, 88,

GABERT.
    Jacob 15, 36, 55, 89,
GALFORD.
    Thomas 43, 75,
GAMBLE.
    Isabella (Widow) 43, 75,
    John 10,
    Robert 10,
    Robert (Colo.) 55, 63, 88,
    William (Son of Isabella, Widow) 31, 43, 75,
GARBER.
    Michael 88,
GARDNER.
    Ensign 10,
    Francis 55, 88,
    Francis Junr. 11,
    Francis (deced) 11,
    James 10,
    John 36,
    Samuel 55, 89,
    Samuel (Heir to Francis, deced) 11,
GARRISON.
    John 11,
GARRIX.
    William 41, 42,
GARVIN.
    Thomas 36,
GAY.
    James 42,
GEENS.
    John 43, 75,
    William 43, 75,
GERARD,
    William 74,
GIBSON.
    Alexander 55,
    Alexander Senr. 11, 88,
    Davis 11,
    Robert 10, 55. 88,
    Samuel 10, 55, 88,
GILESPY / GILLASPY
    Hugh's Estate 42, 74,
    James 11,
    John 42, 74,
    Thomas 42, 74,
    William 11,
GILIKSON.
    Archibald 10,
    Hugh 10, 55. 88,
    William 10, 55. 88,
GILMORE / GILMER
    James Senr. 10, 55, 88,
GIVIN(S)
    David 42, 74,
    George 11,
    James 11, 35,
    John (Capt.) 11,
    John Senr. 11,   (Givins, contd.)

GIVINS (contd.)
    Joseph 37, 42, 74,
    William 43, 75,
GLAVIS.
    Mathew 36,
GLEAVES.
    Mathew 36,
GLENN.
    George 11,
GOODPASTURE / GOOPASTURE
    Abraham 10, 38,
GRAGG.
    Robert 10,
    Thomas 10,
GRAGORY / GRIGORY
    Mary 43, 75,
    Jacob 75,
    John 75,
    Samuel 43, 75,
    William 75,
GRAHAM.
    Christopher 74,
    Elizabeth 31,
    Elizabeth (Widow) 75,
    John 31, 37, 75,
    Robert's Estate 75,
    Thomas 11,
    William 11, 55, 89,
GRAM.
    John (B. Pasture) 75,
GRASS.
    Jacob Senr. 11, 55, 89,
    Peter 10, 11,
GRAY.
    Robert 28,
GREAVES.
    William 55, 88,
GREEN.
    Hugh 11,
GREENWOOD.
    Joaiah (deced) 11,
    Margaret (Widow & Heir of Josiah) 11, 55. 89,
GREGORY.
    John 43,
GREHAM.
    Christopher 42,
    Elizabeth 42,
    John 42,
    John (B. Pasture) 42,
    Robert's Estate 43,
GRIFFETH.
    Able (Dickey's Co.) 10,
    James 36, 43, 75,
GRIFFIN.
    John 55, 63, 88,
GRINER,
    David 55, 63,
    David's Heirs 88,
GROIN.
    Joseph 31,
GRONDER.
    David 11,

GROVE.
  Windle 11, 55, 89,
(? GRUVIR)
  William 10,
GUM.
  Abraham 43,
  Isaac 43, 75,
  John 31, 43,
  John Junr. 43, 75,
  John Senr. 75,
GUTHRY.
  William 11, 55. 89,
GWINN
  Joseph 33, 38,
  Robert 37, 38,

HAGAN.
  Arthur 57,
HAGHTHORN.
  James 12,
HAIR.
  John Junr. 12,
HAISE.
  James (Son of Moses) 12,
  Moses 12,
HAKE.
  Henry 12,
HALL / HOLL.
  Adam 76,
  Edward 14, 39, 56, 90,
  George 43, 76,
  Henry 9, 54, 87,
  Jacob 76,
  John 12,
  Patrick 14, 56, 90,
  Peter (Capt.) 43, 76,
  Robert 36, 43, 75,
HAMILTON.
  Alexander 44, 76,
  Andrew 43, 75,
  Archibald 11,
  Arthur 12, 55, 89,
  Audley 11,
  Charles 44, 76,
  James 55, 89,
  John 55, 89,
  John (L. Meadow) 13,
  Ozburn 33, 35, 44, 76,
  Robert (Doctor) 14, 57, 90,
  William (C. Creek) 13,
HAMMER.
  George 35,
  Palzer 75,
HANDLEY / HANLEY
  John Junr. 12,
  John Senr. 13, 56, 89,
  William 37, 44, 57, 76, 90,
HANDREL
  George 55, 89,
  Lawrence 55, 89,
  Philip 55,

HANGER.
  Frederick 12, 55, 90,
  Frederick Senr. 89,
  Peter 12, 13, 32, 39, 56,
  Peter Senr. 89,
HANKEY
  Simon 12, 55, 89,
HANNA(H)
  Robert 12, 55, 89,
HARBURN
  David 13,
HARLES.
  Emanuel 13, 35,
HARNESS.
  George (Harrison Co.) 34,
HARPER.
  Adam (Hampshire) 43, 76,
  John 13,
  Nicholas 31, 43, 76,
HARRIS.
  Robert 13, 56, 90,
HARRISON.
  David 56, 90,
HATTON.
  Mark (for Samuel Blackwood's Heirs) 14, 57, 90,
HAUPE / HAUPH
  Randolph / Randle 36, 57, 90,
HAWK.
  Henry 55, 89,
HAWTHORN.
  James 55, 89,
HAYES.
  Hugh 11,
  Moses 11, 55,
HAYS.
  A. 96,
  Hugh 14, 37,
  James 56, 89,
  Moses 35, 37,
  Patrick 14, 56, 90,
  Samuel 14, 56, 90,
HEATH.
  Henry (Fort Pitt) 43, 76,
HEIZER / HIZER
  John 38, 57, 90.
  Samuel 12, 55, 89,
HEMPINSTALL
  Abraham 31, 44, 76,
HENDERSON.
  Archibald (deced) 8,
  David 56, 90,
  David (S. River) 30,
  David Esqr. 13,
  David Senr. 14, 56, 90,
  James Senr. 13,
  Jones 43, 75,
  Joseph (near Town) 12, 55, 89,
  Samuel Junr. 13,
  Samuel Senr. 13,
  William 13, 56, 90,
HENEMAN.
  Andrew 13,

HENRY.
  James 35, 37,
  James (B. Smith) 14, 56, 90,
  James (Weaver) 14, 56, 90,
  S. 87, 97,
  Samuel 14, 56, 90,
HENSHAW.
  John 44,
HICKLAND.
  Thomas (Capt.) 31,
HICKLEN.
  Hugh 43, 75,
  John 43, 44, 75, 77, 81,
  John Junr. 76,
  Thomas 43, 75,
HICKMAN.
  Roger 43, 76,
  Thomas Junr. 44,
HIGANS.
  Arthur 38,
HILL.
  James 12, 56, 89,
HIND(S)
  Edward 43,
  Edward's Estate 75,
  John (deced) 13,
  Samuel 11, 37,
  Thomas 56, 89,
  William (Admr. of John) 13,
HINES.
  John 76,
  Thomas 13,
HINGE.
  Thomas 32,
HINKLE.
  Paul 43, 75,
HINSDALE.
  Philip 12,
HITRIGHT.
  John 39,
HODGE.
  John 43, 75,
HOG.
  Capt.'s Widow 11,
  James 39,
HOGSHEAD.
  David 12, 30,
  David Junr. 12,
  James Junr. 12,
  John's Widow & Heirs 12,
  John Senr. 12,
  Michael 12,
  William (Rockingham) 13,
HOOFMAN / HOFFMAN
  Gasper 56, 90,
  John 57, 90,
HOOKE.
  John 13,
HOOVER.
  Bostian 43,
  Bostian's Estate 76,
  Jacob 43, 76,

(Hoover, contd.)

HOOVER (contd.)
  Michael 43, 76,
HOPKINS.
  John (Rockingham Co.) 39,
HORNBACK.
  Benjamin (Harrison Co.) 34,
HORRIS.
  Hugh 39,
HORYNE.
  Rhandolp 37,
HOUGHT.
  Hezekiah 39,
HUDSON / HUTSON.
  George 12, 55, 89,
HUFF.
  Francis 12,
HUFFMAN.
  Gasper 14,
HUGHES.
  13,
  Euphemia 13, 55, 63, 89,
  Thomas 14, 57, 90,
HUGHART.
  James 35, 36, 43, 75,
  Thomas (Colo.) 43, 75,
HULL.
  Francis 13, 56, 90,
  Peter 38,
  Peter (Capt.) 31,
HUMPHREY
  David 14, 90,
  Jonathan 44,
HUMPHREYS.
  Jonathan 31, 76,
HUNT.
  Charles (Doctor) 13, 56, 90,
HUNTER.
  John 14, 57, 90,
  Samuel 14, 90,
  William 13, 56, 89,
HUPMAN
  John 35,
HUTCHISON.
  George 14, 56, 90,
  Sarah 13,
  William 44, 76,
HYNES.
  John 43,
HYSKILL.
  Peter 38, 55, 63, 89,

INGLEMAN.
  Peter 57, 91,
  William 14, 57, 91,
INGRAM / INGREHAM.
  Abraham 44, 76,
  Abraham Junr. 44, 76,
INMAN.
  Lazarus (deced) 15,
  Sarah & Heirs of Lazarus 15,
  William 57, 91,

IRWIN.
  Charles 31,
  James 31,

JACKSON.
  John (Doctor) 14, 57, 91,
JAMES.
  Daniel 14, 36,
JAMESON.
  G. 84,
  George 14, 57,
  John 36, 57, 91,
JASPER.
  John (Black Smith) 15,
JERVIS.
  Thomas 44, 77,
JOHNS.
  Isaac 37, 44, 76,
JOHNSON.
  Anthony 76,
  John 14,
  William (Brinkey Neck) 14,
  William (Stiller) 14,
  Zachariah (Capt.) 14,
JOHNSTON.
  Andrew (Rockingham Co.) 39,
  Anthony 44,
  Zacharia 36, 38, 39,
JONES.
  Eniss 14, 36,
  Gabriel 15, 31, 44, 57, 77, 91,
JOSEPH.
  Daniel 14, 35, 36, 37,
JORDAN / JOURDEN
  Andrew 76,
  John 31, 44, 71, 76,

KEILLER.
  Michael 30,
KELLY.
  John 44, 77,
KENNEDY / KENADY.
  James (Rockbridge) 16, 57, 91,
  William 15, 58, 91,
KENNERLY.
  James 15,
  James Junr. 15,
  Reuben 15, 38,
  Samuel 15,
  Thomas 15, 35,
  William 38,
KENNY / KINNEY
  Bryan 15, 36,
  Matthew 15,
  Robert 15, 33, 37,
KERR.
  Gilbert 15, 37,
  James 16, 57, 91,
  James (B. Smith) 15,
  John 15,
  John (Trimble's Co.) 15,
  William 16, 57, 91,

KIDD.
  D. 6,
  Daniel 15, 27, 57, 63, 91,
KILHENNY.
  John 35,
KILLER.
  George 15, 57, 91,
  Michael 57, 91,
KILLINGSWORTH.
  Richard 31, 44, 77,
KILPATRICK.
  Andrew 44, 77,
  James 44, 77,
  William 31, 44, 77,
KING.
  Henry 30, 32,
  John 57, 91,
  John (B. Creek) 16, 30,
  John (M. River) 15,
  John Senr. (N. Creek) 15,
  Susannah (Wife of Henry) 30, 32,
  William 15,
KINKEAD./ KINKADE.
  John 38, 77,
  John Esqr. 44,
  John (S. River) 44, 77,
  Thomas 44, 77,
  William (Capt.) 44, 77,
  William (Stiller) 44, 77,
KIRK.
  James 15, 57, 91,
  John 15, 57, 91,
KIRKPATRICK.
  John 15, 57, 91,
KITTLE.
  Abraham (Harrison Co.) 34,

LACKEY.
  Andrew (Weaver) 16,
LAFERTY./ LAUFFERTY
  Ralph 44, 77,
  Rebecca 44, 77,
LAIDCHEY.
  George 58,
LAIRD.
  David 30, 33,
  David (Capt.) 16,
LAMB.
  John 37,
LAMBERT.
  John 44, 77,
LAMME.
  James 16,
  Samuel 16,
LANCE.
  Barnard 44, 73, 77,
  Coonrod 77,
  George 77,
  Joseph 77,
LANSDALE / LANGSDALE
  William 45, 77, 81,

LASSLY
  Samuel 16,
  Sarah (Widow) 16,
LAW.
  Robert 16,
LAWELLS.
  Andrew (deced) 33,
LAWYERS.
  Alexander 38,
LEDGERWOOD
  William 16, 58, 91,
LEDICK.
  George 16, 92,
LEEZER.
  Joseph 44, 77,
LEMONIS.
  George 16,
LEREW
  Abraham 16, 58, 92,
LESLIA
  Jacob 33,
LESSLEY.
  Thomas 16, 91,
LESTER.
  Robert 16,
LIVINGSTON.
  William 58,
LEVRNGOOD
  Harmon 16,
LEWIS.
  Andrew (Rockingham) 39,
  Charles (deced) Estate 44, 77,
  George 16,
  John 31, 45,
  John (Capt.) 77,
  Samuel (Colo.) 16,
  Thomas 45, 77,
  William 16, 44, 77,
LEWISTON.
  William 16,
LINER.
  Henry 16,
LINK.
  Matthias 16,
LIPEN.
  Frederick 38,
LISTER.
  Robert 33,
LIVINGSTON
  William 91,
LOCKHART.
  James 16, 58, 91,
  Sarah 16,
  William 17, 58, 92,
LOCKRIDGE.
  Andrew 44, 77,
  John 44, 77,
  William 44, 77,
LODOWICK.
  George 58, 91,

LOGAN.
  John 16, 91,
  William 16, 58, 91,
LONG
  Alexander 17, 58, 92,
  David 17, 58, 92,
  Francis 17, 58, 92,
  James 17, 58, 92,
  Joseph 17, 58, 92,
  Samuel 17, 58, 92,
  William (deced) 17,
  William (Legatee of Wm.) 17,
  William (Majr.) 16,
LOUGHRIDGE.
  John 31,
LOVINGOOD
  Hermon 39, 58, 91,
LOWRY.
  Alexander 31, 45, 77,
  John 16,
LYLE.
  J. Junr. (Deputy County Clerk) 66.
LYONS / LIONS
  Henry 39, 58, 92,

McCANTREE.
  Richard 20, 60, 94,
McCARTY.
  James 45, 78,
McCASTLAND / McCASHLIN
  John 31, 45, 78,
McCHESNEY.
  James 19, 36, 39, 59, 93,
  Robert 19, 59, 93,
  Samuel 45, 78,
McCLANACHAN(D).
  Alexander 35,
  Alexander (Colo.) 18, 59, 92,
  Elijah 29, 94,
  Elijah (Commissioner) 1,
  Heirs 58, 92,
  John (deced., Heirs of) 17,
  Robert 18, 59, 92,
McCLARY
  Hugh 60, 94,
McCLEREY.
  James 36,
McCLINTUCK.
  William 18,
  William Junr. 59, 93,
  William Senr. 18, 59, 93,
McCLOUGHLIN.
  James 46, 79,
McCLUNG.
  James 18,
  John 45, 78,
McCLURE.
  Andrew 17, 38,
  Andrew Senr. 19,
  Eleanore (Widow) 19,
  James 20, 67,
  John 60, 94,

(McClure, contd.)

McCLURE (contd.)
John Junr. 19,
John Senr. 20,
Josiah 19, 33, 66.
Samuel 19,
William 17,
McCOLLOCK.
Thomas 19, 66.
McCOLLOM
John 45, 78,
McCOMB.
Andrew 19, 33, 66,
McCORCLE
Samuel 58, 92,
McCOY.
John 31,
John (Capt.) 45, 78,
William 46, 79,
McCRAY.
Robert 46, 79,
McCREA.
Robert 33,
McCREREY.
Robert 31,
Robert (Capt.) 45, 78,
McCROSKEY.
David 59, 92,
McCUNE.
John 19, 34,
McCUTCHAN / McCUTCHEON
C. & Compa. 4,
John 19, 30, 31, 37, 39, 45, 59, 60, 78, 93,
Joseph 19, 36,
Robert 31, 33, 37, 46,
Samuel 37, 59,
Samuel (Capt.) 19, 60, 93,
Samuel the Elder 18, 92,
William 20, 35, 37, 46, 59, 60, 78, 79, 93, 94,
William Senr. 20, 60, 94,
McDANNALD.
Samuel 46,
McDAVID.
Patrick 19, 59, 93,
William 19,
McDONALD
Anguish 35,
John 45, 77,
Samuel 78,
McDONOUGH
John 19,
McDOUGAL / McDOUGHULL
John 20, 38, 67,
McDOWEL / McDAWILL
Hugh 19, 33, 59, 93,
William 33, 38, 59, 63, 93,
McFADEN
John 60, 94,
McFARLAND
Duncan 31, 45, 78,
McFEETERS / McPHEETERS
Alexander 17, 36, 58,
Alexander Junr. 92,   (McFeeters, contd.)

McFEETERS / McPHEETERS (contd.)
Alexander Senr. 92,
John 18, 58, 92,
William 18, 30, 59, 93,
William (Commissioner) 29,
McGIBBINS
James 59,
John 59, 63, 93,
McGLAMERY
John 36, 67,
McGONIGAL.
James 59, 93,
McKEE.
Alexander 18, 59, 92,
Samuel 19, 36, 66.
McKEMY
John 33, 37,
McKENNY.
Alexander 18, 59, 92,
James 18,
John 60,
John (Capt.) 94,
John Junr. 18, 19,
William 17, 18,
William (Admr. of Charles Floyd) 54, 88,
McKETRICK.
Robert 17, 58, 92,
McLARRY.
Hugh 19,
McMACHAN.
John 19, 66.
McMULLIN
Robert 45, 78,
McNEIL.
James 19,
Robert 19,
McNUTT.
Alexander 38,
James 60, 94,
Robert 60, 94,
McVAY.
John 18,
McVEAR.
Daniel 17,

MADISON.
Richard (Clerk Augusta Court) 29,
MALCOM
John 18,
Joseph 45, 78,
MARA.
Francis 37,
MARROW / MARRO
Francis 18, 19, 59, 63, 93,
Samuel's Heirs 17,
Samuel (deced) 17,
MARSHAL.
George 20, 60, 94,
John 17, 58, 92,
MARTIN.
Adam 45, 78,
Joseph 16, 57, 59,   (Martin, contd.)

MARTIN (contd.)
Lewis 45, 77,
MATEER.
James 20, 60, 94,
William 45, 78,
MATHEWS.
Adonijah (supposed Greenbriar Co.) 38,
George 35, 38, 78,
George (Colo.) 17, 45, 58, 92,
Richard 17,
S. 88,
Sampson 35,
Sampson (Colo.) 18, 45, 59, 63, 78, 93,
MAULENAX
John Junr. 46,
(?) MAURAH
Henry 17,
MAURY.
Samuel 60, 94,
MAXWELL.
Robert (Harrison Co.) 34,
MAY / MAZZE
Joseph's Estate 45, 78,
MEEK.
Daniel 45, 78,
John 45, 78,
Thomas's Estate 78,
MENIS.
Thomas 18,
MERRIT.
Samuel 59, 63, 93,
MERTIN.
Joseph 18,
MIERS.
Ludwick 18,
MILLAR.
Henry (I. Works) 35,
Jacob 39,
John 35,
MILLER.
Gasper 19,
George 37, 92,
Henry 20, 30, 33, 34, 38, 66, 67,
Henry (I. Works) 19, 37,
John 31, 45, 78.
John Senr. 18,
Patrick 45, 77,
MILLS.
Robert 17,
MINER.
Thomas 38, 59, 92,
MINGS / MINGA
Henry 19, 60, 93,
MIRES.
Frederick 35, 66,
MITCHEL.
Alexander 20, 36,
James Junr. 20, 60, 94,
James Senr. 20, 60, 94,
Thomas 20, 60, 94,
William 20, 60, 94,

MOFFETT.
G. 9,
George (Colo.) 17,
James 18, 59, 92,
John (Exr. of John Vance) 27,
John Senr. 18, 59, 92,
William 93,
MONTGOMERY.
John 38, 45, 78,
MOODY.
Andrew 45, 78,
Robert 19,
MOORE.
Levi 45, 78,
Mary (Widow) 46, 79,
Moses 33, 34, 45, 78,
William 20, 45, 60, 78, 94,
MORRISON.
Hugh 46, 79,
MORTON / MORTAN
Edward 39, 46, 79,
MOSES / MOSSES.
Samuel 46, 78,
MOUROW
Henry 38,
MOWRA.
Lewis 17,
MULLONIX / MULLENEUX,
John Junr. 78,
John Senr. 31,
MURPHY.
William 19, 60, 93,
MURRY.
Thomas 38,
MUSTER.
Anthony 59, 63, 93,
MYRES.
Lewis 38,

NEAGLE.
George 46, 79,
NELSON.
Alexander 38, 39, 60, 63, 67, 94,
James 27,
Thomas 60, 88,
Thomas (Admr. of Robert Eager) 36,
Thomas (Admr. of Thomas) 20,
Thomas (deced) 20, 61,
NEWILL.
William 34,
NICHOLAS / NICOLAS
George 31, 79,
NICKLE / NICHALL
John 20, 67,
NORTH.
Phillip 60, 94,
Phillip (Orphant) 20.
NOTINGHAM / NUTINGHAM
William 46, 79,
NULL.
Henry 46, 79,

OLINGER.
Phillip Junr. 20, 94,
Phillip Senr. 20, 94,
OLIVER.
James 20, 67,
John (N. Creek) 30,
John Senr. 20,
OTT(S)
John 21, 37, 94,
OWENS.
Owen 20,

PACKETT.
Lewis 81,
PAGE.
Thomas 60, 67,
PAINTER.
John 46, 79,
PALMER.
William 21, 61, 94,
PARIS / PARRISS
John 60, 94,
John (Taylor) 21,
William 61, 94,
PATRICK.
John 21, 67,
PATTERSON.
James (S. River) 21, 67,
James Senr. 21, 67,
Deaf John 21,
John 36,
John (below Staunton) 21,
John (Deaf) 67,
Joseph (Capt.) 21, 67,
Robert 94,
Robert (N. Mtn.) 21,
Thomas 21, 33, 67,
William (Dumb) 21,
William (Rockbridge) 94,
William (S. River) 21,
William Junr. 38, 67,
William Senr. 38,
PATTON.
Hance 21,
Jacob 61, 94,
Mathew 38, 46, 79, 80.
(?) Phillip 36,
PECK.
Garrit 46,
Gerard 79,
Jacob 21, 33, 35,
Jacob (Tanner) 67,
Stephen 21, 35,
PEEBLES.
John 31, 46, 79,
PENINGER.
Henry 31, 46, 79,
PENN.
Mathew 31, 37,
PERREY. / PEARY
George 21, 60, 94,
James 21, 60,

(PERREY, contd.)

PERREY / PEARY (contd.)
John 21, 67,
Joshua 21, 63,
Joshua (Capt.) 61, 94,
PHILLIPS.
John 21, 30, 60, 94,
PICKLE.
Christian 46, 79,
PILSON.
Samuel 21, 67,
PLUNKET
John 46, 79,
POAGE.
George (Capt.) 31, 46, 79,
John 29, 46, 68, 68,
John (Commissioner) 1,
John Esqr. (Admr. of Mathew Reid) 22,
John Gent. 31,
R. 18,
T. 93,
Thomas 21, 63,
Thomas (Admr. of Mathew Read) 61, 95,
William 61, 95,
William (at Pollock) 21,
PORTERFIELD.
Robert 36,
Robert (Major) 67,
POTTER / POTTARF.
Philip 61, 95,
PULLIN.
Lofty 31, 46, 79,
PURVIS.
William 21,

RALSTON / ROLSTON.
John 22, 68,
Samuel 22, 68,
William 22, 68,
RAMSEY.
Andrew 23, 68,
James 79,
James (Commissioner) 49, 83.
James (of John) 46,
John Junr. 23, 69,
John Senr. 23, 68,
Robert 80,
William 46, 79,
RANDOLPH.
William 33, 35, 61, 95,
RANKIN.
James 22, 33, 68,
John 22, 68,
Richard 22,
Richard Junr. 33, 69,
Richard Senr. 68,
Thomas 14, 68,
Thomas (Capt.) 22,
William 22, 68,
RAY.
Daniel 23, 61, 95,
Joseph 47, 79,

READ.
  Mathew (deced) 61, 95,
  Robert 61, 63,
  Robert (deced) 95,
REAUH / REAH
  John 79,
  William 61, 79, 95,
REBURN.
  John 68,
  John Senr. 22,
REDMAN / RADMAN
  John 46, 79,
  Samuel 47, 80,
REDNOUR.
  Joseph 22, 36.
REED.
  Alexander 68,
  George (Harrison Co.) 34,
  Robert (S. M.) 68,
REID.
  Alexander 22,
  Mathew (deced) 22,
  Robert (Shoemaker) 22,
  Robert (Staunton) 22,
RHEA.
  John 46,
  William 46,
RICE.
  John's Estate 47, 80,
  William 23, 61, 95,
RICHARDS.
  William 36,
RICHARDSON.
  Phillamon 23, 61. 95,
RICHEY / RICHIE
  Hugh 37,
  Hugh (Doctor) 61, 95,
  John 37,
  John (Black Smith) 22,
RIDDLE.
  Cornelius (Capt.) 23, 61, 95,
  John 25,
RIDER.
  William 47, 80,
RISK.
  Robert 30, 32,
RITCHEY.
  Hugh (Doctor) 22,
  John 36,
ROBERTSON.
  George (deced) 27, 65,
  James 69,
  James Junr. 23,
  John (deced) 22,
  Mary (Widow to John) 22, 68,
  Mathew 21, 32, 68,
  William 46,
  William Senr. 23, 69,
ROBINSON.
  G. 98,
  William 76,

ROBISON.
  Petter 80,
ROCKEY.
  Henry 46, 79,
RODGERS.
  Seth 22,
  Robert 36,
  Thomas 22,
RODMAN.
  Samuel 39,
ROGERS.
  Robert 23,
ROWAN.
  James (Tanner) 23, 61, 95,
RUCKER.
  James Junr. 47, 80,
  James Senr. 32, 47, 74, 80,
  John Senr. 80,
  Samuel 80,
RUNKLE.
  Samuel 22, 38, 68,
RUSK.
  David 22, 61, 95,
  Margaret (Widow) 22, 61, 95,
  Robert 22, 47, 61, 80, 95,
  William 22, 61. 95,
RUSSELL / RUSSLE.
  Andrew 21, 68,
  Joshua 22, 68,
  Robert 22, 68,
RUTLEDGE.
  Edward 21, 37,
  George 68,
  James 37, 69,
  Thomas Senr. 23, 61, 95,

SANCEBAK.
  John 96,
SAWYER.
  James 62, 96,
  James Junr. 23, 24,
SCOTT.
  Andrew 23, 35, 61, 95,
  Archibald (Revd.) 24, 36, 62, 96,
  James 37, 64, 97,
  John 24, 62, 96,
  Thomas 23, 61,
  Thomas Junr. 23, 33, 62, 95,
  William 38,
  William (Sadler) 25, 63, 97,
SEAWRIGHT.
  Alexander 25, 62, 96,
  George 30,
  John 69,
  John Senr. 24,
SEEMAN / SEIMAN / SEIMONS
  George 47, 81,
  John 47, 81,
  Leonard 32, 47, 80,
  Leonard (S. Fork) 47, 81,
  Leonard Junr. 32, 47, 80,
  Mark 80,   (Seeman, (contd.)

SEEMAN / SEIMAN / SEIMONS (contd.)
Michael 47,
Petter 80,
SHARP.
John Junr. 24, 62, 96,
John Senr. 24, 62, 96,
William 48, 81,
SHAUNDS. / SHOUNDS
Leonard 24, 62,
SHEETS.
Jacob 37, 39, 69,
Jacob (Black Smith) 24,
SHEITZE.
George 48,
SHIELDS.
John 27, 39, 63. 97,
John (Pine Run) 25,
Margaret (Widow of Thomas) 25, 63, 97,
Robert 47, 80,
Thomas 25, 62, 97,
Thomas (Major) 48,
Thomas (deced) 25, 63, 97,
William 62, 97,
William (Ch. Creek) 25, 63,
William (Miller) 25,
William Junr. 24, 96.
William Senr. 24, 62, 96,
SHIRES / SHIERS
John 23, 69,
SHIRLEY.
Valentine 69,
SHOEMAKER.
Henry 39,
SHOLTS.
George 25, 62, 96,
SHULTS.
David 33,
SICKAFORIS / SIGAFOOSE
Peter 47, 80,
SIGLINGTON.
Andrew 32,
SILLEN.
Gasper 23, 69,
SIMMONS.
George 39,
SINK.
John 25, 62, 96,
SINKLER.
Alexander (Marcht.) 24,
SLATERY / SLATORY
Patrick 32, 47, 48, 81,
SLAVENS.
John 48,
John Junr. 81,
John Senr. 81,
SLUSHER.
Conrod 24, 62, 96,
SMITH.
Abraham (Rockingham) 24, 69,
Daniel Junr. 48, 81,
John 24, 62, 95,
John's Heirs 24,   (Smith, contd.)

SMITH (contd.)
John (deced) 38,
Lewis 23, 69,
Nicholas (Harrison Co.) 34,
Peter 47, 76, 81,
Robert 39, 47, 80,
Thomas 37, 38,
Thomas (Major) 38, 81,
William's Estate 47, 80,
Zachariah 24, 69,
SNARE.
Michael (Hampshire) 47, 80,
SNIDER.
John 47, 80,
SOMMERS.
Paul 32,
SPOTS.
George 24, 62, 64, 96,
SPRING.
Nicholas 35, 70,
SPRINGSTON.
Abraham (Harrison Co.) 34,
SPROUL / SPROWL
Alexander 24, 62, 96,
James 24, 36,
William 24, 62, 96,
Zachariah 24,
STARRETT
Robert (Back Creek) 25,
William 24,
ST. CLAIR.
Allexander 37, 62, 64, 80, 96,
Robert 47,
STEEL.
Andrew 24, 69,
David 25, 62,
David (Miller) 96,
David Senr. 24,
James 25, 62, 96,
James Esqr. 25, 62, 96,
Frederick 24,
Nathaniel 25, 62, 96,
Robert Senr. 25, 62, 96,
Samuel 62, 96,
Samuel (Black Smith) 24, 62, 96,
Samuel (Taylor) 25,
Samuel (Holster) 25,
Samuel Senr. 24, 25, 70,
STEPHENSON.
James 48,
STEVEN.
Robert 24, 69,
STEVENSON. / STEPHENSON
Adam 24, 33, 69,
David 35,
David (Major) 70,
James 38, 81,
John 24, 69,
Thomas 25, 35, 38,
STEWART.
Alexander 35, 38,
Alexander (Majr.) 25, 62, 96,   (Stewart, contd.)

STEWART (contd.)
  Archibald 38, 62, 96,
  Benjamin 25, 62, 96,
  Edward 81,
  Elizabeth (Widow) 24, 62, 96,
  John 23, 35, 47, 69, 80,
  John (M. River) 30,
  Ralph 48, 77, 81,
  Robert 47, 80,
  Thomas 63, 64, 97,
  Thomas (S. River) 25,
  William 33, 47, 80,
STINETT
  William 62, 96,
STIRLING.
  John 25, 63, 97,
STIRRETT
  Robert 63, 97,
STONE.
  Henry 48, 81,
  James 47, 80,
  Pastian 48, 81,
STORY.
  Ann (Widow) 23, 69,
  James 23, 69,
  John 69,
  Thomas 23, 69,
STOUT.
  Daniel 48, 81,
  George 32, 48, 79,
  Zachariah 47, 80,
STRICKLING.
  Joseph 61, 95,
STULL.
  Frederick 69,
STUNKARD.
  John 38,
  William 38, 69,
SUCK.
  Jonis (Hampshire) 48, 81,
SUMMERS.
  John 24, 62, 96,
  Paul 47, 81,
SUMWALT / SOMWALT
  George 47, 80,
  John 47, 80,
  Stuffell / Stophill 48, 81,
SUNKARD.
  John 24,
SURSASS / SURTICE
  John 23, 69.
SUTTELINGTON / SUTLINTON
  Andrew 47, 80,
  John 47, 80,
SUTTON.
  Joseph 48, 81,
SWADLEY.
  Henry 48, 81,
SWALLOW.
  Jacob 23, 62, 95,
SWARINGIN
  Van 47, 80,

SWINK.
  Henry 23, 61, 95,
  Larance 23, 61, 95,
SYBERT.
  Henry 48, 81,
  Nicholas 35, 47, 80,
SYLOR.
  Jacob 24, 62, 96,

TACKET(T)
  Christopher 32, 48, 81,
  Lewis 48, 75, 81,
TAIT(E)
  John 38,
  Robert 36,
TALLMAN / TALMON.
  Benjamin 26, 30, 32, 36,
TANDY.
  Smith 26, 64, 97,
TANNER / TANER
  James 48, 71, 81,
  John 70,
TATE.
  John Senr. 30, 64, 98,
  Robert 26, 64, 98,
  Sarah (Widow) 26, 64, 98,
  Thomas 64, 98,
  William (Capt.) 64, 98,
  William (Commissioner) 29,
TAVENBOUGH / TEVENBOUGH
  Palzer 36, 70,
TAYLOR.
  Joseph 26, 37,
TEAFORD.
  Jacob 26, 64, 97,
TEAS.
  Charles 25, 35,
  Mary (Widow) 26, 64, 98,
TEAT.
  John Senr. 26,
  Thomas 26,
  William (Capt.) 26,
TEETER.
  Abraham (Rockingham Co.) 39,
TELFORD.
  James 65, 98,
THOMPSON.
  Alexander 27, 38, 48, 65, 81, 98,
  Alexander (Colo.) 26, 64, 97,
  Andrew 26, 70,
  Edward 48, 81,
  John 27, 98,
  Joseph 26, 64, 98,
  Margaret 26, 36,
  Mathew 27, 65, 98,
  Robert 97,
  Robert (Capt.) 26, 64,
  William 26, 48, 64, 65, 97, 98,
  William (W. Creek) 26,
  William (Elder) 30,
TIPTON.
  William 34,

TORBIT / TARBET
  Hugh 26, 39, 65, 98,
  Robert 98,
TOWNSEND / TOWNDSEND.
  Ezekiel 48, 81,
  James 48, 81,
TRIMBLE.
  David 26, 64, 97,
  James 26, 64, 97,
  James (Capt.) 26, 64, 97,
  John 64, 97,
  John (Son of David) 26,
  John Senr. 26, 64, 97,
  Robert 26, 59, 64, 93,
  Walter 26, 64, 97,
TRINGAR
  Peter 35,
TROPOAGH.
  Nicholas 70,
TROTHER.
  William (Mid. R.) 25,
TROTTER.
  David 26, 38,
  James Esqr. 26, 37,
  James Junr. 26,
  James Senr. 64, 97,
  Joseph 26, 35, 64, 97,
  William 35,
TURK.
  Thomas (Capt.) 70,
  Thomas Junr. 25,
  Thomas Senr. 25,

USHER,
  Robert 70,
  William 27, 36,
UTT,
  John Senr. 27, 65,

VACHUB / VACOB
  John 48, 82,
  Joseph 48,
  Robert 48, 82,
VANCE,
  David 70,
  Henry 98,
  John 34,
  John (deced) 27, Estate -48, 65, 98,
  Samuel (Colo.) 48,
  Samuel (Commissioner) 71,
VANLEAR.
  Jacob (Exr. of George Robertson) 27, 65, 98,
VENUS,
  Henry 65,
VERNER.
  Ada, 48,
  Adam Senr. 32,
  Henry 27, 65, 98,

WADDLE.
  James 27, 70,
  James (Minister) 28, 39, 66, 99. (Waddle, contd)

WADDLE (contd.)
  John 28, 65, 98,
  Joseph 70,
  Joseph Junr. 27,
  Thomas 70,
  Thomas Senr. 27,
WAGONER.
  Christopher 49, 82,
WAIDE.
  John 49, 82,
WALKER.
  Andrew (deced) 28,
  Alexander (Connely's Exr.) 70,
  Alexander's Heirs 70,
  Alexander Junr. (deced) 28,
  Alexander Senr. (deced) 28,
WALLACE / WALACE.
  Jean (Widow) 27, 70,
  Jennett 27, 35,
  John 65,
  John (B. C.) 98,
  John Senr. 98,
  Rachel 27, 35,
  Robert 27, 48, 65, 82, 98,
WALTER,
  Henry 27,
WARD.
  William 49, 82,
WARDER.
  Jeremiah 28,
WARREN / WAREING
  Abijah 49, 82,
WARRICK / WARICK
  Jacob 48, 82,
  John 32, 49, 82,
  William 49, 82,
WASON.
  Robert 28, 65, 99,
WEAVER,
  George 28, 65,
WHITE.
  David 27, 70,
  Isaac 98,
  Isaac Junr. 27, 65,
WHITEMAN.
  Henry 32, 49, 82,
WHITREL.
  Martin 65, 98,
WIDEMAN.
  Peter 27,
WILEY.
  Alexander 49, 82,
  John 28, 65, 99.
WILFONG / WOLFONG
  Michael 49, 82,
WILLIAMS.
  David 27, 70,
  John 27, 28, 65, 98,
  Moses 27, 65, 98,
  Richard 28, 65, 98,

WILSON.
  Andrew 28, 65, 99.
  David 28, 65, 99.
  Elizabeth 48, 82,
  James 27, 70,
  John 48,
  John (Major) 82,
  Martha 27,
  Mathew 27, 65, 98,
  Ralph 32, 36,
  Robert Junr. 27, 65, 98,
  Robert Senr. 28, 65, 99.
  Stephen 48, 82,
  William 27, 32, 48, 65, 82, 98,
  William (Revd.) 28, 70,
  William (B.
WIMERT.
  Jacob 49, 82,
WIMOUR / WIMORE
  Philip 49, 82,
WISEMAN.
  Peter 65, 98,
WOLF.
  Nicholas (Harrison Co.) 34,
WOODS.
  James 48, 76, 82,
  Mary (Widow) 27, 70,
  Steven 27, 36,
WORMSLEY.
  John 32, 49, 82,
  Thomas 49, 82,
WRIGHT.
  James 28, 65, 99.
  John 38,
  Joseph 49, 82,
  Samuel 27, 38,
  William 48, 82,
WYMER.
  Jacob 32,
  Phillip 32,

YEAGER.
  Andrew 49, 82,
YEARACIT.
  Charles 28,
YOOL / YOLL
  William 38, 49, 82, ·
YOUNG.
  James Junr. 28, 71,
  James Senr. 28, 71,
  John (Lieut.) 28, 36,
  John (Capt.) 28, 66, 99.
  Robert 28, 71,
  William 28, 33,
  William (Black Smith) 28, 36, 71,
  William Senr. 28, 71,